HOODS

THE GANGS OF NOTTINGHAM
A STUDY IN ORGANISED CRIME

Carl Fellstrom

MILO BOOKS LTD

First published in hardback in December 2008 by Milo Books

This paperback edition published in September 2010

ISBN 978 1 903854 94 5

Typeset by e-type

Printed in Great Britain by
Cox & Wyman Ltd, Reading, Berkshire

MILO BOOKS LTD
The Old Weighbridge
Station Road
Wrea Green
Lancs PR4 2PH
United Kingdom

www.milobooks.com

HOODS

For Mum, Dad and CMS, without whom this
would not have been possible

Hood[1]

• a covering for the head and neck with an opening for the face.

Hood[2]

• a gangster or violent criminal.

Hood[3]

• a neighbourhood.

(source: Oxford English Dictionary)

Robin Hood:

Legendary outlaw, hero of a series of English ballads, some of which date from at least as early as the fourteenth century. Robin Hood was a rebel, and many of the most striking episodes in the tales about him show him and his companions robbing and killing representatives of authority and giving the gains to the poor.

(source: Encyclopaedia Britannica)

CONTENTS

FOREWORD

This has been a long journey, for myself and for all of the people touched by this depressing, brutal saga. Though we have still not reached the end of a dark passage for the city of Nottingham, there are chinks of light to look forward to. Perhaps we are nearing the final chapter of a story that the people of this city will never wish to visit again.

It has been all too easy to forget that things were not always this way. In the eyes of the victims who have trusted me enough to be interviewed for this book, the first thing that always struck me was the look of fear. Could they trust me? How much could they safely say? What might be the repercussions for those who speak out? Few of these people are angels; many have been born from the underbelly of our city and have helped to propagate criminality themselves. But the brutality of the Bestwood Cartel, as it became known, has shocked even those criminals to the core.

Take one example. For safety's sake we shall call him Peter. He, his wife and two young children ended up travelling around Britain for two years, hopping from place to place in fear of their lives. They left their home in Nottingham because associates of Colin Gunn, a violent gangster later to be jailed for conspiracy to murder and who is one of the main characters in this saga, had made it clear their lives would be worthless if they continued to stay in the city. Gunn's so-called Bestwood Cartel had discovered they were on the point of giving information to police about a robbery carried out in the city centre. Peter was also a witness to a murder which, six years on, no one had been charged with. Peter and his family uprooted themselves from their house when the police said they could not safely live in Nottingham any more. Then their rented home, under the care of the authorities who had told them to leave, was ransacked by the villains once they had left.

I met Peter and his family at a caravan parked in a desolate field on farmland in the north of England in 2007. The couple's lives, and those of their two young children, aged ten and eight, had been turned upside down. They were living a subsistence life, just existing, with no roots. The children had not been to school for two years. They had slipped through the protective net of police, council and social services support were now in a Kafkaesque nightmare failing to meet the criteria needed for a new home because they had 'intentionally' made themselves homeless even though they had tried to get help from all three agencies. They were living an utterly miserable existence, unable to return to see relatives or friends for fear of receiving a bullet from the Bestwood Cartel as a greeting.

'We just need to be safe and stable,' said Peter. 'Our kids need to get some schooling. What can you do to help?'

They had no money, and it would be another day before a social worker could visit. I felt embarrassed that Peter was so grateful for the £20 I gave him to buy some food. Standing before me was an intensely proud man who felt ashamed that he had been reduced to this, helpless to protect and look after his own family. What had they done to deserve this? Of course, it would be easier to evoke sympathy for more deserving characters. Peter has a long history of petty criminality, and though his family entered protective custody for a time, they then threw it back in the face of the police. It hadn't helped that just a few months after trying to begin a new life in the north-east, bills from Nottingham began arriving at their supposedly secret address.

The police had wanted a full statement from Peter about the unsolved murder, but after the episode in Newcastle he became distrustful – not without reason – of the police's ability to protect the family. They told him they could not provide new identities for all the family. Peter told them he would find his own way out of the mess. In truth there was no way out. Above all Peter had tried to do the right thing; a very brave thing, from which there was no immediate return. He wanted to tell the truth, but the reality was that the authorities were not geared up to deal with the likes of Peter and his family. The city council maintained he had made his family intentionally homeless and the police would not vouch for him with the council unless he gave them his signed statement. The family were caught between a rock and hard place and eventually they split up. With Peter's reluctant consent, his wife Mary took the two children away to her own relatives, in tears. They felt it was the only option to keep the children safe; extract them from any connection with Peter's world.

Corruption and complacency within agencies like the police and local authorities are cancers that significantly blight the fight against crime and at the heart of the problem there is another unpalatable truth: we are now running out of people like Peter who are willing to stand up and speak out today, because they simply don't trust our public institutions any more, let alone believe they can protect them. They have all seen what happens when you 'grass' on someone. There is no place to hide. Many choose not to risk it; some have no other option because they have already been tainted as grasses by the criminals who assume they are talking to police because they have fled their homes. A former police officer who knew the Bestwood Cartel well told me of one instance where a man suspected of grassing them up was taken to a remote area, where his hand was nailed to a wooden bench. He was then saturated in petrol while Colin Gunn tormented him with the promise of a naked flame. When the police found the victim he was barely able to speak his own name, let alone name his attackers.

What surprised me more than anything else while researching *Hoods* was the discovery that some of the major criminal figures, who have been enforcing the rule of not grassing up your own, have been informants for the police themselves. But these people have no interest in making things right, they have been cleverly using the system to their own ends, feeding information into the police to take out their opponents while creating for themselves a protective zone courtesy of the authorities. These are the same criminals who would have you believe that grassing somebody up is a heinous crime, worthy of the most severe retribution. And police officers, some of whom have tried their hardest to bring down the gangsters, have themselves been faced with very real threats, even contracts being placed on their lives.

At the height of the Bestwood Cartel threat, senior officers at command level within Nottinghamshire Police were given exit strategies designed to get them safely out of their homes should the mobsters pursue them. Sometimes fear of the violence that may be visited upon you is as devastating as the real thing – this is what urban terrorism is really all about and this is what happened to communities in Nottingham as the twenty-first century dawned. Was this really the Nottingham I knew and had come to love? The city that had one of the highest university applications from students or that had attracted thousands of new residents eager to relocate to the city of Robin Hood in the late 1980s and early 1990s?

I came to live in Nottingham in 1995. It was a place I had fallen in love with during many weekend visits over the preceding years. The adjective 'vibrant' was a favourite word used to describe the atmosphere of those weekends and rarely in my first few years here did I see any real trouble in the city centre. Between 1994 and 1999 there were only two recorded murders involving firearms. Neither was drug-related. However, change was on its way. Cocaine began to blow like an indiscriminate blizzard. With it came crack and huge profits to be made. With huge profits came the need for the gangsters to enforce and protect their material wealth and their standing. With that came guns and knives. In the past seven years I have seen lives battered by use of crack cocaine and heroin, but cocaine more than anything else. It is arbitrary in its social networking – I have seen accountants, barristers, financiers, footballers, factory workers, students and villains take the drug and seen the impact on their ego. Long before night leads into morning they are babbling and railing at the world and before they know it they've burnt wads of money and can't function as responsible human beings any more. And I've seen the families mourning the loss of their loved ones, murdered victims of the profits to be made from these drugs.

In 1995 you could go into most city centre bars and the most aggressive behaviour you encountered was the result of revellers drinking too much alcohol. Cocaine was simply not available on the scale it is now and, if it was, the price, at £60 per gram, was prohibitive. Now you can go into those same venues and more besides and, uniformly, there is the depressing sound of young and middle-aged people, men and women, snorting lines of cocaine from any flat surface they can find inside the cubicles. The same person who was worse for wear for drink in 1995 is now, in 2007, with a few lines of 'Charlie' down them at £30 a gram, able to drink twice the volume of alcohol as their 1995 counterparts and is standing up and spoiling for a brawl, or worse. It was no surprise to me that when police carried out their own tests, in 2006, they found traces of cocaine in the toilets of twenty-four out of twenty-eight of the bars they checked in the trendy Lace Market area. The depressing truth is that evidence of this scale of drug taking would be found in every city in the UK on Friday or Saturday evenings in 2008. This commodity is one of the products that has been fuelling the violence in our cities and the Bestwood Cartel was one of the groups at the heart of it in Nottingham. I asked a villain what changed between 1995 and 2000 and, ultimately, what led to the orgy of violence that Colin Gunn presided over from 2000 onwards.

'It was the powder (cocaine), mate, everyone has been on it,' he said. 'And they all want to use a gun these days and you mix up cocaine with steroids and guns and all this gangsta rap stuff and it's like "boom". It all kicks off. The powder made them think they were in some kind of *Sopranos* show. Too much powder, mate, that's what it is.'

And so it goes on, like a runaway train. What has also struck me about this episode is the response of the police and the city authorities, some of whom ultimately failed in their work. Organised crime was staring them in the face and had the city in a clench-fisted grip before they really began to take action. I asked a senior police officer about Colin Gunn and the Bestwood Cartel in 2005, at the peak of a massive operation to nail them. I was stunned to learn that plans had been in place to take out the Bestwood Cartel as early as 2001 as part of an ongoing operation against major drug dealers in the East Midlands.

'What happened?' I asked.

'Well, it's like this,' he said. 'We had the operation ongoing and had taken out the middle tier and Colin and his associates was the next tier. Everything was in place. It was just a question of moving up a gear and we would have had them within four months. Some people in authority didn't want to spend the resources needed on it. We had just finished another big job [against drug baron Robert Briggs-Price, see Chapter Five] and the top corridor said, "We are not doing any more jobs like that. Too expensive, we need to tackle volume crime, show we are tackling the figures.'"

Eventually, money and resources were thrown at the problem. But by then the Cartel had become a stronger entity and a number of people had lost their lives. Those lives cannot be brought back, nor can the ripple effects on the lives of those directly affected by those tragic deaths be diminished. I hope more than anything else that those that bear responsibility directly or indirectly for those deaths – from the criminals who pulled the trigger to those who valued their budgets more than someone's life, to those who sold their souls to the dark side when they knew they were doing wrong – will one day comprehend the damage they have done. Perhaps they can learn to be more courageous in the future and put right the wrongs they encounter instead of adding to them. A civilised society, and one which everyone should aspire to if we are caring people, cannot function where a culture of revenge and violence is allowed to prevail. To an extent the Bestwood Cartel, under Colin Gunn's leadership, was allowed to perpetuate a Robin Hood image on the Bestwood estate, a 1950s housing scheme two miles north of Nottingham city centre. The Gunn brothers were almost latter-day Kray Twins, 'looking after their own', keeping petty crime down in their area while controlling it with extreme violence.

Hindsight is a great thing but it has often seemed to me that the authorities have found it far easier to get hot under the collar about the media's portrayal of Nottingham than proactively dealing with the reality of the problems which created those headlines. If we really want to rid the cancer of organised crime from our streets then we need to nurture a caring society, something that has been too often absent from British life in the past three decades. Above all our recognised institutions, and those who are influential within them – from police and prison officers to council officials and social workers – must be more vigilant. They must be unwavering in cracking down on corruption within their own ranks. And we need those people to be fully supportive and, above all, compassionate towards those, both within and outside the petty criminal fraternity, those disconnected from society, who are brave enough to come forward to try to put things right. They deserve our protection, regardless of the cost, and they deserve our respect. If we don't strive to accommodate them, we may wake up one day and the mob, as it has already shown itself capable of doing, will be ruling the roost.

What I have set out to do in *Hoods* is try to provide some sort of context to what has happened in Nottingham. The serious criminality exposed here is a microcosm of criminality in every other city in the UK and if the right ingredients are mixed together the same results unfold. The same characters can be recognised in Manchester, Birmingham, Liverpool, London, Newcastle, Glasgow, Leeds, Sheffield, et al. More than anything else, the alarming expansion of this country's black economy – an expansion fuelled by materialism and the social chasm that now exists between the haves and have-nots – is something that must be combated. This black economy, particularly the drugs trade, has created some of our most violent criminality and diminishes respect both for our law-abiding citizens and morality. The more it grows, the smaller the number of people there are who are impervious to its infections; it breaks down their ability to see what is right and wrong, their moral immune system against bad faith. It is a global business in its own right, now worth some $320 billion according to conservative estimates. In Britain alone, the illegal drugs trade has a turnover of at least £8 billion, according to 2005 Government figures. It has been breaking down parts of our society slowly but surely for over four decades now, pitching community against community, individual against individual and, in the case of the illegal drugs market, has been leaving young people dying on our streets – sometimes explosively in a hail of bullets, sometimes silently with the blade of a knife.

Why is this happening? How, in one of the richest and most advanced nations on earth, can it be tolerable to have twelve-year-old children selling crack cocaine or heroin on the corner of our streets in broad daylight? It should be a grave cause for concern among those sections of society who so often ignore what is going on around them until it touches their family or friends. We need a serious and comprehensive debate about the drugs issue before the problems associated with the culture lead to further avoidable tragedies. Does that mean we should be considering legalising recreational drugs? I don't have the answer to that, but I know that there is a trail from all the tragic deaths that are contained within these pages which lead all the way back to this problem and that must surely be our first concern.

Hoods is by no means a comprehensive account of recent events in this city. It does not purport to be a pure historical record. History, as we have learnt, is constantly being rewritten, updated and is ultimately flawed as a fixed entity to be relied upon. What I hope is to provoke some thought. In order to create a picture of certain significant events I needed to dramatise some episodes. Though these vignettes are dramatisations, they are based firmly on the factuality of those events derived from interviews with those involved and details from the resulting court cases. To that end this is a faithful and true account of how crime can destroy communities. As such I am indebted to the many people who have helped me try to understand what has been going on. Most of these people have chosen to remain anonymous for a myriad of reasons, ranging from fear of retribution to professional pride. Aside from the research I have undertaken myself, I can't thank enough the former head of Nottinghamshire CID, Peter Coles, for his willingness to pick up the phone for hours on end and explain some of the history of crime in this city. I am also indebted to Nick Davies's brilliant book *Dark Heart*, which I would recommend to anyone seeking to understand how impoverishment on a financial and moral level can create such darkness in the human soul. I should also thank the *Nottingham Evening Post* for some of the images reproduced here and Jacqui Walls and Steve Fletcher on the news desk for their help in tracking down material. Similarly Alistair Jackson at the BBC deserves my thanks. Above all I can't thank enough all those anonymous and often very brave people who took the time out to tell me their own stories, or spare the time to help me formulate my own thoughts and give them purpose and conviction – they all know who they are and this is their story. I hope I have done them justice. Finally, if there are errors, they are, of course, all my own.

Carl Fellstrom

PROLOGUE

The summer sun was already warming the flat landscape of the Lincolnshire coast when Joan and John Stirland awoke on 8 August 2004 in the modest bungalow they had made their new home. The middle-aged couple were both from Nottingham, but recent unpleasant events had forced them to move to the quiet village of Trusthorpe, near Mablethorpe, on the east coast of England. John, aged fifty-five, had retired as a machine operator in the traditional Nottingham industry of lace-dyeing. He was generally an outgoing man, the sort who would go out of his way to give a lost stranger directions, but had recently become less open and more suspicious. Joan, aged fifty-three, had worked as a cancer nurse and had known troubles in her life – a broken marriage, a tearaway son.

John, shirtless and in his summer shorts, flicked through a Sunday tabloid filled with more revelations about the private life of Sven-Goran Eriksson, the England football manager. Occasionally he looked up at the television, which he liked to have on all the time. Despite her husband's nonchalant protestations that she should enjoy the weather, Joan was feeling anxious. The day before, one of her daughters had left with the grandchildren after a wonderful few days' stay. Life appeared to be getting back to normal. But then that very morning, one of the neighbours had called round to tell them she thought she had seen a tall, shadowy figure jumping over a fence and prowling in their back garden the evening before. Joan wanted to play it down to her neighbour. No need for them to know more than they have to, she thought.

'Probably just kids messing about but I'd better tell John,' she said. 'Thanks for letting me know but probably nothing to get worried about.'

But Joan was worried – very worried.

'I'm going to ring the police at Nottingham in a bit, just to be on the safe side,' she told John.

'Okay, love, but I'm telling you you're wasting a lovely day getting all het up about it. Get it out the way and then we can have a walk on the front.'

Joan had every right to be scared. The past year had been a living nightmare as they moved from place to place, looking for sanctuary. Michael O'Brien, her son from a previous relationship, had shot dead a young Nottingham man, Marvyn Bradshaw, in a pub car park. Bradshaw had some very dangerous and powerful friends and this had put not just O'Brien but anyone related to him at risk. Even though Joan and John deplored the murder, they had since spent months looking over their shoulders and tensing at every knock on their door.

Michael's trial for the shooting had recently concluded and he had been jailed for life. Joan was ashamed of what he had done and even more ashamed that he had hurled a tirade of abuse at the victim's family. When he was sentenced, he threw a cup of water in the direction of the victim's family and taunted them. That was two weeks ago and Joan had since heard that Marvyn Bradshaw's best mate, Jamie Gunn, had also died. Jamie had cradled his friend's bloodied head in his arms as he lay dying. Unable to cope with his friend's death, his life had collapsed into a haze of drugs and drink and his own body had given up. It was the worst news possible and was bound to reopen old wounds – Jamie Gunn's uncle, Colin, was an infamous ganglord and Joan rightly feared that he would want revenge yet again.

On 16 September 2003, two weeks after Michael had shot Marvyn Bradshaw, Joan and John had been forced to flee Nottingham. A few days after Michael was arrested, Joan and John were watching television in the home they rented in Carlton, Nottingham, when they heard the unmistakable blast of gunfire and the sound of shattering glass. Someone was shooting up their home. They both hit the floor, ducked down and lay quivering with fear as they heard the sound of a motorcycle revving and speeding off. Eventually they crawled up the staircase of the house where Joan got to her mobile to dial 999. It was a while before they felt safe enough to get up and assess the damage.

Joan had told police after the attack: 'I heard a series of about seven bangs. I was standing up in the living room when the window went in and can only describe it as like a rush of wind past my arm. Having bullets fired at the house has left me and John very, very frightened. We fear for our safety. It is only luck that we weren't both killed.'

The next morning they moved out of the house and went straight to the Crescent Hotel in Bridlington, on the Yorkshire coast, without telling the police. They were soon traced and offered witness protection, but Joan was told she would have to make a full statement about Michael and the phone call he had made to her admitting his role in the murder if the police were going to help them fully. She would also have to cut all connections with her two daughters because police would not provide them with protection. It was a step too far for Joan. She wanted protection for the whole family: her daughters and John's son and daughter. The police would not justify such a move; the costs were prohibitive.

'We will look after ourselves in that case but we want you to keep us informed about what is going on in the meantime,' she told officers.

Joan was close to Michael. His alcoholic father had died from cancer when Michael was just thirteen and his passion in life – he had been a promising footballer who dreamed of a professional career – disappeared. Michael never got on with his stepfather. He resented the loss of his natural father and the harder John tried to be a replacement the more Michael rebelled. He refused to take up the Stirland name, preferring O'Brien, and by the time they left the St Ann's estate to move to neighbouring Carlton, Michael was a runaway train. Eventually he even sucked his mother into his criminal world. A few years earlier she had stupidly concealed some cannabis in her bra to give to him on a prison visit and was caught. Michael had been serving time in Swinfen Hall Young Offenders Institution and had asked her to bring the cannabis in after he was slashed with a razor blade by a fellow inmate, resulting in eighty stitches to his face. But sniffer dogs caught her as she went through security at the prison. She was lucky to escape a jail term herself. She shuddered as she remembered standing before the stern judge who had told her, 'Stand up, Mrs Stirland. It is with considerable hesitation that I have not sent you to prison.' Instead he suspended her nine-month sentence for two years.

Joan had admonished Michael many times for his criminal ventures. She knew he was capable of bad things but the murder cut deep into her heart. Where had she gone wrong? Had Michael really become a monster? She had seen no such signs in him when he was a toddler and though she loved him as any mother would love their child, she now felt deep shame that she had brought him into a world where his mark had been made for all the wrong reasons. When he had first gone on the run he had even threatened to have his stepfather kneecapped if Joan refused to help with food and clothes. She had told the police all this and more. What else was there to tell, that they didn't already have from other witnesses, about Michael's role in the murder?

After a week in the Crescent Hotel, the couple moved to Old Goole, in Humberside, for a few months. It had been their dream to live on the coast but this still didn't feel like home. The small flat became a prison. Then, in the New Year of 2004, the opportunity of a bungalow came up in Trusthorpe. Joan's daughter Rosie rang to tell her she had seen an ideal place to rent in the classified section of the local newspaper. It was perfect, and just a few yards from the seafront. Joan told the police they had moved and they weren't happy.

'Joan, you are moving into an area that the Gunn family have serious connections with, they have all sorts of contacts in the area. All it takes is a slip of the tongue to the wrong person and they will find out where you are,' a detective told her.

'I think we will be all right but just keep us informed,' said Joan.

That was eight months ago. Now the very thing the police feared might be coming to pass, thought Joan. Her mind raced through the possibilities. Had someone said something at the wedding of John's son Lee, which they had attended to a few weeks earlier at Newstead Abbey? John had been very worried when three car tyres had blown on the way to the wedding – he thought it was more than just a coincidence. 'I mean, what are the chances of all three tyres going at the same time,' he had confided to one of the guests. Despite all the precautions they took, maybe someone had followed them back from the wedding or had followed her daughter when she had come to visit.

By about 11am, Joan had called the number she had been given by her police contact. She got through to Tony Webster, the duty inspector on call, and explained her concerns. DI Webster was well aware of the Stirland case – and of the Bestwood Cartel.

'I'm worried because my neighbour said she saw someone in the back garden last night. What with Jamie Gunn dying and the end of the trial I'm worried they might have found us. Maybe I'm just being paranoid but can you look into it for me?' she asked him.

'Okay, Joan. Leave it with me,' the officer replied.

DI Webster contacted Detective Chief Inspector Paul Cottee, who had been dealing with the Stirlands' concerns. Cottee was at the airport, picking up a friend, when he received the call and but arranged for a detective sergeant to call Lincolnshire Police. At 2pm, the bungalow telephone rang. Joan picked it up. It was a detective from Nottinghamshire Police.

'I don't want police cars screaming up here but if you can do something it would put my mind at rest,' she told him.

'Joan, I'll get Lincolnshire to send someone over. We'll keep it low key, don't worry,' he replied.

Joan put the phone down, feeling slightly more reassured. It was almost 2.15pm.

No one paid much notice to the two workmen in blue boiler suits wearing caps and silver gloves going in through the door of the bungalow – or the car parked on the kerb with its hazard lights on. Joan heard the pleas of her husband John from the other room and the sickening sound of gun fire. She rushed into the living room and saw John slumped on the sofa with six bullets in him, two in his neck.

The two Beretta-carrying gunmen moved swiftly and backed her into the bedroom. She realised the end was near but knelt down, pleading with the gunmen. 'Please don't do this, I've got grandchildren,' she screamed. Four bullets hit her; the fatal wound was to her neck. She slumped down into the narrow space between the side of the bed and the wall. Nearby was a picture of her son Michael; just below that was a bullet mark.

The shooting was neither heard nor reported, and it was seven hours before the first police officer arrived, in belated response to Joan's earlier call. John's body was slumped on the sofa, newspapers still by his side and the flickering television screen illuminating the now darkening room. John had been hit by six bullets, three from each pistol. PC Kevin Jackson didn't spot Joan's crumpled body lying between the wall and bed in their bedroom. It would not be discovered until CID officers arrived at the murder scene another three hours later. She had been hit by four bullets, three from one of the assassins and one from the other.

It would not be long before detectives realised the painfully sad and violent scene before them bore an indelible, blood-soaked label: Made in Nottingham.

CHAPTER 1
MADE IN NOTTINGHAM

AS THE A453 carves its way between the flood plains either side of Kegworth and Wilford, leading towards the Clifton estate, the first clue that a visitor is about to enter a city with a rich history is the welcome sign: a Robin Hood motif. This is Nottingham, a city where, for some, the myths are intrinsic to and inseparable from the reality. A city that feels like a village, where everyone seems to know everyone else and people are not slow to update each other on the latest gossip or fable. Thousands of tourists arrive every year to seek out the legend of Robin Hood and, of course, that is all it is – a legend. A fable borne from writings some 600 years old and revolving around two characters: the Sheriff of Nottingham and Robin Hood: one a cynical, overbearing, authoritarian figure whose main task is to round up outlaws, the other an outlaw whose aim is to take wealth from the rich, by violent means if necessary, and distribute it to the poor.

Nottingham dates back to early Saxon times. In 600 A.D., it fell under the control of a Saxon chief known as Snot, whose people populated the ancient caves which still permeate the city and its Lace Market area today. It quickly became known as Snottingham, which means the 'homestead of the people of Snot'. In more recent years, headline writers in London would revive the use of the 'S' and label the gun-plagued city 'Shottingham'. It evolved into a centre first for the manufacture of religious artefacts during the fifteenth century and then, by the time of the Industrial Revolution, for the making of lace. The River Trent, which runs through the city, was crucial to its development. Marking the divide between northern and southern England, it linked Nottingham with the Potteries to the west and the Humber to the east. It was on the Trent, navigable for some 117 miles, that King Canute purportedly attempted to turn back the tides, near Gainsborough in Lincolnshire.

The textile industry brought prosperity. The area's lace-making became internationally renowned and by 1831 the population had swelled to 51,000. But this rapid expansion also resulted in what were reputed to be the worst slums in the British Empire outside India, and this in turn led to the riots of 1831. The first Reform Bill, which sought to end some of the abuses and corruption of the electoral system by giving more people the right to vote, was rejected by the House of Lords, and those living in poverty took up arms and burnt down the Sheriff's lair, Nottingham Castle. Then owned by the pompous, anti-reformist Duke of Newcastle, whose surname still adorns streets in the nearby Park area of the city, the castle bore the brunt of several days of rioting; it was another forty years before it received a replacement roof.

From the midst of this angry, dispossessed mass emerged a gang called, rather inappropriately in the circumstances, the Nottingham Lambs. They were anything but lambs. Originally the name was applied to early nineteenth century gangs who fought on behalf of rival political masters: the Yellow (Whig) 'lambs' taking on their Blue (Tory) rivals. Eventually it came to apply to the ale-swilling brutes who followed renowned bare-knuckle fighter William Thompson, commonly known as Bendigo, who became Champion of England in 1839. Such was Bendigo's reputation that Sir Arthur Conan Doyle penned an ode to him entitled *Bendigo's Sermon*;

> *You didn't know of Bendigo?*
> *Well that knocks me out!*
> *Who's your board schoolteacher?*
> *What's he been about?*
> *Chock a block with fairy tales;*
> *Full of useless cram,*
> *And never heard of Bendigo*
> *The Pride Of Nottingham*

Bendigo became an icon to the poor of Nottingham as he demolished opponents across the country. He spent spare hours fishing by the Trent, on one occasion rescuing three people from drowning. Though he eventually turned to God, preaching fire and brimstone in the streets, he was also a terrible drinker and incorrigible brawler and frequently appeared before the courts. He eventually became a figure of fun, taunted by small children. He died in 1880, aged sixty-nine, after falling down the stairs at his home in Beeston. His funeral procession, one of the biggest ever seen in Nottingham, was a mile long, with thousands lining the streets to pay tribute. In Bestwood Park is a small wooded copse known as Bendigo's Ring, where, it is said, he fought some of his matches and where his restless spirit lays in wait ready to exact revenge upon the children who taunted him during his final years.

By the beginning of the twentieth century, the city population was 240,000 and Nottingham was a major centre of commerce. The majestic Council House, which looks out over the Market Square, known as 'slab square', was completed in 1928, causing the famous

Goose Fair to be moved to its present location on Forest Fields. But by the Second World War, profits to be made from the lace industry were dwindling and the city began to rely on other industries for employment, such as the Raleigh bike and Players cigarettes factories, the mining industry, and the chemist chain Boots, which had been built into a national chain by Jesse, the son of founder John Boot.

Some of the worst crimes in the city were not of a human but of a planning nature. The demolition of the Black Boy Hotel in Long Row in the late 1960s was one such misdemeanour. It was a hugely popular watering hole, crafted by the renowned Victorian architect Watson Fothergill and incorporating a huge tower and Bavarian-style wooden balcony. One of the most striking landmarks in the city centre, it made way for a dull shopfront eventually occupied by Littlewoods and later Primark. By 1969, some of Nottingham's older homes had been deemed unfit for habitation by the local housing authority. Despite the protests of many families living in them, including those in the terraced houses of the St Ann's district, they were bulldozed and replaced with modern houses and flats. However, the open plan St Ann's, with its narrow interlocking alleyways and poor lighting, soon became was a mugger's paradise. Having failed to learn from their mistakes with the St Ann's estate, the planners went on to design the huge Meadows estate in much the same fashion.

Nottingham was no different to many other urban centres in the post-war period, built upon a strong ethic of work hard, play hard. The factories boomed, as did the hard-drinking image of the city portrayed in Alan Sillitoe's groundbreaking 1958 novel *Saturday Night and Sunday Morning*, later filmed starring Albert Finney. It was the first in a series of 'kitchen-sink' cinema dramas focusing on the boozing, street-fighting, womanising, white working-class male and his view of the world. It encapsulated his schizophrenic existence, the Saturday night alcoholic haze contrasting with the sobriety of the Sunday, which preceded the start of the working week.

The no-frills hero of the story, Arthur Seaton, is a man who coins a phrase for his and subsequent generations: 'Don't let the bastards grind you down.' Set in the terraced Victorian 'little palaces' of Radford, where much of the later movie was filmed, it captures his life working at the local Raleigh factory where, just as at the nearby Players cigarettes factory, thousands of Nottingham workers would clock in and out during the week and await the weekend. It doffed the cap to the country of D.H. Lawrence's miner, but now instead of working at the coalface he was sweating over a lathe to bring home his wages. It was also the age of the Angry Young Man and the whiff of revolt was in the air, but what Sillitoe, Nottingham and the rest of the country had missed was that this would realise itself, initially, in antagonism from within the indigenous white working-class community towards the communities who had migrated to Britain in the post-war period.

After the Second World War, many communities within the British Commonwealth and Europe, which had been allies in the war effort, saw in Britain a chance to throw off the shackles of the old world and embrace a new life in a new country – the mother country. The loss of a large proportion of the young, white population of working age during the war created a demand for labour. Among those who took up the challenge and sailed from Jamaica were two brothers, Vincent and Wellesley Robinson. In Nottingham and further afield, they would eventually become known by their respective nicknames: 'PG Man' and 'Douggie Man'. The story of their extended family is a microcosm of some of the roots of social and crime problems besetting the Afro-Caribbean community in Britain today. The Robinson family were to become infamous in Nottingham, their story eventually emerging in Nick Davies' ground-breaking book *Dark Heart*. But to understand what was happening we must go back to 1950s Britain and the new immigration.

By the late 1950s, many Afro-Caribbean families had made the trip to Britain. Some Caribbean men had already experienced the UK, having been stationed as servicemen, mainly airmen, in the country during the war. They found in Britain a chance of prosperity unavailable back home. On 22 June 1948, the steamship *SS Empire Windrush* docked in Tilbury, Essex, carrying nearly 500 people from Jamaica and Trinidad, many of them ex-servicemen. Though it amounted to a mere trickle of migrants, those who made the transatlantic voyage were pioneers, setting in motion a myriad of social changes in post-war Britain.

Steve Mitchell, a former serviceman and passenger on the *Windrush*, later described the alienation that he and other male Afro-Caribbeans encountered when they reached British cities. 'People just took their chance,' he told the radio journalist Alan Dein. 'I suppose what was the biggest stumbling block to them was being refused accommodation in houses that had vacancies. You could see notices in the windows, they have vacancies, and as soon as they ring the bell or knock the door, they would shut the door in their face. This was the mother country and they expect it to be motherly to them but they were disappointed. All I had was my bit of clothing, nothing else. I landed with £5 and no tools, nothing else, couple of suits, few shirts, no overcoat, no nothing, wasn't prepared for the cold weather. I was given a little job, pick-and-shovelling to fortify myself for the winter to come, so in that sense I was lucky.' Mitchell described another integration problem which would later lead to Britain's first major race riots: black men meeting white women at dances. 'There was a lot (of white women) who would willingly dance with you so it was mostly the men who caused the problem, not the women. Black fellas never had no problem getting white women, it was the men who was making all the problem. You'd go to dances [and] very few women would refuse to dance with you.'

With Britain ill-prepared for integration, it was this tension between the white working-class male portrayed in *Saturday Night and Sunday Morning* and the new immigrants from the Afro-Caribbean which led on 23 August 1958 to an outbreak of sustained violence in the St Ann's area. There are two different stories about what sparked the riots that night but both involved the perception that a black man should not be with a white woman. 'There were two accounts,' said the late Eric Irons, who became Nottingham's first black magistrate in 1962. 'One was that a West Indian was in the pub chatting up a white young lady and, when he left the premises, he was assaulted. The other was that someone insulted a West Indian man out with his white girl-friend. I think the police and everybody were shocked by the speed and ferocity of the West Indian response. There was no nonsense about it.'

At 10.20pm, police received a 999 call from a pub in St Ann's Well Road after a black man was severely beaten by several youths with his own walking stick. Hours later, the city was recovering from the devastation caused by more than 1,000 young men – mostly Teddy Boys and West Indian males going on the rampage. As running street battles continued throughout the night, young men were bottled, beaten and, in several cases, men, mostly white males, were stabbed. 'The whole place was like a slaughterhouse,' said the *Nottingham Evening Post*. It was clearly an overstatement, yet it captured the feeling of shock that the whole city felt. The following weekend a larger crowd of 4,000 gathered in St Ann's Wells Road but the Afro-Caribbean males stayed away. More violence erupted as the white Teddy Boys turned on each other, creating a turf war between young gangs from St Ann's and those who had dared to venture into the city from the Bulwell area.

As Mike and Trevor Phillips point out in their illuminating book *Windrush*, the second outbreak of violence was more significant. 'At the time, nearly all the commentators, focused as they were on race, missed the point, which was that if there were no black people available on whom to focus their rage, the crowds were equally willing to fight each other. In that sense it was apparent that the riots were as much about the feelings of exclusion and deprivation experienced by a wide section of the English population as they were about the presence of black migrants. The attention that the disturbances claimed for the conditions in which the people lived was, in itself, a factor calming the city.' It was also about young people defining themselves by the area into which they had been born or, as the young black males from the estates in St Ann's or the Meadows would later describe it, life in the ghetto.

By 1958, the belated post-war boom which had brought many Afro-Caribbean immigrants to Britain was drawing to a close and cultural tensions, which had been hidden to some extent, began to surface. Many West Indians found themselves facing a closed door when applying for jobs in Nottingham factories or even when buying a half of their favoured stout at the local pub. On the other hand, life for everyone in St Ann's was tough, with poor housing conditions for white and black neighbours alike.

As Milton Crosdale, another Nottingham black rights campaigner, pointed out, the riots led to a change in public housing policy. 'Up to 1958, you had a number of people from Caribbean countries in Nottingham,' he said. 'They had jobs but they had difficulty finding a place to live or they were in multiple occupation. People from the Caribbean were being shepherded into St Ann's and the Meadows. You had people crowded into old St Ann's, most of them living in multiple occupation. Nottingham, unlike other cities, went on to knock down major estates. Derby didn't knock down whole areas and rebuild them. Leicester didn't do it. It had a significant effect on the redistribution of people in the city. For me, the most significant thing was about how the employment market was being opened up. People began to realise that there was a serious problem. Who would have thought there would have been riots in Nottingham? Riots on their doorsteps? You can talk about prejudice but if it doesn't affect them in their front rooms, it doesn't matter. You can get away from it. It's like famine in Africa. It's only when it's on a TV picture and you're eating a meal in your front room that it affects you.'

A week after the riots in Nottingham, the Notting Hill area of west London erupted in an orgy of violence that made headlines around the world.

Into this cauldron of racism and lack of opportunity dropped Vincent and Wellesley Robinson when they arrived in Nottingham from their homes in Spanish Town, Jamaica, in the early 1960s. The story has it that Vincent was born on the day in 1938 that the Governor of Fiji made an official visit to Jamaica, and so was nicknamed 'Fiji Man' by relatives, which over the years became mispronounced as PG Man. Vincent was around twenty when he arrived in Nottingham, while Wellesley was a couple of years older. Before long, any aspirations they held were dashed when it became apparent just how difficult it was to get a steady job if you were black. Every time they went to the factory gates with a vacancy sign on it, they were turned away with the words, 'Job filled, sorry.' They became worn down by the sheer repetition of the rejections, although Vincent, who was a dapper dresser, managed to get a tiny part as an extra in the film *Saturday Night and Sunday Morning*. He appeared on screen only briefly, seen in the background in a scene involving Albert Finney near the city's castle, but such was his pride that he spent a week polishing his shoes for the part.

Many of the new immigrants identified not with England, which had held out a hand of false hope to them, but with their Jamaican homeland, and they began to import a bit of Caribbean sunshine into those dark days. Shebeens, or illegal drinking and gambling houses, began to spring up in Nottingham and Vincent and Wellesley saw this as a way to provide for their growing families. There would be classic ska music, soul and blues playing through the distorted sound system, which was always cranked up high enough to vibrate through the neighbours' floorboards, and there would be rice and peas, yams and curried goat and other tasty Jamaican food. And, of course, there would be 'a bit of smoke'. Cannabis was as essential to the Jamaican soul of the sixties as the music which boomed from the sound systems. The rude boy was born.

While most of the drug-taking white youth of Nottingham were downing amphetamines – for the most part taken from chemist shops which had been burgled – and staying up all night to listen to The Who and the Rolling Stones, their Jamaican counterparts were easing back into their chairs for a smoke of ganja, playing cards or dominoes and listening to the ska of Prince Buster, the blues of Jimmy Cliff and later the reggae of Bob Marley and the Wailers. Prince Buster's hit *Big Five* in 1968 would almost certainly have been banned if the controllers of the nation's radio airwaves had understood the lyrics. They also illuminated the baser instincts of the Jamaican male, which would cause a host of social problems in later years.

> *Right now I'm feeling irie*
> *Want a big, fat pussy this December night*
> *Today I smoke an ounce of weed*
> *Tonight I'm gonna plant a seed*
> *In her wump, alright.*

By the late 1960s, Nottinghamshire Police had concluded that it was easier to bust Jamaicans for cannabis than it was to bust white youths for popping pills. They only had to follow the pumping sounds coming from the shebeens and smell the acrid smoke wafting out from the houses to know they could make a quick bust. The sound systems were a product of the ghettos of Kingston and Spanish Town, where DJs would load up their trucks with a generator, turntable and huge speakers and set up impromptu street parties. By the early 1960s, Jamaican MCs such as Count Machuki were pumping out music through wardrobe-sized speakers capable of delivering 30,000 watts of sound.

PG Man and Douggie Man were soon running regular blues nights at their homes in Nottingham, initially using a fifty-watt speaker. Once they had a little money, they invested in a sound system they named the V Rocket. It would become well known throughout the UK over the following three decades and even now tapes from the V Rocket are much sought after. V Rocket would vie with the sound system called Saxon run by a Birmingham crew, and there would be many times in the 1980s and 1990s when guns were let off into the ceilings of shebeens to salute the DJs from the two sound systems.

With cannabis readily available, it was a safe bet that they would be busted sooner or later. When they were, it triggered a chain of events that would lead, eventually, straight to the front pages of the *News of the World*, the country's most lurid, and popular, Sunday tabloid. PG Man was living in Querneby Road, near to what would become the St Ann's estate, when things started to get hot. PG Man had already had a few encounters with the police. He spent three months in prison in the early 1960s after he was caught with a small amount of cannabis. Douggie Man, who lived nearby in Alfred Street North, had also been busted for a small amount of cannabis in August 1966, which resulted in a £100 fine. Then things started to get much worse: PG Man began working for the police. After his last bust they had told him that he would be able to run his shebeen, sell cannabis and stay out of prison if he started informing on his friends and family. Police raids started to occur regularly and PG Man's friends and neighbours all told the same story: drugs were being planted and were nothing to do with them. They were people like Keith Ansell Maclean, nicknamed 'P Sun', whose home in Truman Street was raided in September 1968 for a small amount of drugs. PG Man testified against him in court for the prosecution, saying that he got drugs from him, and P Sun went to prison for twelve months.

In the end, even Douggie Man was busted. Despite his daughter Elaine claiming she had spotted police planting the drugs on top of a radio, the courts did not believe he was an innocent man. He faced a three-year prison sentence and it became apparent to everyone that mattered that PG Man was working for the police. By now he had acquired another nickname: 'Judas'. Yet he was sick with remorse that he had sold his own brother down the river to save his own skin and vowed to get his revenge on the cops who, he felt, had forced him into a corner. He went to London to see if he could get a gun and planned to come back and use it on the officers who he felt had used him. But one of PG Man's friends, Adam Foster, had a better idea. He knew a *News Of The World* journalist, Simon Regan, and was sure that he could expose what had been going on and hurt the police officers on PG Man's back without resorting to violence. Regan listened to PG Man's woes as he detailed the troubles of a black man living in a white man's world. Then he set up PG Man up with several job interviews in the Nottingham area, including at the Player's cigarette factory. He watched how each job vacancy disappeared once PG Man showed his face for interview. Altogether, he was turned away from more than forty vacancies. Next Regan moved onto PG Man's story of planting drugs on his neighbours for the police. By the summer of 1969, Regan had a wealth of covert tapes which he believed were enough to show that certain police officers had acted corruptly. They apparently included PG Man going into the police station, being given cannabis and then arranging to call the police once he had been able to plant it.

In August 1969, the country's biggest-selling newspaper ran the story under the headline 'Police Plot to Plant Drugs'. It detailed, in full, PG Man's allegations and caused a sensation. The tapes landed on the desk of the then Home Secretary, James Callaghan, who had helped draft the Race Relations Act of 1968. He wasted no time in appointing a senior officer from Manchester and Salford Constabulary to investigate. The officer listened to the tapes, interviewed PG Man and many of his friends and associates, and believed what they had to tell. The inquiry sent shockwaves through the corridors of Nottinghamshire Police and three officers were charged with conspiring to pervert the course of justice. PG Man was cock-a-hoop, as were his relatives and friends.

The officers went on trial at Nottingham Crown Court in October 1970. Opening the prosecution case, Cyril Salmon, QC, told the jury they were about to hear 'a saga of corruption' which revolved around Jamaican immigrants being 'bullied, coerced and intimidated' by police officers into giving false evidence against family and friends. Police officers, he said, had threatened to arrest and prosecute Jamaican males who refused to become informants, had turned a blind eye to the illegal activities of others involved in prostitution and shebeens, on the basis that they became informants and had given drugs to others to plant on the targets of their crime-busting activities.

However, the jury were to be denied access to the damning tapes made by Simon Regan and PG Man. The judge, Mr Justice Kilner-Brown, decided that there was no proof that the voices on the tapes belonged to the police officers, and ruled them inadmissible. The jury then heard witness after witness describe how police had coerced them into informing after their homes were raided by officers looking for drugs. They included Victor 'Speck' Brown, who was arrested over non-payment of a fine and sent to prison for ten weeks. He told the court, 'A vice squad officer said to me: "Tell us about anyone who is selling cannabis and you walk – otherwise you is going to prison."' Seymour Oliver said police had planted cannabis on him as well. Then it was thirty-two-year-old PG Man's turn. He described how he had been forced to write a statement implicating Ansell 'P Sun' MacLean in dealing cannabis, resulting in MacLean being jailed for a year. He said police had told him, 'Vincent, you can continue to deal in cannabis and run a shebeen if you inform on other Jamaicans.'

The witnesses went on and on, all telling broadly the same story. But sometimes there were inconsistencies in their testimonies, which were pounced on by the defence barristers. The all-white jury found it difficult to follow the Jamaican accents and, after only thirty-eight of the planned eighty-seven witnesses for the prosecution had been called to give evidence, they sent a confidential note to the judge. It was the thirty-third day of the trial and the judge ruminated for a while on what the jury had said in the note. Finally Mr Justice Kilner-Brown announced, 'I agree with you, members of the jury. It seems to me it would be an absolute waste of time to produce any more witnesses who may be regarded as rubbishy by you.'

The trial was abandoned and, on Monday, 23 November 1970, all the police officers were cleared. The judge thanked the jury and commended them, saying that the trial had at the very least proved that 'the coloured community had nothing to fear' from a British jury. Nottinghamshire Police Authority was quick to tell the local paper what a travesty it had been that any police officers had had to face charges. 'It is regrettable that the force has been deprived of these officers for so long on the evidence of people who have never done a day's work since they came to this country,' said the authority's vice chairman.

PG Man and his friends and relatives had been publicly humiliated, and through successive generations the resentment that built up around the case would prevent many in their community trusting authority in any meaningful way again. Some of the young Robinsons were more convinced than ever that the way to live their lives was to be the 'bad black man' and the second and third generations would embrace that role, as epitomised by Jimmy Cliff in the cult 1972 film *The Harder They Come*, the story of a Jamaican anti-hero who shoots a police officer. 'I'd rather be a free man in my grave than living as a puppet or a slave,' sang Cliff in the title track. By the late 1970s and early 1980s, some of PG Man's and Douggie Man's numerous offspring were caught up in crime. PG Man alone fathered seventeen children, while by the time Douggie Man's eldest daughter Elaine had reached twenty, she had five children all by different fathers. One of Douggie Man's sons had fathered seven children by five different women by the late 1980s. It seemed to the women that that was how many young Jamaican males behaved: they spread their seed and then abandoned you with a pile of dirty nappies and no money to bring up the children.

The British ska revival of the late 1970s, spearheaded by Jerry Dammers' 2 Tone record label, and the popular reggae sounds of the Rastafarian movement gave Douggie Man's V Rocket sound system a boost and some welcome earnings but some of the family seemed to see criminality as their only route to financial survival. The young rude boys of the second generation were of a grittier character than their fathers. PG Man and his peers had been happy to deal in cannabis and take in a bit of cash by running blues nights, but they generally eschewed violence. Some had put a few white women onto the streets but they looked after them better than the Glaswegian pimps they had taken over from. The next generation, though, were carrying knives and even guns, robbing people and trafficking prostitutes all over the country. If you were in London and picked up a prostitute near Paddington or King's Cross during the late 1980s, there was a good chance that they had come from Nottingham. And then crack cocaine burst into the ghetto.

By 1989, Nottinghamshire Police had begun to see the symptoms of this new cocaine derivative on the streets of Radford, St Ann's and the Meadows. It wasn't that they were arresting more people or busting the crack houses which had begun to spring up, or that they were making huge seizures of the drug; it was the sinister breakdown of morality. Crack left an indelible trail everywhere its users went: prostitutes beaten black and blue by their cane-carrying, crack-smoking pimps; men willing to sell their own girlfriends on the streets to buy more crack, and the girlfriends willing participants because they needed their crack pipe full too; robbers who previously drew the line at stealing a handbag from a pensioner now not only robbing them but beating them black and blue when there wasn't enough money in the stolen purse to get a rock. It was not just that this drug left the rude boys unable to pay their debts, it was morally bankrupting sections of certain communities in Nottingham, Bristol, Birmingham, Manchester and London.

In June 1989, the Nottinghamshire drug squad made its first major seizure of crack. Roy Scott, aged thirty-six, a small-time street dealer from Denman Gardens, Radford, was stopped in the street with more than 120 rocks after a tip-off. Each rock of crack, from which you got about five smokes, was then selling at £25-£30. Scott was jailed for seven years. It was the largest single seizure of crack cocaine in the country that year and it came straight off the street; crack didn't hang around in lock-ups for weeks like cocaine, heroin, speed, ecstasy or cannabis might, with dealers waiting for the right moment to shift it wholesale. Crack, by its nature, is consumed rapidly by its users and when it's gone they crave more. It was a high-turnover trade. Mobile phones had also made dealing easy and the dealers distanced themselves from potential arrest further by corrupting the local youth. At the bottom of this huge business pyramid, permeated with crack and heroin, the twelve- and thirteen-year-olds who rode around St Ann's on mountain bikes would take the risks. Rocks of crack in pocket, they would make handovers and get paid a few pounds by the dealer. Career paths no longer meant anything to these teenagers; they weren't bothered if the police picked them up. What could the police do when they told officers they had just found the bag of drugs in the street? As youngsters they aspired to be footballers or pop stars, not doctors or police officers, and if they didn't make it they knew they would be able to make it as drug dealers in a few years' time. Then they too could have a BMW and some nice jewellery.

One of the principal reasons that crack cocaine was turning up with the same regularity and volume as in London was Nottingham's links to Jamaica. Even before crack began to appear, Jamaican criminals on the run, often from London, would regularly lie low in Nottingham with a distant relative or friend. But now the violent gangsters known as Yardies were appearing on the streets. Political turmoil in Jamaica caused many to flee for the United States and the United Kingdom. Many gravitated first to London, then began moving to provincial cities like Nottingham. They hung around the Black and White Café on Radford Road and the Marcus Garvey Centre on Lenton Boulevard, and swaggered around in heavy gold selling rocks down at a cavernous late-night drinking hole on Ilkeston Road, the Tally Ho (later called the Lenton, then the Drum). It was popular with some of the black homeboys, but even they knew not to push it when the Yardies were around. They were all unaware that an undercover cop from London was hanging around too, having managed to convince everyone he was a Yardie. The Tally Ho was seen as an ideal shopfront from which to peddle rocks without the potential danger of bumping into rival posse members, as frequently happened in London, often with fatal consequences. In addition, they had a ready-made market, as the Tally Ho was a favourite haunt for white street girls who would sell their skinny bodies every night on Forest Road for the price of a few rocks of crack.

Politically and socially, Jamaica was going through torrid times. The peaceful movement of Rastafarianism, led by Bob Marley, masked deep troubles. Corrupt politicians working for the two main political parties, the People's National Party (PNP) and the Jamaica Labour Party (JLP), were recruiting crack dealers from the ghettos of Kingston and Spanish Town at an alarming rate. These politicians needed the fear the Yardies brought to enforce their will and keep the lid on their own criminal activities. This was complicated further by the fact that Jamaica had become a stop-off point in the shipment of cocaine from South America to the United States. Someone on the island had discovered that if you boiled down the cocaine with some baking soda in a pan you could remove impurities and create a hard rock which, if smoked, could take you to the moon – but only for a brief few minutes. Young Jamaican men soon didn't care if smoking this stuff was like putting a gun to your head; after just a few tokes from a makeshift pipe fashioned from a beer or pop can, they were ready to sell their souls for the next hit. It was just about the most addictive drug that enforcement agencies had ever come across and pretty soon it was making its way to the UK – and taking a leading role in the most violent crimes in this country. The three things you could be sure of if you had bumped into a Yardie in the early 1990s were that they would have a wad of cash on them, some rocks of crack (or access to them), and, most of all, a firearm close to hand.

The Robinsons were caught up in this. The first evidence of the wave of mayhem that crack would bring came in a quiet street in the Wollaton area on 11 October 1991. Ian Bedward, a twenty-eight-year-old homeboy, had succumbed to the drug and the paranoia it brought on made his tempestuous relationship with partner Sophie Robinson, Douggie Man's granddaughter (her mother was his eldest daughter Elaine), with whom he had three children, worse still. Bedward was involved in armed robberies in the city, ran various drugs as a courier, and had robbed some drug dealers of their cocaine. He had armed himself, fearing they would come after him. One Tuesday, after a row, Sophie left their house in Whitby Close for a few days to go down to London, leaving the children with him. Ian, who thought she was seeing other men, consoled himself by writing rambling letters that he hoped would make some sense of his turbulent life. They rambled on about how some of the Robinsons were mixing with Yardies and mentioned a gunman called Eaton Green, known as 'Leon', who was selling crack around the housing estates of St Ann's and Radford like a candy store salesman. Bedward became more and more distraught as the hours ticked by and he sat alone with his thoughts. By the next day he could see only one course of action open to him: he lined up his three children, Lorne, aged four, Loren, three, and Lorene, two, and shot them through the head as they lay on the sofa. Then he sat beside them and pulled the trigger of the Colt 45 resting against his head. The bodies were discovered on the Friday when neighbours, worried they hadn't seen the children and unable to get an answer from the house, called the police. Sophie arrived home the same day, just as police made their grim discovery, and ran down the street screaming hysterically. Two of the children had been killed by the same bullet. One part of the letter Bedward left said, 'See you in heaven cos down here is hell.'

Detective Peter Coles, who later became head of CID, said the horrific scene was one of the worst he encountered in his police career. 'It really was truly sad and shocking and just so distressing seeing these little bodies. It was really the first time we had also come across the Yardie phenomenon in terms of violence in the city. We had the letters examined for intelligence purposes, some information was extracted which proved useful. It was the first time we encountered Eaton Green's name but they were such rambling letters it was hard to make much sense out of them. What we did have was the first bit of information that there was a connection between the Robinsons and Eaton Green.'

Next it was PG Man's family who had tragedy knocking at their door. Some of his sons had formed a gang with friends from the St Ann's estate, now known in ghetto terms as the Stanz, and they called themselves the Playboy Posse. In the early 1990s they got into a war with the Meadows Posse, who would also become known later as the Waterfront Gang. It was the beginning of the black-on-black gang violence that was to blight the city intermittently over the next fifteen years. At the heart of it was the territorial drug business and, in particular, cocaine and its derivative crack. A number of the Robinson clan had succumbed to crack by the early 1990s and turned to crime to pay for their drugs. Some of the Robinson girls took to street robbery and prostitution as a means to buy their next rock, organising gangs of shoplifters who would fleece designer ware from the city's fashion houses or carry out street robberies. The rude boys of the 1980s, with their neat clothes and flash cars, who had earned a significant living off the street girls and weed they traded in, were now virtual down-and-outs, like the prostitutes who worked for them. Crack had created a major economy in its own right as the consumption of the little brown rocks spread like a cancer through the ghetto. One of Douggie Man's sons, Easton 'Bubsie' Robinson, went to prison for six years for robbing women on the street to fund his crack habit (twenty-three years after tasting his first crack pipe, Bubsie was still at it: in 2008, at the age of fifty-seven, he pleaded guilty to shoplifting from the Gap and Madhouse clothes stores to buy crack). Another son had been lifted by the police for attempted murder after violence erupted in a black club where two Birmingham dealers had stolen crack from one of the Robinson's dealers. Then the third generation of Robinsons started to succumb to crack. Douggie Man's granddaughter Sophie, who had had the life sucked out of her when her three children were murdered, became a crackhead and began to sell her body on the streets.

Against this backdrop, the men were still able to maintain some semblance of togetherness and organisation through membership of the posses. These small, tight-knit groups gave those living in the ghettos of St Ann's and the Meadows a sense of meaning; an order among all the chaos that surrounded them. They knew what constituted their patch and who to be wary of, and the Playboy Posse knew they had to be on the lookout for the Posse from the Meadows. No one knows quite how it all started, but by the early 1990s gang life within St Ann's and the Meadows estates was flourishing. One of the major flashpoints between the gangs, which acted as a catalyst for the war, was ignited when some of the Playboy Posse were ambushed and one of PG Man's sons was slashed and needed sixty stitches. Four weeks later the Playboy Posse took retribution and attacked five members of the Meadows gang as they came out of a club, leaving one with his skull fractured in two places. Then the rape of a fourteen-year-old girl was alleged against three of the Playboy Posse. More violence followed.

Finally, on 1 August 1993, PG Man's twenty-one-year-old son Lloyd, who had taken to carrying a machete for self-defence, got into a dispute with some of the Meadows gang. One of Lloyd's friends had stolen a bike from a youngster and the Meadows crew were not happy about it. They considered it to be disrespect of a grave nature and someone had to pay for it. PG Man's family had gathered at his house to celebrate the birth of his latest grandson and, after a while, Lloyd and his brother Daston, aged nineteen, went off to the nearby Afro-Caribbean Centre, near Hungerhill Road. Just after midnight, the pair were about to leave the club when they were confronted by around fifteen youths looking for a fight. Daston went to raise his father from bed, but before PG Man could intervene, the Meadows gang had attacked Lloyd, striking him so hard with a baseball bat that the force almost split his head in two. He died three days later in hospital.

PG Man was a broken man from that day on. 'I saw a boy holding a baseball bat walk behind the crowd, come up behind Lloyd and whack him on the head,' he later told the *Nottingham Evening Post*. 'As he collapsed to the ground, I fell to my knees and put my hands on my head. From that lick I knew he must be dead because it went right through me. I can still hear the crack of the baseball bat against my boy's head. I was broken down bad by Lloyd's death. I am not the same person no more.' The young man who struck the fatal blow, Gary Mayor, a nineteen-year-old amateur boxing champion, was jailed for life for the murder in November 1994. Three more gang members, Sean Cope, aged twenty, Dean Johnson, nineteen, and Simon Rowbottom, twenty, received between three and six years for manslaughter.

CHAPTER 2
SEEK AND DESTROY

In the early hours of 30 May 1993, a blues party was well underway in a disused warehouse in Ashforth Street, St Ann's. Among those who had been forewarned about the event was the Yardie Eaton Green. Green had fled to the UK to escape an attempted murder charge in Jamaica and to elude fellow Yardies who had scores to settle. By the age of twelve, he had left school in downtown Kingston and was mixing with gangsters who had affiliations with the PNP. They ran areas of the city with the help of corrupt politicians and policemen. By the time of the 1980 elections in Jamaica, the criminal gangs were merging almost seamlessly with the politicians. Green was at the vortex of it, now a gunman doing the bidding of corrupt PNP leaders who wanted to take down rivals working for the JLP.

Green became part of the Tel Aviv Crew, named after the slum area of Kingston where he was brought up. These were government housing projects built around yards, hence the name 'Yardie'. The Tel Aviv Crew was divided into a number of posses or gangs, including the Rapid Posse, the Kremlin Posse and the Desert Posse, to which Green belonged during the 1980s. Before the decade was over he had been involved in a number of murders, which he would later confess to, spent four years in prison and been arrested for a multitude of crimes, from murder to armed robbery. Reluctance on the part of witnesses to come forward shielded him from several life sentences in Jamaica. In 1991, awaiting trial for a shooting, he jumped bail, booked a flight to the UK and walked through immigration to begin what he hoped would be a new and prosperous life.

Green was a dangerous man who was known to use a firearm at the slightest provocation. He became a frequent visitor to Nottingham from London and was soon known to the police. Nottinghamshire Police intelligence picked up information that Green was selling crack cocaine in the city: his name had cropped up in the letters written by Ian Bedward which were seized by police. In fact Green was only one of a small but growing number of Yardies branching out from the capital and selling drugs in the major provincial cities of Bristol, Manchester, Birmingham and Liverpool.

According to testimony at a later court trial, two brothers from Birmingham who had recently fallen out with the Robinsons in an apparent turf rivalry were expected at the blues party, which began on the night of 29 May. Police suspected these brothers were ferrying large amounts of cocaine into Nottingham. At a party two weeks earlier, two of the Robinson clan, Peter and Ricky – Douggie Man's grandsons – had been severely beaten up. Another of the family, Leslie, who was working as a clerk at a law firm and would later become the main organiser for the Nottingham Afro-Caribbean Carnival, had his car torched in an attack police believed was linked to the feud. Eaton Green, who had been partying at the Marcus Garvey Centre in Nottingham the same night with some Yardie friends, had also been 'dissed' by some of the locals. One of them had saluted Asher's sound coming from the speakers with a volley of gunfire into the ceiling, which had almost deafened one of Green's associates, Rohan 'Bumpy' Thomas. Bumpy wasn't happy.

By 3.30am, the Ashforth Street party was in full swing, with around 200 punters enjoying heavy bass sounds from the booming speakers. Then chaos erupted. Five men – one dressed in a bandana and brandishing a Luger pistol, two others with handguns and another with a shotgun – burst into the building and switched the lights on. The music ground to a halt. The silence was broken by two blasts as a shotgun was fired into the ceiling by one of the raiders. Next, they began to strip customers of their money and jewellery. Their leader, Eaton Green, brandished his Luger in the face of a number of the men present, taking interest in one in particular, Michael Johnson, who had refused to hand over anything and made to run away. Green took aim and fired. The bullet missed Johnson and instead hit twenty-year-old Leibert 'Bubbler' Henry in the foot. Two other men who refused to take this disrespect without a fight were beaten up by Green and his associates.

'We are the Seek and Destroy Posse and this is a robbery,' Green screamed at the terrified partygoers. Leibert Henry, blood pumping out of his damaged foot, pleaded to be let out of the building to get medical help but Green refused, taunting him with the words, 'Bleed, pussy, bleed.' The gunmen then demanded that the men be separated from the women and began to remove jewellery, money, credit cards, mobile phones and drugs. The incident was over within half an hour but in that time Green and his gang robbed more people in one go than at any other recorded British crime scene. The Birmingham brothers Green was looking for did not appear to be among the partygoers but he evidently felt some part of his mission had been accomplished by robbing the locals and 'dissing' them.

At first Operation Warehouse, as the police investigation was called, dug up few leads to the gunmen's identity. But gradually a picture began to emerge of some of the assailants. The main protagonist was a slim, young black man in his late twenties with a large scar across his right cheek wearing a bandana and had answered to the name Leon, which Nottinghamshire detectives knew from recent intelligence was Green's street name. Another man had the nickname Bumpy, according to some of the witnesses. The vehicle Green and his associates had driven from London was found to be a hire car booked from a company based at Heathrow Airport. CCTV images obtained from the company showed Green and two of his gang meeting Elaine Robinson at Heathrow. Nevertheless, for Nottinghamshire Police the biggest revelation was yet to come.

Over the subsequent weeks, officers began to piece together more information about Green. They found an address he had been staying at where there was further evidence of a connection to Nottingham: photographs of Elaine Robinson and her daughter Sophie, along with Green's mobile phone number. Information from the Jamaican authorities revealed Green to be a dangerous Yardie wanted for involvement in several brutal murders. How then had he managed to slip into Britain without being arrested or turned back? In fact, as police in Nottingham were to discover, Green had been helped in avoiding deportation back to Jamaica. Not only that, he had brought two violent associates over from Jamaica on false passports with a little help from 'friends' in high places – friends specifically in the Metropolitan Police and the Immigration Service. They in turn were acting with the consent of the top brass at Scotland Yard and the Home Office. Eaton Leonard Green was a top-level Yardie informant playing a double agent role within the Metropolitan Police S011 Intelligence Unit. His code name was Aldridge Clarke.

By July 1993, some resourceful Nottingham detectives were closing in on Green, despite a lack of assistance from Scotland

Yard. At around 2pm on 8 July 1993, after tracking him through several addresses they had gained from social security details, they finally located their man walking down Mandela Road in Newham, East London. He was handcuffed and led to a car that would take him up the M1 to be questioned about the blues party robbery. But, as the Nottinghamshire officers were soon to discover, this was far from an open-and-shut case. The Metropolitan Police work ended up hampering the progress of their provincial colleagues, perhaps on the basis that the 'ends justify the means'. Ultimately the criminal trial would descend into chaos.

As Nottinghamshire Police began to question Green, a complex story began to unfold. Green said he was not at the blues party but could identify the assailants. He told them to check in with a constable called Steve Barker at the Metropolitan Police's SO11 Intelligence Unit, and all would be explained. Green insisted he was working for the Met and had become involved in gaining intelligence on the local drug scene, particularly as a man with the street name 'Pepsi' had relocated to Nottingham from London to sell crack cocaine. Pepsi was supposedly one of the leaders of the Tel Aviv Crew based in Kingston, Jamaica. The Nottinghamshire detectives were highly sceptical. Nevertheless they would have to check out the story before they could carry on with any questioning, particularly as the repercussions could prevent them from charging him for the offences he was suspected of in Nottingham.

What they began to uncover, through little help from the Met, was that Green and two of the other men believed to be involved in the robbery, Rohan 'Colonel Bumpy' Thomas and Cecil Thomas, were being actively shielded by Scotland Yard detectives because of their value as informants. Indeed, Green had been deemed so important to the Yard that he was given an A grade informant tag, denoting an agent whose information was prized at the highest possible level. He had his own code name to prevent his identification, a specialist handler who would meet him at prearranged secret locations to pay and debrief him, and a two-year history of providing top intelligence on the Yardies – who had become a serious problem for Scotland Yard in their fight to prevent crack cocaine taking hold in deprived inner-city areas. He was, in fact, Scotland Yard's most prized asset in the battle against the unpredictable Yardie gangsters. Perhaps the Met thought that Green was an asset worth sticking your neck out for, as they proceeded on a path that seemed to break the conventions of policing, justice and the law.

The detectives from Nottinghamshire were unimpressed. The more they discovered about the nature of Green's relationship with their London counterparts, the more it strengthened their resolve to see Green put on trial for the robbery on their patch. They did not doubt that he had provided good information on the movement of firearms around the capital and the arrival of Yardies in London, but to turn a blind eye to an armed robbery of 150 out of 200 people at a party was not something they were prepared to do, or to try to justify to the victims. As far as they were concerned, Scotland Yard had effectively done nothing to help with Green's arrest after the robbery. Moreover, some individuals had effectively helped Green avoid arrest, not least his handler, who had met him during the weeks after the robbery and allowed him to walk away despite the Yard having been told by Nottinghamshire that he should be arrested.

Detective Inspector Michael Leyton was among the senior Nottinghamshire officers trying to track down Green and his accomplices. The team had been given full authority by their bosses to nail the gang, putting them on a collision course with Scotland Yard that would serve neither justice nor the public.

They were still in the dark about the extent of Green's role as an informant even as they tried to solve a major case, and the economy of truth displayed by their fellow agencies was something they could never have predicted. Indeed it would take a court case to flush out the truth.

By July 1993, Green, along with Rohan Thomas, Cecil Thomas, and Steven Crossdale and Errol Lynch, alleged to be the fourth and fifth members of the gang, had been charged with robbery. Three Robinsons from Douggie Man's side of the family were also arrested: sisters Elaine and Valerie and their brother Leslie. Detectives were convinced some of the Robinsons had played a role in sponsoring Green's gang to carry out crack cocaine business in the city and, ultimately, exact revenge on the two Birmingham brothers for humiliating members of the Robinson family. The three Robinsons were charged with conspiracy to cause grievous bodily harm.

Right up to the start of the trial, at Leicester Crown Court, Scotland Yard concealed the importance of Green's role as one of their most prized agents. In October 1994, after a few weeks of the trial opening, tactics that seemed almost Machiavellian were used to protect Green, who was pleading not guilty. First a mitigation text, a method sometimes used by police to tell a judge that a defendant has provided crucial information to help solve crime and should be sentenced leniently but without telling the barristers or the jury, was received by the judge from the Metropolitan Police. It indicated that Green had been very helpful in the arrests of a number of cases and should be given credit with a reduced sentence, should he be found guilty. Defence barristers, tipped off about Green's role in the arrests of his co-defendants, demanded the informant be identified. The prosecution barrister also indicated that senior officers from Scotland Yard were imploring him to abandon the trial. On 14 October, with the truth in danger of coming out, an officer went to the court to see Judge Richard Pollard and ask him not to reveal Green's identity

Faced with some unpalatable questions, the judge halted proceedings as top-level discussions took place between Nottinghamshire Police, Scotland Yard, Barbara Mills, the Director of Public Prosecutions, and Sir Nicholas Lyell, the Attorney General. Nottinghamshire Police were astounded to discover that Green had given the Met information about the weapon used in the robbery, who the assailants were, where they were holed up and where some of the jewellery had been fenced. They also learned that the Met's intelligence report stated that all this information had supposedly been passed on to Nottinghamshire Police during the first few weeks of the investigation, which was news to them. It was suggested that there had either been a calamitous breakdown in communication between the two forces or that the Met was lying. The trial judge also felt that the Met had misled led him and the CPS about Green's relationship with SO11, and that a senior Met officer had made inappropriate approaches to the judge and counsel in an apparent attempt to scupper the trial. After batting the issue back and forth over a number of weeks, the Director of Public Prosecutions and the Attorney General ruled that the Met were in the wrong, the role of Green would have to be revealed in court and the trial should continue. After a month away from the courtroom, however, Judge Pollard had no option but to discharge the original jury and call for a retrial. The defendants were remanded in custody.

Faced with nowhere to hide, Green now changed his story once more and began to admit to a catalogue of crimes in Jamaica – eleven murders – as well robberies, shootings and cocaine deals while in London on the payroll of Scotland Yard. He described in graphic detail to Metropolitan Police officers how he had murdered, on behalf of a senior PNP politician, three Yardies suspected of snitching to the Jamaican authorities. He went on to explain how he was spotted carrying out the killing by a passing taxi driver and so executed him too, along with his passenger. Crucially, he was prepared to plead guilty to the robbery in Nottingham and implicate the three members of the Robinson family in the process.

By the time the case finally came to retrial in June 1995, again at Leicester Crown Court, Green had already pleaded guilty and been sentenced to six years in prison. The new trial judge, Mr Justice Smedley, fully aware of what his counterpart Judge Pollard had been put through during the original trial, had some choice words to describe the conduct of the Metropolitan Police. 'I am very disturbed at the way in which those responsible for handling Mr Green as an informant appear not only to have failed to cooperate but possibly to have impeded inquiries, and that causes me alarm,' he said. Meanwhile, SO11 had given Green a new identity and placed him in the witness protection prison wing at Parkhurst Prison on the Isle of Wight. It was an area reserved for just a handful of supergrasses, including Darren Nicholls, the main witness in the 1998 Essex Range Rover murders fictionalised in the film *Essex Boys*. The Met clearly still believed Green could be of use to them if he went back to Jamaica.

The retrial jury was told the events at the Ashforth Street warehouse were like a 'Hollywood-style robbery'. Barristers for the Robinson trio argued forcefully that their clients knew of no bad blood between them and the two Birmingham brothers, and that the gang was simply doing what all Yardie gangs do at blues nights: rob fellow partygoers. By the end of the retrial, the jury was unconvinced that any of the Robinson family had been involved in a conspiracy to commit violence against anyone at the party. Though it was clear from the CCTV images at Heathrow that Elaine Robinson knew Green well, and that a phone linked to her sister Valerie had been used to contact Green right up until the minute the robbery was taking place, all the Robinsons were cleared of the GBH conspiracy charge. The alleged gang members did not fare so well. Rohan 'Colonel Bumpy' Thomas was convicted, along with Steven Crossdale. Cecil Thomas and Errol Lynch were cleared but were deported back to Jamaica. Crossdale was eventually cleared on appeal and Thomas, who had been faced with a fourteen-year sentence, had some of his convictions quashed as a result of an appeal which ruled that Green's evidence could not be relied upon.

Meanwhile Hampshire Police's Chief Constable, Sir John Hoddinott, was given the role of carrying out a major enquiry into the Metropolitan's Police handling of Eaton Green and another Yardie, Delroy Denton, who had murdered a woman while on their informant payroll (Delroy Denton was jailed for life in 1996 for the killing of Marcia Lawes). The story of Green's recruitment emerged from 15,000 pages of evidence collected by Hampshire Police. The report, published in 1999, revealed just how far the authorities were prepared to go in allowing a gun-toting killer to help them in the battle against the Yardies.

Green had arrived on British soil in February 1991, and quickly immersed himself in the Yardie hotspots of Brixton and Hackney, where he found former associates from Jamaica doing a roaring trade in crack cocaine and robberies. By 21 May he had been arrested for a traffic offence by a young constable, Steven Barker. Following a 1am chat with Barker in Brixton Police Station, Green took the only available option to avoid extradition back to Jamaica: he turned grass. Over the next two years he was to provide detailed information to Barker of murders and robberies in London, New York and Jamaica, the traffic of cocaine and firearms into the UK and the movement of Yardies through immigration desks in the UK and United States. He was paid up to £1,000 a time for the 170 detailed reports he gave to Barker, though their sheer scale meant there were rarely the resources to act upon them. But all this time, Green was himself dealing in cocaine and robbing other dealers – with a firearm by his side almost everywhere that he went. 'Everybody carry gun in Jamaica so we do the same in England,' he told detectives who would later question him. 'Sometime we whip it out and shoot up the roof. We just saluting the music.'

During his time as an informer, Green was arrested on three separate occasions by other Metropolitan Police units for possession of crack cocaine but each time his crimes never reached court – until the audacious robbery in Nottingham. Despite this, he was allowed to bring his own associates into the UK, including Rohan Thomas, who had served fourteen years in a Jamaican prison for shooting a policeman, and Cecil Thomas, another Yardie. Both came in on false passports despite the fact that it was known by both Metropolitan Police officers and immigration officials that they had violent pasts and were wanted by the Jamaican authorities. 'Colonel Bumpy' alone was believed to have been involved in around ten murders. Two weeks after the robbery in Nottingham, and despite knowing he was on the run from their Nottinghamshire colleagues, the Met's S011 unit sanctioned a visit by Green to Holland, where he promptly robbed some local dealers at gunpoint with an Uzi machine pistol. Later Steve Barker, after specifically being asked by Nottinghamshire officers and agreeing to help find Green, met the fugitive. Whatever was said during the meeting, Barker did not arrest his informant, allowing him to walk off.

Sir John's report, which went to the Crown Prosecution Service, stopped short of recommending criminal charges against police and immigration officers involved in the handling of Yardie informers, including Green, even though there seemed to have been possible breaches of the Immigration Act. To prove a misconduct charge, 'deliberate failure' or 'wilful neglect' would have to have been shown. What did result from the report, however, were sweeping changes in the way informants were handled by all law enforcement agencies. The recommendations resulted in the new Regulation of Investigatory Powers Act (RIPA) of 2000, which specifies a large number of rules to be followed during the handling of 'human covert resources' – not least that those recruiting informants should be kept away from those handling informants – and that the informants themselves would have to sign a far-reaching contract which lay them open to prosecution if it was not followed. It would inevitably mean that the Green episode would be harder to repeat but it would also mean fewer officers recruiting informants; ultimately, the intelligence which had been pouring in to those fighting to keep drugs and firearms off the streets would often now come only from criminals hoping to take competitors and opponents out of the game. Officers became reluctant to handle informants, fearing they could be prosecuted themselves if their snitches ran riot, as Eaton Green had done.

By 1997 Green, still in his cell on the Isle of Wight, was fighting a deportation application from Nottinghamshire Police. He was already eighteen months past the time when he could have been freed from his six-year sentence, but found the cell walls at Parkhurst more inviting than freedom on the streets. His lawyer argued that a 'very senior' officer from the Met had promised Green, his wife – a British citizen – and his mother protection for the rest of his life and that if he was sent back to Jamaica it would be sending him to certain death, as his status as an informant was now well known due to media coverage of his case. This time the Home Office was not prepared to play ball with Green and the Home Secretary, Jack Straw, took the personal decision to rubber stamp the deportation order. Green was sent back to Kingston a few months later.

John Grieve, head of the S011 team that handled Green, seemed unperturbed. He did, however, apologise for not sending Nottinghamshire the 'right information in the right format at the right time'. He told reporters, 'Green was well worth the investment. It is extremely unfortunate and to the detriment of the people of London that we no longer have him.' Nottinghamshire Police's Head of CID, Phillip Davies, took a different view. 'Informants are essential,' he said. 'However, there are stringent guidelines and procedures which must be observed if the integrity of the system is to be maintained.' No doubt his officers wouldn't disagree with the sentiments of using informants like Green in the ongoing battle against such seemingly impenetrable problems such as Yardie gangs – after all, they have used many such duplicitous informants themselves. Years later, in February 2006, a man whose identity they protected as a witness in a murder case, Trinidadian Trevon Thomas, shot and seriously injured one of their own officers, Rachel Bown, as she investigated a burglary in Lenton. What angered Nottinghamshire Police was that their Scotland Yard counterparts had failed to control their source and then, when presented with the unpalatable truth, tried to protect his identity and stymie the work to arrest him by withholding information. The fallout led to poor relations between the two forces for years. It also led to tensions between local police and the victims of the blues party robbery, who felt Nottinghamshire and the Met were using the black community as pawns in a game between each other.

For Eaton Green it was to be, predictably perhaps, a short-lived existence in Jamaica. On 20 April 2005, police were directed to his Mitsubishi car close to the Central Sorting Office in Kingston. In the boot they found Green's body, wrapped in tarpaulin and riddled with five bullets, signifying a Yardie execution. Green had been lured from his Craig Town home along with two other men, who were also shot dead. It seems that Green, who had been back for more than three years, had carried on his trigger-happy exploits. Police suspected him of a number of crimes, including the murder of a young woman found dumped at Constitution Hill the previous year. Green was the 508th murder victim in Jamaica in a year that was not even four months old. He was thirty-seven, having passed the average life span of a Yardie criminal by some five years. The scale of the death toll demonstrated just how cheap life in Jamaica had become. The ripple effect, seen in Britain with Yardies like Green and his associates, carried with it a cut-price attitude towards life. By the turn of the century, black-on-black violence had become an everyday occurrence in Nottingham, London, Bristol, Manchester and Birmingham. The difference was that the crimes were being committed by a new generation of criminals: so-called homeboys, born and bred into British life who were now setting up their own posses, rapping in patois, dripping in gold jewellery and carrying guns.

CHAPTER 3
HOME BOYS AND POSSES

y the beginning of the 1990s, as the Robinsons fell under the spell of crack cocaine, a new drugs king emerged who would rise to such an influential level he would be feted by politicians in Westminster and police officers alike. I met David St Anthony Francis at a hospital next to Nottinghamshire police headquarters. The meeting had been arranged as part of research into a television documentary about the drugs, gangs and firearms problems being faced by the city in 2004. Francis, by then a veteran of the crime scene, had been out of prison for a few years – urban legend has it that on his release a friend arrived at Derbyshire's Sudbury Prison in Francis' favourite Porsche to pick him up – but the only way I could make contact with him was to visit his jewellery shop in the Sneinton area and drop off a message.

He responded promptly, partly because the message had contained a letter from a former police officer who knew Francis well and had effectively used Francis, albeit unwittingly, as an informant. He arranged to meet me at the private Nottingham Park Hospital, as he was undergoing treatment for diabetes. The hospital is just a stone's throw from police headquarters at

Sherwood Lodge, a place Francis was very familiar with. He was not at the hospital when I arrived, but shortly afterwards a phone call came through. He apologised. 'I'm down at the Ferrari dealership having a look at a car but I won't be long,' he said. I wondered if this was some sort of joke but then, while having a coffee in the hospital's cafeteria, I saw a car draw up. It was a new Bentley. From the driver's side a bulky white man in his late fifties, reminiscent of a minder, got out. There was a pause of a few minutes, then Francis appeared, stepping almost regally out of the passenger door. It transpired that it was his own vehicle and the Bentley dealership had provided him with a driver for the day so that he could browse some new cars down at the Ferrari showroom.

After waiting a few minutes for him to make his way into the building, we wandered down towards his room. The forty-one-year-old Francis, bespectacled and with long dreaded hair, lay himself on his hospital bed, kitted out with his own Versace bedspread, ready to hold court. He was keen to give very little away but exuded a kind of enigmatic charm which you couldn't help but admire. I can't better the description of him by investigative journalist Nick Davies in his book *Dark Heart*. 'Dave positively breathes money,' wrote Davies. 'He wears diamonds in his teeth. They have been drilled into the enamel by a specialist dentist – half a dozen sparkling advertisements for his success in life. When Dave smiles, the rest of the world sees his wealth winking back at them. In his ear, he has another diamond, on his wrist he wears a heavy gold Rolex with diamond studs which he says cost him thirty grand. There is gold around his neck, more gold around his wrists.'

I mentioned to this black Goldfinger the media coverage he had received and in particular Davies's book, in which he prominently features. 'Just as well I'm not the sort of person to bear a grudge, eh?' he said, pointedly. When I raised the subject of wanting to do a documentary with him, he was less than enthusiastic. 'Why would I want to do that? There's nothing in it for me. My days of all that [crime] are over. I'm a grandfather now, I'm just getting on with things at the shop and keeping out of trouble.'

I was interested in his views on white criminals, particularly as the vacuum created by his own arrest and conviction for supplying heroin had been filled by the mob known as the Bestwood Cartel, and signs were that the police were about to bring them down. 'It's taken them long enough,' he said. 'I mean do you think they would have got away with it for so long if they had been black? That's Nottingham Police for you. I'm black so they make me out to be this big dealer. I'm just another nigger dealing drugs to them.' Francis was always quick to play the race card. When I raised the subject of a friend of his who had been forced to quit a high profile job because of allegations of impropriety, he said, 'Ah well you see, he's got his troubles now just because he was trying to help out a few brothers. Don't tell me it's not because he's black.' The fact was, as I was to discover, that Dave Francis had done more to damage the black community in Nottingham than possibly any other individual.

He grew up in Arnold, a leafy suburb to the north of the city. By the time he was fourteen, he had already come to the attention of the police for handling stolen goods. He was, as a youth, very much feared at school, taking on pupils much older than him in the playground and often leaving them bruised and battered. By the time he was a young man he was beating up hardened thugs twice his age. The playground fights didn't always go his way though. One fellow pupil remembered an incident in which Francis almost came off worst – to a girl. 'Dave had these huge hands which gave him the tools to be a formidable fighter. One day this girl, who was very hard and very useful with her fists, got into an argument with Francis and launched at him. As the fight went on the classroom resembled a warzone, there was blood and desks and chairs strewn everywhere and the teacher just ran off because she couldn't handle it. In the end, after her beating seven shades of shit out of him, they called it a draw. Francis so respected her that he then asked her out, even though she had left him battered and bruised.'

By his early twenties, having moved to the Meadows estate, he was a prolific young offender and was on his way to heading the Meadows Posse. This gang of black criminals, which was highly organised by four main leaders, specialised in armed robberies, burglary, handling stolen goods and drugs. To avoid detection they wore Jackson Five-style afro wigs and used stolen cars. If stopped by police they would admit to taking the car but could claim that any evidence found in the vehicle, such as a firearm or overalls that matched the description of the armed raiders, must have been in the car when they nicked it. When a burglar cleared out a gun shop in Carlton, the Meadows Posse took control of the haul of firearms. These guns would regularly turn up at crime scenes over the next decade. Later, Francis even admitted to officers that he had control of the distribution of firearms across the city. 'Guns are fine if they are in the hands of people who know how to use them,' he told officers.

In July 1989, the gang came a cropper after a painting was stolen from the house of an eighty-three-year-old woman in the Bilborough area of Nottingham. Believed to be a Gainsborough worth £1 million, it passed through the hands of Francis and his Meadows Posse; they were arranging for it to be handed over to some unscrupulous art dealers for £300,000. In fact, they were dealing with undercover police officers. Francis stayed on the periphery of the sale and let two other Meadows Posse main men, Tony Slacks and Alvin Henry, arrange it. Slacks met the 'dealers', who included an undercover police officer and a police informant, at the city's Albany Hotel and said he was willing to sell the painting for a discount price. It had been almost a year since the burglary and the Posse were keen to shift it. Slacks and Henry arranged to meet the 'art dealer' himself at a Gamston Airport, near Retford in Nottinghamshire, where the exchange would take place. An undercover officer flew up from London in a light aircraft. While the Meadows gang had no inkling they were dealing with undercover officers, the police were also unaware that the gang planned to rip them off. Henry and Slacks were armed with sawn-off shotguns and had brought flex to tie up their victims. When it came to the exchange, Slacks became suspicious and asked to see the money again. Then he realised it was a set-up. 'We're both playing same game,' he told the undercover officer. 'That's not the money. I was going to rip you off but you are doing the same.'

The incident descended into chaos as police moved in to arrest Slacks and Henry. Slacks was apprehended as he tried to run off, but Henry threatened to shoot some of the unarmed officers and managed to escape. He was arrested a few days later. Despite feeling he had been fitted up, Slacks was given twelve years for his part in the crime, which included possession of two firearms. Henry was cleared of conspiracy to rob but convicted of firearms offences and sentenced to three years. The painting turned out to be a fake and was probably worth just a few hundred pounds.

The case dealt a severe blow to the Meadows gang and, though they had all grown up together, they began to distrust each other. Then they were caught up in another case, after attempting to rob a store in Nottingham. Again, police seemed to have inside infor-mation and the robbery went wrong, resulting in the arrest of one of the Posse, Godfrey Hibbert, an ex-boxer from the Meadows. A white man called Kevin Morledge, who had acted as a dogsbody for the gang – Francis called his white helpers 'tampaxes' because they were on a string controlled by him and would absorb any unwelcome problems around him – had been approached by the police after he was arrested on burglary charges. Francis evaded the police and was busy devising a cunning plan to destroy the police case against the Posse. He gained access to the depositions in the attempted robbery case and knew who was saying what to their solicitor and what evidence the police had. In Morledge, he saw an opportunity to wreck the police probe. Officers had been to see Morledge in Lincoln Prison after he let it be known that he wanted to speak to them about a deal. Before they could make a follow-up visit, Francis smuggled a tape recorder to Morledge. When two officers from Nottinghamshire Police arrived again at Lincoln Prison, they outlined the help Morledge might receive if he gave evidence that Hibbert and Francis were involved in armed robbery. Morledge secretly taped the conversation, and then got the tape out to Francis, who edited the recording to make the case against the detectives even more damning.

By the time the case came to trial, in December 1989, Morledge was claiming the police had tried to get him to make a false confession in return for immunity against prosecution. The judge at Nottingham Crown Court dismissed the jury and then heard, in closed sessions, about the tape recordings. Though the police denied making the offers and said the tape should be scrutinised forensically to see if it had been tampered with, the judge had little option but to dismiss the case against both Hibbert and Morledge. Five years later, Morledge received £10,000 from Nottinghamshire Police as compensation. Dave Francis was once again safe, and as Hibbert had ended up going to prison anyway after being convicted of a separate drugs offence, could now crown himself King of the Meadows Posse in his own right.

But the fact was that by 1991, there really was no Meadows Posse left, or at least not as it had been. Francis was still organising the movement of stolen jewellery and gold but had moved into the drugs business in a big way by 1990. Though he owned a gold shop, he still made regular trips to Birmingham to see two contacts who were prepared to melt it down for him, no questions asked. Still, Francis saw that the drugs business was where the money was to be made. There were two drugs which were bringing in colossal profits for those wanting to trade. Ecstasy sales were booming. It was clubland time in Nottingham and people were coming from London, Manchester, Sheffield, Leeds and Birmingham to enjoy the sounds and hedonistic nightlife at venues like Venus, as well as at illegal raves. Francis organised security for some events, along with nights at the Marcus Garvey Centre, which would spill over into violence when rival gangs fought it out on the neutral turf of Radford.

Controlling the doors at large raves effectively meant control of the drugs going into the venues. Francis's street dealers could sell the pills without any worries and he could cream off the profits. A genuine ecstasy pill, most of which were coming in from factories in Holland, sold for around £20 in the UK at the time, and dealers were making huge profits. Speed was also still one of the main drugs of choice in Nottingham. Some said it had been around since the days of the miners, who would take doses to stay awake on long shifts underground. By the late 1980s, the mines were all but gone and the speed culture became a recreational one. The rate of consumption during the late 1980s and early 1990s was such that police were often baffled when they came to make busts. Frequently they would discover that in the few days it had taken it to organise the raid, kilos and kilos had already been sold off and consumed, suggesting a quick turnover.

Cocaine was also increasing in availability. It was already destroying the Robinson family, some of whom were members of the St Ann's Crew (or St Ann's Massive or Playboy Posse). During his trips to Birmingham to melt down the gold he was accumulating, Francis hooked up with the two Birmingham brothers whose feud with the Robinsons had led to Eaton Green's infamous blues party robbery. Francis believed he could help the brothers make inroads into the Nottingham drug scene and at the same time gain help in distributing cocaine with some heavy backers who would not fear other traders from the St Ann's estate. But this move, together with potential flashpoints at the nights he ran at the Marcus Garvey Centre in Lenton, meant trouble was always just round the corner. It ultimately brought him into conflict with the Yardies and Francis decided to strike out further on his own.

By 1993, Francis had served a number of spells in prison and had thirty-odd convictions dating back to 1976. They included possession of a firearm, actual bodily harm, unlawful sexual intercourse and possession of drugs. Now he embarked on a new criminal project, building up a network of contacts who ranged from the influential within local politics and the police to the useable young wannabes who saw the chance of a career doing the bidding of Nottingham's premier gangster by becoming street dealers. Francis was to achieve this partly by getting himself a proper job. He applied for, and amazingly landed, a posting as the manager of a local drugs charity project which specialised in 24/7 outreach work for addicts, particularly those ravaged by crack cocaine. The charity, the Association for the Prevention of Addiction (APA), later to become Addaction, was setting up units across the country and Nottingham addicts were to be among the first outside London to benefit from its Open Doors crack awareness team. Francis, despite his convictions and his flamboyant lifestyle, was the ideal candidate as far as the APA was concerned. Here was an intelligent, streetwise black man with whom drug users could identify. He breezed through the interview.

Former CID boss Peter Coles remembers Francis visiting him at the time. 'He had just been to the interview and he drove down to Central Police Station and parked his Porsche up in the garages there. He was keen to stress his life of crime was over, he said he had made four million pounds by that time and he was going to be a Good Samaritan now and help the community. I was aghast. I couldn't understand how this man who was wearing an Armani suit, driving a Porsche and had all these convictions could have got the interview, let alone the job. Didn't anyone think to ask why this man, dripping in jewellery with a Rolex watch worth fifty thousand pounds on his wrist, would want a job as a minor social worker? These crack awareness teams were beginning to spring up all over the country and ironically there was another individual who had done a similar thing down in north London. Francis knew this man well through the national drug supply network. He was higher up in the chain than Francis and I think Francis aspired to be someone like him and I think that's where he got the idea from. It was a perfect cover for him to branch out into large-scale dealing.'

With Yardies seemingly attracted to Nottingham likes bees to honey, Francis was keen to avoid street dealing and the hassles it could bring. He embraced his new role with gusto, raising his profile as a bona fide drugs worker, attending Home Office select committee hearings at Westminster on the crack cocaine problem and appearing in an ITV television documentary to talk about the problems facing crack users. During this time he was in fact building up his power base and recruiting people who would later become his dealers. As the main CAT worker, he would be in and out of police cells on an almost daily basis to offer 'advice' to addicts who had been arrested. He also had access to depositions in criminal cases. This all provided him with useful information, particularly when it came to who was grassing up who and the police's weak points. Francis's advice to those languishing in a cell and dreaming of weaning themselves off heroin or crack was, 'Come and work for Dave, I'll look after you.'

Francis told newspapers the Government was not doing enough to solve the cocaine problem that was blighting the city – and he sounded convincing. He waxed lyrical about what needed to be done and how the work carried out by him and his band of followers was an essential part of that process: 'Crack cocaine users are people who have lost their houses, their jobs, sold most of their possessions and are no longer capable of looking after their children,' he told reporters. 'Their lives are chaotic. There is not a lot of point in giving them a nine-thirty appointment for four weeks' time because they are never going to make it. For years they virtually denied that there was a crack problem. Most of the calls we get are at about two or three in the morning when people are on a down. The two things we don't give them is drugs or money. But we can give them food, liquid if they're dehydrated and we can listen. At other times we can help them sort out court problems, warrants, Aids tests.' He wasn't afraid to be controversial in his interviews either. 'The fact is that there is a good side to most drugs. If you're telling people it's all bad they are bound to start looking up to people who look as though they are having a great time. The issue is that there is a downside as well and to show people that side and make it clear to them where they are likely to end up,' he said.

It was the perfect ruse to cover his tracks, for Francis was dealing in heroin, cocaine and crack cocaine, ecstasy and weed. He was, in fact, one of the biggest dealers in the Midlands. He also had a job which paid him £21,000 a year from the public purse, which he drove to in a Mercedes convertible worth £50,000. He also changed his BMW every year. He kept a beautiful mistress who earned a living from high-class prostitution; a house in

Jamaica in his mother's name which resembled the White House; several properties in Nottingham, including a three-bedroomed house in Compton Acres, a stone's throw from his Meadows home turf and kitted out with the latest Bang & Olufsen hi-fi; a flat in the appropriately named Francis Street in Hyson Green; diamonds drilled into his teeth and gold dripping from his fingers. He was sitting on anti-drug and child prostitution problem-solving panels alongside the likes of Nottingham South MP Alan Simpson and former Chief Constable Dan Crompton and had influence over the spending of £170,000 a year from the likes of the Department of Health and other Government bodies.

Francis's deputy at CAT, Henry Warner, was his first lieutenant in this booming drugs empire and Francis had also bought the loyalty of many of those going through the Open Doors offices, or working alongside him, by selling them gear or getting them to sell for him. He was fast becoming out of reach from the authorities, not least because he had built up a wide network of influential people who would tip him off about any investigation into his activities. And he was clever. He knew the road to power and people's weaknesses and he exploited them ruthlessly. Each time the forces of law and order got close to him, there were people willing to help him. Some were in lowly places, like the young white 'tampaxes' who served him; others were in high places, some of them white, middle class individuals willing to cry racism if Francis was criticised and to say, 'This man is a good guy, he is doing great work. We should be applauding him, not doing him down.' Others began asking themselves: what does Dave Francis have on these people? What power did he wield over them that they felt an obligation to support him when many knew or suspected he was one of the bad guys?

So frustrated were the police by the lack of evidence against him that some even resorted to illegal tactics to try to nail him. On one occasion, an officer arranged for a stolen credit card to be placed inside Francis's car overnight. The following day a call was made to local traffic police to pull over his vehicle. It resulted in his arrest and detention in a cell for a few hours, which enabled a warrant to be obtained to search his house and safe – which in turn helped police to gather intelligence about where Francis was keeping his money. But it was still not enough to nail him. He had to be caught red-handed if anything was to stick.

During 1997, Francis came to the attention of the local health authority after complaints were lodged by some fellow workers who had not been corrupted by his charm and wealth. They were prepared to stand up and be counted, even if it put their careers at risk. Sue Loakes and Tony Herbert were among a number of ex-workers and clients who knew what Francis was up to and could not stand to see what was happening any longer. In November 1996, they went to Nottingham Health Authority, which partially funded the crack awareness programme, to complain that Francis was actually selling large amounts of crack cocaine, heroin and weed. Not only this, some alleged he was dealing in firearms and prostitutes. He was, they said, nothing more than a charlatan who was using the CAT project as a prop to hide his drug-dealing empire. The APA launched an inquiry, but by the following March Francis had been exonerated. Worse still, he was taking retribution against those who had spoken out against him. Tony Herbert found his car vandalised and several clients who had been brave enough to speak to the inquiry received anonymous telephone threats. It was clear that dark forces were at work. How could the APA committee reject over-whelming evidence from more than twenty professional workers whose clients were on the frontline, witnessing Francis in action every day? Most had never even met each other and so could clearly not be tainted by association.

When material started to leak out to the *Guardian* newspaper, it became clear just how much power Francis had accumulated. Among those speaking up for him were MP Alan Simpson and the chairman of the APA, Sir Geoffrey Errington. Sir Geoffrey told the *Guardian* that not a scrap of real evidence had emerged which could be backed up and that critics were tainting Francis's character unfairly. 'He's a good guy as far as we are concerned and he is a jolly worthwhile employee,' said Sir Geoffrey. 'We couldn't find a spark of evidence to back up any of the allegations. These things were rumours. I don't think we have been fooled.' Simpson also spoke to the inquiry, telling them Francis was the victim of malicious gossip at the hands of people who had their own agenda. Staff that had made the allegations about Francis were threatened with legal action by the APA if they were repeated. However, by 1997, faced with a particularly damaging article in the *Guardian* which 'outed' him as a drug dealer, Francis decided to resign from Open Doors. Nottinghamshire Police meantime had launched a secret operation against him, convinced there was truth in the allegations and determined this time to nail him.

By 1998, Operation Odin was well underway. A meeting took place in a car park off the M1. In a car were two detectives from the Major Crime Unit and they were waiting for a man who would help unlock some of Francis's secrets. The silent stranger who greeted the two officers looked more like a down-and-out than the specialist operator that he was. He got into the back of the car with stealth-like ease, the two detectives jumping with a start. The mystery man sported a tattoo on his wrist, a snake entwined around a dagger. The symbol could mean only one thing to the detectives babysitting him: he was either a serving, or former, Special Forces operative. The car weaved its way back towards Nottingham, taking the ring road past the Queen's Medical Centre and out towards leafy West Bridgford.

Detectives knew that Francis would be out of the way for only a few hours. He had taken his mistress to Luton Airport, where she would make one of her regular flights to Switzerland. Officers had also carried out research on all Francis's properties to determine which one was most likely to provide the wealth of intelligence they needed to bust him – and what sort of security they needed to bypass. They already knew they would have to get past a highly sophisticated alarm system. Then there was the small problem of the Doberman guard dog. Their target was his home in Maythorn Close, Compton Acres. Their plan was to break in, immobilise the dog temporarily and plant a device which would allow investigators to hear his conversations. It was, of course easier said than done, unless you had a bit of help from some extremely talented individuals. Arriving at their destination, the mysterious tattooed man was out of the car and up the street almost before the detectives had a chance to pull up. He disappeared around the corner. Within fifteen minutes, a call from the senior detective in charge of the operation made it clear that the man was on his way back to the car, the bug having been planted safely. These were pieces of equipment which could break down at any time. Every month the batteries had to be changed and, at the conclusion of each operation, the equipment had to be retrieved. These mysterious specialists were invaluable. 'These were guys who could tell the type of key and lock needed for a property and any security systems to bypass with a mere glance,' one senior Nottinghamshire officer told me. 'They could also break into the most difficult locations and you just knew they would leave not so much as a strand of hair behind.' In Francis' case, detectives would eventually bug a passenger seat on a jumbo jet carrying him to Jamaica in a bid to learn more about his conversations. According to one very senior officer, this may be the only time a police force in the country has undertaken such a radical move to monitor a criminal target.

Months of surveillance work would now be undertaken, but the validity of the material coming through on the bugs would have be tested every month in order to get ongoing Home Office approval. If there was no incriminating material on the bugs, there would be a problem gaining the authority to use the devices the following month. The officers listened in as Francis briefed his foot soldiers. 'Be very paranoid, don't trust anybody. There are people out there who would love to destroy us so keep your eyes and ears open and don't say anything unless you have to,' he told them. 'We can't fuck around. We've got to be the best team, the cheapest and the quickest to get the gear out, otherwise the other crews will be on top. I don't want us getting into a warzone with any Yardies.'

Francis's and Henry Warner's mobiles were bugged and every day, against the background noise of the repeated cable TV soap operas that his crew seemed to be avid fans of, they heard him organising kilo after kilo of the brown heroin. Francis was only just keeping up with demand as sales soared, partly as a consequence of the crack epidemic sweeping Nottingham. Crackheads found that one way to reduce the drop from their cocaine high was to smoke or inject heroin. Many were therefore fighting two addictions at the same time. Prostitutes, some of whom Francis was pimping, were among his best customers. The crack kept them working through the night and the 'brown' comforted them when they eventually got back home. It took the pain away for a brief few hours, until they woke and needed a toke on their crack pipe, starting the cycle all over again.

Francis was making extraordinary profits and the police knew it. Six officers monitored conversations round the clock from the listening post in Wilford as Francis organised his shipments. He was talking to dealers in London, mainly Nigerian contacts he had built up over the years, and was dealing with people like Ramzy Khachik, a major supplier from Leicester, who had made some of his wealth from the city's notorious 'hotdog wars'. Khachik would later be jailed for nineteen years for conspiracy to supply class A drugs. In addition, Francis had contacts in Manchester, Newcastle and Birmingham. Meanwhile, officers on the ground were taking out Francis's troops. A number of his key street dealers had already been taken arrested as part of Operation Odin and its forerunner, Operation Diamond Back, and he was clearly starting to feel vulnerable. That would mean, it was hoped, that Francis would have to start taking more risks and ultimately get his hands dirty, which might just result in them catching him with drugs – they could only hope for such luck

By February 1999, the end was approaching as the accumulation of material indicated that he was clearly selling heroin and cocaine on a large scale. In the final weeks of the operation more than seven kilos of heroin alone passed through Francis' hands. After allowing four kilos to go through in less than two weeks, the team was ready to move. They picked up information through the bugs that there was to be another kilo delivery of heroin that evening coming in a hired VW Golf from south London, which Francis had had to organise himself. Better still, Francis – running out of troops he could trust or who had not been arrested – would be at his flat in Francis Street, Hyson Green, to take stock of what had come in, weigh it and help bag it up. Alongside the bugs, Nottinghamshire Police had also brought in a black undercover officer a year earlier who was so convincing he had been accepted as a trusted Yardie drug dealer by the local criminal underworld and local police officers. The *pièce de résistance* was that Francis's inner sanctum had been penetrated: Nottinghamshire Police had 'turned' one of Francis' loyal crew, a heroin addict they had busted during a low-key operation. The tactics that won him over were reminiscent of the TV series *Life on Mars*: according to one of the officers involved, he was taken to a desolate area in the dead of night by two detectives, who then retrieved a spade from the boot of their car, pulled the petrified young man from the car and told him to start digging his own grave. He later provided important information about Francis and his movements.

On 23 February, police made their move. After the VW Golf arrived carrying the heroin from London, they waited until they were sure Francis was inside his flat before they burst in. Their startled target was standing at the top of the staircase, mobile phone in one hand and thousands in cash spilling from his pockets. Shocked he may have been, but to the officers he appeared his usual confident self, almost as if it was all some silly misunderstanding. After all, he was Dave Francis, King of the Meadows, the man everyone looked up to.

Francis initially tried to make out that the drugs were nothing to do with him and that he was renting out the flat to someone who had brought the drugs in. He was already aware that he would be one of the last to face the courts out of an army of some 150 soldiers he commanded; most of them had been removed from circulation over the previous nine months by Operations Diamond Back and Odin. Nottinghamshire Police had managed to get to Francis only because he had believed his own invincibility and because they had painstakingly removed the tentacles of his operation from the foot soldiers up to the man himself by removing, brick by brick, the business pyramid which Francis oversaw. This was a tried and tested technique against large-scale drug dealers which usually resulted in the 'main man' being flushed out from his or her safety zone. If the tactic worked it would result in the target being left isolated; all around him the network of street dealers who had previously hidden, supported him and ultimately protected him, left in tatters. There was also the issue of the assets Francis held in various parts of the world. There was at that time no assets recovery unit to track down ill-gotten gains and, even if there had been, it would still have had to prove in court that Francis was the true holder of those assets.

It would be a further year before any kind of case came to court. In the meantime, Francis converted to the Islamic faith while in prison. It meant that he could order his own prison food and have some time on his own set aside for prayer. It could also become a useful tool in mitigation should he face conviction at Crown Court. He had used the technique once before, converting to the Christian faith while on remand previously. Nevertheless, Francis also believed he held good information that he could trade with the police to reduce his sentence if he were convicted or forced to plead guilty through the weight of evidence against him. His trusted lieutenant, Warner, had already pleaded guilty at the first chance that he got, which lengthened the odds on Francis being able to squirm his way out of trouble. 'Whenever Francis had been arrested and he knew he was in trouble he would always contact his favourite solicitor,' said former CID head Peter Coles. 'He would then let it be known he wanted to do a deal with the police. In reality all this meant was that he wanted us to talk him through a deal and then he would hope that he could make some use of it in the courtroom to try to sully the case against him. We got very wise to that though after a while.'

By the time he faced Nottingham Crown Court in March 2000, charged with conspiracy and possession with intent to supply class A drugs, Francis was ready to accept some guilt, but right up until his last day in court he told officers he wanted a deal. The full details of that deal are not known but Francis had planned to reveal some of the police's covert tactics in open court, which could have damaged future operations and may have led police to considering a deal. There is also speculation that he provided information on drug consignments being awaited by other major dealers in the city. Whatever the truth, in the end Francis pleaded guilty to possessing half a kilo of heroin with intent to supply. Another charge which could potentially have added another seven years to his sentence was ordered to lie on file by Judge Dudley Bennett. Jailing him for seven years, Judge Bennett summed it all up in a sentence: 'I have to deal with people day after day in this court who appear before me after committing crimes to fund their drug habit. Because of your involvement in the past with trying to stop all that in your work, you more than anybody else should have known the misery of people who had become addicted.'

Francis, his dreaded hair cut short and tipping his glasses back towards his face, looked like a trendy academic trying to make sense of a spurious argument. He would be able to do this stretch standing on his head. But the Operation Odin team were ecstatic. Regardless of the sentence, they were proud that the case had stuck and they had nailed their man. The command team of Nottinghamshire Police lost no time in helping the headline-makers turn Francis into the city's premier black criminal. There were red faces in Westminster too, with MP Alan Simpson admitting, 'Those who said he was bad have been proved right and I was wrong.'

Francis had claimed to speak for the black man in the street and to want to help drug addicts. It had been a sham. He was dealing addictive illegal drugs to his 'brothers' and used women without remorse. 'His runners have the rocks that the working girls want, so he has power over them,' wrote Nick Davies. 'Sometimes, he sends them down to London where he has friends who run brothels. Sometimes, he keeps them for himself.' He was the worst thing that could have happened to Nottingham's black community. He was concerned only with power and wealth. Yet despite trips to Jamaica and investigations in Switzerland, Nottinghamshire Police were unable to trace the millions that Francis had told Peter Coles he had gained. Once out of prison in

2004, he would enjoy plenty of trips to Jamaica to the white house he had bought with his sullied profits.

There was a price to pay for the success of nailing Francis and his foot soldiers: the vacuum left by the removal of his operation would ultimately lead to the worst sustained outbreak of territorial violence ever seen on the streets of the city, pave the way for the growth of a white crime gang whose proclivity for brutality eclipsed even that of the Yardies, and ultimately would shatter the reputation of Nottingham.

CHAPTER 4
TURF WAR IN THE NG TRIANGLE

The death of Lloyd Robinson failed to bring peace. Gang conflict, particularly between the St Ann's and Radford Posses and the Meadows, continued unabated and firearms became a regular feature on the city's streets. Previously their use had been largely confined to the occasional armed robbery crew hitting a security van. The Yardies changed all that, importing the capricious violence of the Jamaica slums. 'Shoot or be shot' became their motto. The homeboys from St Ann's, Radford and the Meadows – known as the NG Triangle after the 'NG' postcode – embraced the Yardie gun culture and accompanying gangsta rap lyrics, and soon a firearm was a must-have fashion accessory. Using it was an even greater measure of street status. There was almost a mathematical equation to it: the juice of the firearm equalled the respect you received from fellow gang members, so some of them would arm themselves with rapid-firing Uzi or Ingram Mac 10 submachine guns. Gang members tried to justify it by saying that they needed the gun to protect themselves from rivals who would otherwise rob them; the truth was that many of them got a kick from carrying a gun.

Weapons were easy enough to get hold of but varied in quality. You could pay more than £1,000 for a smuggled, new Beretta handgun that had no ballistic history, but others favoured cheaper, older firearms that were supposedly decommissioned but had been reactivated by someone with basic engineering knowledge and tools. These sold for less than £100. There were other guns, such as the Brocock, that was essentially an air-pressured weapon which, with a bit of DIY engineering, was capable of firing live rounds. The ammunition was difficult to get hold of at first but soon manufacturing live rounds became a mini-cottage industry in the cellars of houses. In Derbyshire, a small family-run farm selling eggs developed a highly profitable sideline – it sold thousands of decommissioned guns throughout the 1990s, all quite legally, until its owners began telling customers how they could reactivate the weapons to working order, firing live rounds. This little shop of horrors, run by William Greenwood and his son Mitchell in Little Eaton, sold more than 4,000 deactivated guns, from Uzis and Kalashnikovs to Lugers and Berettas, and with a nod and wink they would tell purchasers how the weapon could be restored to full utility. They even sold the engineering kits needed to reactivate the weapons for as little as £45 and offered their own DIY advice.

UK restrictions on gun ownership had been tightened considerably after the massacres perpetrated by Michael Ryan in Hungerford in 1987 and Thomas Hamilton in Dunblane in 1996. And a working Uzi was a prohibited weapon in Britain by any criteria. But such weapons could be imported by registered dealers who pledged to 'de-act' them. This involves cutting away seventy-five per cent of the firing pin, welding up the chamber mechanism, then plugging the barrel with a steel ball to ensure it can't be drilled out again. The gun would then be sent away to a proof house. There a certificate guaranteeing that it was useless could be acquired. However, the same 'useless' firearm could be reactivated using the basic engineering skills.

One drug dealer I met in the summer of 2001 bragged obsessively about his guns. He said he kept them in a secret compartment in the boot of his car, and knew all about reactivating weapons; he had bought an Uzi from a dealer in east London. He was paranoid about Nottingham criminals catching up with him and said he needed a firearm around him at all times to protect himself. He was known to police in both his home county of Lincolnshire and in Nottinghamshire and had passed over information about the gangsters he mixed with. His name was Jeremy Earls. Earls was a thin, wiry man in his thirties whose temperament could change like Dr Jekyll's. One minute he seemed haunted, the next he was a wild-eyed paranoiac bursting with energy. He often used the word 'suicided' and said this was how gangsters made murders look like suicides in order to get away with them.

Shortly after I – and the two police forces – lost contact with him in August 2001, he shot dead two young men in Lincoln. They were half-brothers who had been living in Earls' old home after a flat swap. One was a talented, twenty-six-year-old poet, Andrew Walker, the other a seventeen-year-old A-level student, Alexander Woodcraft, who had never even met his killer until his death. Earl, a paranoid schizophrenic, had become obsessed about the flat swap, feeling he had got the worst of the deal, and confided in friends that he wanted to move back to his old address because he didn't like the place he was living at in Cambridge. He also believed that a major Nottingham gang boss, referred to later in this book as the Taxman, was trying to kill him. In his warped mental state, Earl shot the half-brothers through the head as one of them lay in the bath and the other slept, then drove to an isolated area of Lincolnshire, took a large number of tranquillizers and turned the gun on himself. He tried to make his suicide appear as a murder, positioning the gun to make it look like someone else had shot him, and left a tape recording with his solicitor predicting his own bloody end, saying the tape should be played only in the event of his violent death. It was a bizarre attempt to engineer a fake conspiracy around his death and those of the two innocent young men. The weapon which ended all three lives was a reactivated Uzi submachine pistol, probably bought for less than £400.

The police were aware of the reactivated gun problem as far back as 1994, when Sir Paul Condon, then Metropolitan Police Commissioner, raised the issue. Yet between 1990 and 1994 alone, the Greenwoods of Little Eaton sold thousands of guns to a former Sussex special constable, Anthony Mitchell, who in turn sold them to other middle men, who in turn sold them to criminals. Ballistics evidence of these weapons turned up at crime scenes across the UK and Ireland: often the evidence would be a body torn apart by bullets. William and Mitchell Greenwood, partly due to evidence from Anthony Mitchell, who was himself convicted at the Old Bailey and who gave evidence against the father and son, were sentenced in March 2004 at Derby Crown Court to seven years in prison. Derbyshire Police could account for only twenty per cent of the weapons they sold and by 2008 there were still 3,000 unaccounted for, though a huge investigation continues through the auspices of the National Ballistics Intelligence Service into their whereabouts. By 2008, these weapons had been positively linked to eight murders and numerous shootings. Current estimates as to the numbers of deactivated weapons range between 80,000 and 140,000 nationally.

In August 2002, police raided two houses in the Sneinton and Sherwood areas. The homes belonged to twenty-two-year-old Michael Westwood. Officers found equipment to manufacture home-made ammunition and conversion equipment to turn harmless replicas into lethal weapons, as well as empty boxes that contained a number of Brocock weapons, favoured by Yardie gunmen. Detective Chief Inspector Ian Waterfield said Westwood had used premises at Cedar Road, Sherwood, as a mini factory to manufacture bullets from blank rounds of ammunition and convert firearms deemed safe. 'At the end of the day, we have no idea where those firearms have gone,' he admitted. Often the converted firearms did not have proper rifling in the barrel, which would lead to a bullet tumbling from the barrel rather than coming out in a straight line. As firearms expert Mel Musson pointed out, converted firearms can lead to more indiscriminate damage and the potential for innocent bystanders being hit in a gun battle. 'From a tumbling bullet, it is going to be a bigger area hitting you and it is going to cause a larger wound,' he said. Westwood was later jailed for eight years for the gun offences.

The gunslingers, armed by people like the Greenwoods, would hide the weapons at the houses of their 'baby mothers' – down the back of cookers, buried in back gardens, in the toilet cisterns, anywhere with easy access – sometimes without the knowledge of the numerous women they were sleeping with. Dealers were regularly taking their firearms into nightclubs and were getting younger. On a number of occasions, clubgoers fled the dance floor when the gunmen decided to salute the DJ and fire off rounds into the ceiling, a ritual made customary by the Yardies. In November 1999, an eighteen-year-old from Birmingham was arrested after letting off his gun in Beatroot nightclub in Nottingham's Lace Market during a fight. Having the firearm to hand while out on the town gave the gunmen a feeling of having the 'juice', or power, over their rivals. By the time someone had been shot and killed it was too late to see the damage that was being done by becoming a dedicated follower of this fashion.

Black, white and Asian youths were being corrupted by the gang mentality. It started at school, where children as young as five or six were becoming aware that there was rivalry between St Ann's and Radford and the Meadows, the north and the south sides of the city. They even had their own shopping centres marked out as territory. The Victoria Centre was the domain of the St Ann's and Radford crews while the Broadmarsh Centre was Meadows Posse territory. Young gang members had their postcode tattooed on their bodies to mark their affiliations. As one former gang member described it, 'The older youths are always on the lookout for young talent that they can mould into their foot soldiers, the ones who start at the bottom of the ladder taking all the risks. They want youngsters who they can get to be runners for them or to do other work that does not put them in the police's firing line. They start off by giving them a few quid and then that's it, they are in the crew biking some wraps of heroin or coke to some address up the road for the older lads. They could see that in a few years they would be able to command their own lads to do the work they were doing and they would be the ones with the wads of cash and the respect.'

The early 1990s saw very young gangs running amok. One group from the St Ann's estate was dubbed the Brat Pack and became infamous around the city, clocking up crimes and arrests like they had been born for it. The gang was fourteen-strong, ranged in age between twelve and sixteen, and was of mixed race. Between them, they were arrested more than 250 times. One fifteen-year-old leader managed to amass 500 convictions but was still out on the streets ready to 'twoc' (take without consent) his next car. These youngsters had a great deal in common: they had all come from single-parent backgrounds, they all lacked stable male role models in their families, and they all believed that it was their right to take from others what they did not have.

After the demolition of many of the terraced houses in St Ann's and the redevelopment of the area, the city council began to allocate a large number of vacant properties to single-parent families. These parents, almost always mothers, were often living on benefits of around £75 a week and trying to bring up two or more children. It didn't take a mathematician to work out that if the mothers couldn't get the youngsters what they wanted, they would end up, through their own devices, getting it themselves. The Brat Pack was symptomatic of this problem. Members went around the estate taking what they wanted. They craved the best training shoes and the best clothes and saw nothing wrong in stealing. 'It's called taxing,' said one. And it was; just as it had been depicted in the tales of Robin Hood. It was the taking from the haves by the have-nots, and morality did not come into it. The generation of children brought up through the Thatcher years were infected by the materialism of the age; at the same time as the community spirit was dying, the age of the individual was born. These children had quickly worked out that there was no room for any social responsibility towards anyone else: it was dog eat dog and only the strongest survived. More than that, having no conception at all of social discipline, they had within themselves a perverted sense of being society's victims and so, they thought, were justified in doing whatever they liked. The gang would carry out the most audacious crimes, always carrying the business card of their solicitor and demanding the right to silence if they were caught. When they were arrested they were simply recycled back into the same world by the courts on supervision orders and went back to doing what they did best: breaking into houses.

On one weekend in May 1992, four of the Brat Pack, the youngest twelve and the eldest fifteen, set out to rob an old people's home. They planned the job like veterans, cutting the telephone wires to Mellors Court to prevent anyone calling the police, then storming into the building armed with a sword and a plank with nails in it. As staff tried to close the door between them and the elderly residents, the group battered their way through and robbed the terrified staff and OAPs. They rifled residents' handbags and a one-armed fruit machine and made off with a video recorder and television.

In the early hours of 30 November 1997, Shane Thompson, a nineteen-year-old who belonged to a gang from Radford and St Ann's, was beaten to death outside a pub. The attack was sparked by a seemingly innocuous event. Some lads from the Meadows had been in the car park of the Tennyson Centre on Forest Road, where a dance had been taking place. A small number of St Ann's and Radford youths saw one of the Meadows crew spit on their car. This was disrespect and, as far as they were concerned, someone would have to pay. After scouting for the Meadows Posse, the St Ann's and Radford crew spotted them outside a Kentucky Fried Chicken takeaway on Alfreton Road. Wearing masks and carrying baseball bats, Thompson and his crew ran at the Meadows youths and struck an eighteen-year-old on the head. He produced a handgun and fired three shots into the air. The gun was only firing blanks but it caused terror among Thompson's friends and they fled up Alfreton Road. A chase ensued, with around fifteen youths from the Meadows, some now with planks of wood and chains, targeting Thompson and three other youths. Thompson was cornered near a pub, the Two In The Bush. He was struck and careered into a telephone box, startling its occupant, but struggled on before he was felled by several blows. The group then launched into a sickening orgy of kicks and blows with a baseball bat and other implements. Thompson, on his own, could only cry out, 'Stop it, stop it, you're going to kill me.' The youths eventually ran off and left him semi-conscious on the ground, where he was nursed by the pub manager, who had come out to investigate the commotion. He rang an ambulance, which arrived at about 2.20am. Shane was able to say a few words to ambulance staff but his condition deteriorated soon after he was taken for an x-ray. He died at the Queens Medical Centre eighteen hours later.

There were many witnesses to the attack and a large number of youths from both groups were arrested in the immediate aftermath. Predictably, some witnesses began to pull out from making statements after receiving threatening phone calls. Nevertheless, in October 1998, six of the Meadows crew and one of the St Ann's Posse eventually faced a jury. It was a messy trial. It was clear not all the offenders were in the dock and at least one of the Meadows Posse had fled to Jamaica with the help of his influential gangster father. Even though the prosecution had the help of one of the Meadows gang, who was willing to give evidence about who delivered the fatal blows, the trial descended into chaos when he could not identify five of the six charged with murder and violent disorder. On 5 November, trial judge Mr Justice Poole directed that all seven defendants should be cleared.

With some degree of optimism, Mr Justice Poole wasted no time in telling the courtroom that the case should mark the end of the gang violence between the NG Triangle groups: 'The decent people of St Ann's, Radford, the Meadows and adjacent areas are long overdue a rest from the friction between these factions. It brings nothing but misery and unhappiness to all concerned and now would be as good a time as any for calm and common sense to prevail,' he said. The communities involved did try to solve some of the deep-seated problems surrounding the gangs, but those who mourned another victim of the violence knew that justice had let them down once again. The Concerned Citizens Group, as they called themselves, set up a conference at Nottingham's Albert Hall in an attempt to end the postcode division at the heart of the troubles and try to bring the communities together following

Shane Thompson's death. Hundreds of people attended the black youth summit in February 1999. But it didn't stop the violence. It couldn't. Graffiti started to appear on street signs in St Ann's: 'St Ann's r pussies. 2-0'. This referred not to some innocuous football game but to the deaths of Lloyd Robinson and Shane Thompson, and was taunting of the cruellest kind. The prevailing view among many young people was that justice was nothing to do with the system any more; justice was what you meted out in your own way. If the courts could not punish people for wrongdoing then they would take matters into their own hands.

In the intervening period, a youth called Levi Walker, whose uncle Barrington Walker had been murdered in a machete attack outside the Marcus Garvey Centre in April 1996, was himself attacked by a gang wielding knives and a machete. They burst in as he slept at his girlfriend's house in Radford on 21 January 1998. Walker was a regular visitor to Nottingham and claimed that he had been mistakenly identified as one of the killers of Shane Thompson. His attackers had shouted, 'You killed our brethren Shane and you must die.' Walker suffered multiple injuries and went into cardiac arrest. He was in a coma for three months. He later recovered enough to carry on his own violent criminal ventures. As part of the Raiders gang from the West Midlands, he would be jailed for life in 2006 for the murder of twenty-year-old Iraq war hero Narel Sharpe in Smethwick, Birmingham. Sharpe was shot dead by Walker as he strolled home after a night out, simply because Walker, who went by the street name 'Creeper', fancied the gold chain the soldier was wearing. Walker was also one of the gunmen who pumped five bullets, execution-style, into rival drug dealer and former Spurs youth footballer Kevin Nunes in 2002.

In March 2000, one of those cleared of involvement in Shane Thompson's death was severely beaten up: Patrick Wilde suffered a fractured skull when he was set upon by a gang as he walked up Cinderhill Road, Bulwell. Another of those acquitted was soon back in court facing a charge of attempted robbery and malicious wounding after a machete-wielding incident inside a shop on the Meadows estate, while Nicholas Fogo, the St Ann's gang member, later featured in a number of significant city crimes and was convicted and jailed for life with Ashley Graham for the 2001 murder of thirty-two-year-old Roy Henry. Roy Henry was stabbed through the heart as he tried to prevent a friend being robbed outside the Simply Delicious Café on Radford Road, just a few hundred yards from the police station. The police only turned up after four 999 calls had been made. And Makan Dayil, who had also been cleared in connection with the Thompson killing, went on to become a significant drugs dealer on the Meadows estate. In 2007 he was caught in his girlfriend's Fiat Punto with a loaded revolver and five bullets during a police stop and search on Queens Drive. He was sentenced to ten years in prison.

In the aftermath of Shane Thompson's death, firearms became a common tool among the gangs of the NG Triangle.

CHAPTER 5
THE LAW OF THE GUNN

While Nottingham's black gangs succumbed to the lure of crack cocaine, eventually imploding, certain white criminals were making a very tidy profit. One team was led by two brothers Wayne and Dean Hardy, who started off helping to run their father's profitable scrap metal firm and ended up with a multi-million-pound drug-dealing business. These were men who preferred to use their fists than resort to firepower and by staying out of the street gang culture they were able to make millions from a variety of illicit trades. There was also an element of morality to their drug dealing. Cannabis, amphetamines and ecstasy were fine but they never got involved in heroin. Their biggest profits were through the contraband cigarette trade, which at one point was bringing in £70,000 a week. The brothers were always one step ahead of HM Customs – even when a load was busted there were several others going through at the same time, which ensured they were never out of pocket.

Wayne Hardy was helped by an all-powerful figure I shall call 'the Taxman'. During the early 1990s, when ecstasy sales boomed, recreational pills and amphetamines were being downed like candy and Hardy was one of the major suppliers into the city. He came a cropper in 1996, however, after investigative TV reporter

Donal MacIntyre went undercover as a bouncer and exposed the doorman's milieu in a two-part *World in Action* programme. Despite nine months of undercover filming it was not the exposé it had hoped to be, and showed nothing more than doormen dealing in speed, taking steroids and working out in the gym. Ironically the biggest drug deal that takes place on film is when MacIntyre himself splashes out several hundred pounds on a ball of cocaine straight off the block, delivered to him by a nervous-looking black youth. MacIntyre had hoped to entice Hardy into a major drug deal but the drugs went missing when MacIntyre handed over the coke to one of Hardy's associates, who dutifully told MacIntyre he had to throw it out the car window one evening because the police were following him. The impact the programme had was mixed. It didn't bring down Wayne Hardy, though it did put the heat on him. A large number of bouncers lost their jobs, only to be re-employed later, and Hardy carried on his exploits.

A year later, however, the police did catch up with him when he was busted as he drove back to his flat at Aston Hall in Derbyshire with twenty-five kilos of cannabis resin. After pleading guilty in September 1998, he was sent down for three-and-a-half years and a £104,000 confiscation order was placed on his assets. It was pin money to a man who would later have a property portfolio worth millions, with houses in Florida and Cape Town and interests in a diamond mine. After living for a while in South Africa, he returned to Nottingham in 2005 and was approached by Donal MacIntyre to participate in a follow-up programme ten years on from the 1996 sting. But tragedy, which had a habit of pursuing Hardy, struck as talks about the film got underway: he had already had to deal with a girlfriend who killed their young child and then committed suicide, a son with a terminal illness and a daughter who was addicted to heroin. Then his brother Dean, who had also been approached to take part in the programme, was killed by a lorry on Trent Bridge after stumbling into the road just hours after meeting with a film crew. The programme was finally broadcast in 2007 as part of *MacIntyre's Underworld* and was titled 'Wayne's World 2'. It depicted Wayne as a reformed criminal who was now more interested in helping former associates run pubs such as the Carlton Hotel and the Porchester.

A few months before the programme went out, Hardy paid a visit to a man called David Gunn at Full Sutton Prison in North Yorkshire. He was there to ask Gunn if he could spare the £80,000 for the drugs that he had supplied to him before he had been arrested. 'When I get out, Wayne, you can have your money,' Gunn told him. 'I hope you can help me out too when the time comes.'

Another white criminal who became a major player during the 1990s, and who had also been heavily involved in cigarette smuggling, was Robert Briggs-Price. A gypsy, Briggs-Price evaded capture for years even though police knew he was one of the major players in the East Midlands, financing smuggling operations up and down the country. Briggs-Price was a larger than life character. He had grown up with his father's scrap metal business, even using a horse and cart to collect items like a character from *Steptoe and Son*. He could not read or write – at least until prison gave him the opportunity to learn – but he more than made up for it with his sharp mind. He was the life and soul of any party, and couldn't stop boasting, which would be his downfall. By 1999 he had made millions from smuggling cannabis and particularly cigarettes into the UK. He lived in a £500,000 home at Latcham Hall, near Newark, owned the £2.7 million Millgate House Hotel, drove various top-of-the-range cars and sported a wealth of jewellery. He would invite criminal associates round to play snooker or cards at his five-bedroom home, where he felt business could be discussed safely in the relaxed surroundings of a home which boasted a swimming pool and the best security system available.

A customs operation was already underway targeting Briggs-Price's cigarette smuggling enterprise and also Nottinghamshire Police had called in the same mystery experts they had used in Operation Odin to plant electronic bugs in his property – they wanted to nail him for the drug running. In the summer of 1999, police set up Operation Long Island, the beginning of a major probe into Briggs-Price's firm. Special Forces operatives broke into his home and placed a bug in his favourite armchair; devices were also hidden in headrests in his Mercedes and Range Rover. Video surveillance was placed on one of the warehouses he used in Boughton, Nottinghamshire, where contraband cigarettes were being taken, and through one of Briggs-Price's associates they infiltrated his gang with an undercover officer. The bugs caught Briggs-Price boasting about bringing in a ton of cannabis every month as well as other criminal ventures.

Police knew that Briggs-Price was smuggling cannabis but when they heard on the bugs that an associate of his, John Barton, was looking for business partners to help bring in 100 kilos of heroin, they decided they could capitalise on the plan by using an under-cover man. Barton had extensive drug contacts in Holland and wanted to use Briggs-Price's illicit transport network to smuggle £10 million of heroin. An undercover officer, who went by the name of 'Gerry', was introduced to one of Briggs-Price's associates and one evening was invited over to Latcham Hall. Posing as a drug smuggler, Gerry brought with him £200,000 in a bin bag, which he said was to pay off someone in a nearby car park on a deal. At the house, Gerry began counting out the money in full view of Briggs-Price while the others played cards. Briggs-Price's curiosity got the better of him and soon he was asking Gerry whether he wanted to come in on a deal with him to bring some 'hard stuff' into the country. Gerry told him he had good transport connections through an Irishman called Sean, who was in fact another undercover cop, and said he would be interested. More discussion took place over subsequent weeks until Briggs-Price was sold on the idea. He told Barton to get in touch with Sean and to go over to Ireland to sort it out. But someone smelled a rat and Barton told the undercover officers that there were some problems with the shipment at its source in Holland. After weeks of silence, Barton made no further contact.

On 21 June 2000, police decided they could wait no longer and swooped on a number of addresses, arresting forty-nine-year-old Briggs-Price and forty-eight-year-old Barton in the process. Briggs-Price was alerted to the police raid when officers shouted through a megaphone for him to come out. He peered out of the window of his property, looking perplexed. Police had surrounded the place with armed officers, closing off Great North Road, while the rotor blade of a helicopter whirred above. Briggs-Price eventually appeared at the front door, hands above his head, looking tanned in a Hawaiian shirt and shorts – he had just returned from a holiday in Florida. It was like something out of *Miami Vice*, except the weather was not up to scratch.

The case took more than two years to come to court because of the complications over the transcripts of bugged material but, when it did, Briggs-Price felt the full weight of the law. In 2003, he was jailed for seventeen years for the heroin conspiracy and four-and-a-half years for the eight million cigarettes he had brought in. Barton was sentenced to nineteen years for the heroin conspiracy but had amazingly been given bail by a judge and absconded. He is yet to be arrested but was last rumoured to be working alongside a drugs cartel in Spain. Briggs-Price also endured the biggest assets recovery investigation ever undertaken by Nottinghamshire Police. The financial investigators eventually slapped him with a £4.5 million bill, which if not paid would result in extra time in prison.

By now investigators were beginning to make some clear dents in the organised crime structure which had been saturating the city with drugs. Major players had been taken out with the convictions of Dave Francis, Robert Briggs-Price and Wayne Hardy, the threat posed by the Yardie gangs had diminished slightly and some of the posses who had been controlling the NG Triangle were either spent or had taken their eyes off the ball. By 2001, however, a white crime family was slowly building up its influence in the north of the city. This family appeared on the surface to be unsophisticated, lacking the desire to go beyond their geographical boundaries and living up to their image as mere council estate thugs. Yet the fact was, unbeknown to the police at the time, they had already begun to fill the vacuum left by other crime groups which had been dismantled. They had also forged links with another crime family to the north of Nottinghamshire and were about to unleash a wave of violence upon the city. Led by Colin Gunn, the Bestwood Cartel was about to make itself known.

ON A COLD, dark, January evening in 2000, a landlord was called out from his home by a tenant. The landlord, Kevin Musgrove, had been pestered all day by complaints about a broken window to the rear of a property in High Street, Kimberley. His tenant was Godfrey Hibbert, someone Musgrove had got to know through dealings at a garage he owned; Hibbert would pop in to get his car tuned up. But there was one thing Musgrove didn't know: Hibbert, a former heavyweight boxer, was a prolific criminal and had been one of the main players with Dave Francis in the Meadows Posse.

One day Hibbert overheard Musgrove talking in his garage about the problems he was having getting a tenant and said he might know some people who were looking to rent. A deal was done and the tenants moved in, with Hibbert acting as their guarantor. Musgrove thought nothing more of it. He never met the tenants themselves, and there were a few weeks when the rent didn't come through and he had to complain to Hibbert, but Hibbert always sorted it out. Then Musgrove received the call about the window and eventually agreed to take a look to see if it could be easily fixed. When he arrived, Hibbert was waiting outside. Musgrove noticed the broken window and decided to go inside for a better look. The doors proved difficult to open but eventually they got in and were confronted by a property which appeared bare and unlived-in.

'Looks like they've gone,' said Musgrove. 'Done a runner by the looks. But what am I going to do about the rent? You vouched for them, Godfrey, what are you going to do?'

But the rent was not on Hibbert's mind. He was worried about something else. He knew something of great value had gone missing.

Several days earlier, police, supposedly acting on a tip-off from a neighbour who had taken down the registration number of Hibbert's car after seeing suspicious activity at the rented house, had broken in and discovered 300 kilos of cannabis, worth a potential £1.4 million. The cannabis had actually been at the property for several weeks, having been moved there from elsewhere in the city. It had been bought in Leicester from a major dealer called Tony Singh Hare, later jailed in a huge Leicestershire Police operation. The drugs had been bought by Colin Gunn. Hibbert, who was using a man called Kevin (not Musgrove) to babysit the property, was keeping it safe for Gunn until it could be sold. Having discovered the cannabis, the police moved it and placed a covert camera and listening device in the building, hoping to catch the owners of the drugs. Although it has never publicly been confirmed, the police also almost certainly caught someone after they raided the house on the earlier date – perhaps the Kevin who was merely minding the drugs for Gunn and Hibbert – and turned him as an informant to help catch a bigger fish.

Hibbert, who was well known to the police, had already been into the property earlier that day. The video camera showed him clearly walking into the house at around 1.40pm and putting his hand to his mouth once he realised the cannabis was missing. So why did the police wait more than five hours for Musgrove to turn up? They would say later that they had missed Hibbert going into the property and the raid that took place at the first opportunity they had to make arrests.

At around 7pm on 10 January, within a few minutes of the two men going inside, officers from Operation Firecracker swooped. They had no evidence or intelligence that Musgrove was a drug dealer and he answered all their questions dutifully. He was not told about the bug and was not aware of it until a later date but all his answers were honest. Musgrove was, as he was later described in court, a person of good character. However, he was charged with conspiracy to supply class B drugs. Though he was shocked by his arrest and the charges laid by the police, Musgrove at this point still had faith in the justice system. He was sure the jury would be able to see that he was no a drug dealer. But voice analysis experts – at least one of whom was professionally discredited on a later case – were allowed to make claims about the bugged conversations and the jury was allowed to make conclusions about a moment when the two men talk in whispers for a few seconds, implying they both knew there was a bug in the property. Surprisingly, Musgrove was found guilty along with Hibbert. After the High Street bust, officers were immediately able to gain a search warrant for Hibbert's small jewellery shop, Go Fast, in St James Street, where, after a second search (the first having been fruitless despite the presence of sniffer dogs), they found about £200,000-worth of heroin stashed in an alcove. Though he was certainly involved in the cannabis shipment, and had a long criminal record, Hibbert was not known as a major heroin dealer and claimed to believe the heroin had been planted: he suspected someone had set him up. Musgrove received an eight-year sentence at Nottingham Crown Court and Hibbert ten years for the cannabis and thirteen years, at a later date, for the heroin seizure.

After the two were found guilty and led down to the cells, two burly men came to see Hibbert. The pair were heard by people in the custody area thanking him for not saying anything and indicated that they would look after his family while he was locked up. The men were brothers Colin and David Gunn.

After just a few weeks in prison, Musgrove began asking a lot of questions about who was behind this drug shipment. He got some answers and he started to rattle some cages. Meanwhile his wife Dianne, who had no doubts about her husband's innocence, put posters and sheet banners around the local area with the words 'Kevin Musgrove is innocent' to draw attention to the injustice that she had no doubt has been inflicted upon her husband and family. The posters attracted a lot of attention and news of the campaign reached Colin Gunn. He dispatched four men to the Musgroves' home, armed with baseball bats, and Dianne and her teenage son were severely beaten. 'Tell that fat bastard husband of yours to keep his mouth shut,' one of the thugs warned her. 'You put any more banners up, we'll kill the both of you.' The same evening, Kevin Musgrove's garage was razed to the ground. The insurance company later told him that his insurance was nullified because of his recent conviction. A few days later, Dianne Musgrove was summoned to a gym used by her son, where some men were waiting to meet her. She was told to answer a mobile phone which was given to her. On the other end was a voice she did not recognise but she was told it was Colin Gunn.

'Tell your husband to keep his mouth shut or there will be more of the same,' said the voice.

Fortuitously for the police, the raiders left a baseball bat behind, mistakenly picking up one in the house owned by her son as they left. It had DNA on it, and could have identified one of her assailants. After a few weeks the baseball bat went missing from the police's exhibits. No one was able to find it.

Kevin Musgrove eventually served four years in prison. When he came out on parole, assets investigators demanded £200,000 which they said was his share of the value of the cannabis, even though the cannabis never was his and he had made nothing from the sale of illegal drugs. When I met him, he had not long completed his sentence and there did not, on the surface, seem to be a great deal to explore. He had been convicted, after all, by a jury of twelve people 'true and good'. But once he had finished telling me his story I had no doubt that a serious miscarriage of justice had taken place. His greatest crime was to be naïve in not checking out the tenant of his property. The police had asked him why he hadn't checked up on his tenants with regular visits. That may be a priority in the current age of hydroponic cannabis factor-ies in rented properties, but this was 2000 and such checks were only made then by the most circum-spect of landlords. The evidence on which he was convicted was circumstantial at best and, though Musgrove's legal team was given disclosure in the case, they believe that there should have been more video footage from the surveillance bug. They also suspected that there was a participating informant used by the police, which was not disclosed to his defence team.

More information emerged about Musgrove's miscarriage of justice after the first publication of this book. A deal had indeed been done between a police officer and Colin Gunn which was brokered through a solicitor used by Gunn. In essence the deal was this: Gunn would tell them all about the drugs found in the house in Kimberley if he was given a favourable outlook on his own case for which there had been an arrest warrant issued after he failed to answer bail on grievous bodily harm charges over a fight outside the Astoria nightclub in 1998 (see pp118-9). Secondly, questions were also being asked about why the judge who had heard the original outline of the prosecution case against Kevin Musgrove during his first few appearances at Nottingham Crown Court in February and March 2000, and who had told the prosecution in open court he would not countenance the use of a serious drug dealer as an informant, was replaced with another judge before the case went to trial. At the time of writing, a submission regarding these matters and others which raise serious questions over the handling of Musgrove's case was being drawn up for Criminal Cases Review Commission, which will decide whether to refer it to the Court of Appeal. It is hard to see what Musgrove could have done to prevent the catastrophe that befell him. He had to sell everything to pay a drug debt which wasn't his. He no longer has a garage and has to use the facilities of a friend but, more than anything else, he is desperate to prove his innocence.

If Musgrove's case is placed alongside that of another drugs case which took place a year earlier, the injustice seems even more acute. In spring 1999, customs investigators had been tracking a large shipment of cannabis and amphetamines from a French HGV all the way off a ferry at Dover. Part of the shipment had been destined to go to the Gunns and their Bestwood Cartel. Customs men trailed a van which came off the ferry from Calais and watched closely as it made its way to Quarry Farm, off the A46 near Newark. There several men began to load the forty-tonne lorry and place items into a transit van. With the players seemingly caught red-handed, the call sign for the strike was given.

Six men were arrested at the scene and the customs officers then moved in to survey the smuggled goods. At first they believed they had a 300-kilo haul of cocaine and cannabis. Only later, after analysis, were the drugs properly identified. Altogether there were 156 packages of cannabis and 258 packages of amphetamine sulphate with a street value of around £4.3 million. The trial was eventually scheduled to take place in Manchester the following year. All the paperwork was completed and in due course it would be for a jury to decide the defendants' guilt or innocence. The defendants included a former Nottingham police officer who, according to evidence given in court, was seen unloading the lorry and helping to load up the transit along with another local man. Four others from Liverpool, Manchester, West Yorkshire and Blackburn were also in the dock.

The case opened at Manchester Crown Court in September 2000, and all seemed to go well until, on the third day, the prosecution and defence teams asked to see Judge Michael Henshell in chambers. Two days of legal discussions then began behind closed doors. Then the judge called the jury back into court and explained that they would not have to sit through the trial any further or be called upon to make a judgement on any evidence they had so far heard. The prosecutors were throwing in the towel. It was a further day before the Customs investigators had anything to say in public and when they did no one was any the wiser as to what lay behind it all. Peter Hollier, a senior Customs and Excise investigations officer, defended the decision as best he could but some felt there was a hollow ring to his words. 'This is an internal Customs and Excise decision,' he told reporters. 'We have stayed proceedings – this means they will not stand trial. It was a major boost seizing the drugs before they got onto the streets and we put a lot of effort into the case but we are sure this is the right decision.'

Clearly there must have been a good reason why the case of Kevin Musgrove had gone ahead, despite there being no evidence of a business partnership between Hibbert and Musgrove other than through the tenancy of 1 High Street. If any suspicions had been raised about a participating informant then it is unlikely Musgrove would have stood trial. And clearly there was a good reason why Customs chose to stay the prosecution in the case of the Newark drugs trial, but no one seemed able or willing to explain to the general public. The likelihood is that it was also connected in some way with another case or an informant whose position could have been jeopardised by the Newark case going ahead. But there was one other common thread running through this, aside from the likelihood of informants being used. In both cases, the drugs were destined for Colin Gunn, and yet in neither of the cases was anyone from the Bestwood Cartel in the dock. This was to be a story which would be repeated a number of times in the future. When Robert Briggs-Price was under surveillance during 1999 and 2000, a number of calls were intercepted from a phone linked to Colin Gunn, but National Crime Squad operatives, who were responsible for monitoring all the calls going in and out to Briggs-Price, wrote off the material, saying it had not been possible to decipher what was contained in the conversations.

By 2000, there appeared to be some kind of force field around Colin Gunn that prevented the law enforcement agencies getting anywhere near him. The police in Nottingham were also fighting a second front in the form of another outbreak of black-on-black gun crime in the city centre and had set up a specialist team, as Scotland Yard had done with Operation Trident, to tackle the problem. It was called Operation Stealth, and while manpower was concentrated on Stealth, there were few eyes watching what was going on in Bestwood.

DAVID AND COLIN Gunn grew up initially in Eastwood, just outside Nottingham. David was born first, in 1965, and Colin followed on 29 March 1967. In part they were clichéd by-products of a single-parent family, along with another brother, Andy, and a sister, Julie. Their father had left the family home when they were young and they lacked a stable male role model. When the opportunity arose to move to Bestwood, their mother, Carol Mills – who later married a man called Stephen Hudson, grabbed the chance. She had friends on the estate and it was nearer to the city centre.

Bestwood, once a mining village but now a sprawling post-war estate of red brick semi-detached homes properties on the northern edge of Nottingham, would become their fiefdom. Colin, in particular, would come to dislike migrating anywhere outside of it.

One event in their formative years gives an early clue to the contradictions within them. As teenagers they appeared in a local church magazine article which praised their crime-busting heroics. A street robber had attacked a woman and made off with her purse. Colin and David gave chase and apprehended the man before giving the thankful woman her purse back. How accurate the reported incident is must be open to conjecture, but at the same time as they were apparently battling crime on their streets they were known as bruisers in the playground at Henry Whipple Junior School, where David met his future (now estranged) wife Sandie. In those early days, the older David had the more fearsome reputation, though not as far as Sandie was concerned: 'He and his family had moved from Eastwood and I was the gaffer, like the main girl at the school. He was a bit cheeky to me and we had a bit of a fight. I won and we decided that we quite liked each other,' she told the *Nottingham Evening Post*. It was the beginning of what would later become a twenty-year marriage.

By the time they reached Padstow Comprehensive School, Colin was fast catching up. To fellow pupils, Colin Gunn was bully-in-chief, intimidating others with his cold, steely eyes. 'If anyone stared at him too long he would come over and beat the living daylights out of them,' said one ex-pupil. 'Even then he seemed paranoid. If you got on with him then you became part of his gang and he would protect you. He never excelled at anything in school except bullying and fighting in the playground and having his mates around him to show he had a bit of power. I guess even though he came away without any academic qualifications he took some of the lessons he learned in the playground with him. One thing stands out and that is that none of the other kids would ever think to grass him up, not if they wanted to go home in a healthy condition anyway. Even then he knew how to use the power of fear over other people.'

By the time he was only just into his teens, Colin was already carrying out burglaries on the local estate and mixing with older people who were veterans of credit card and cheque fraud. It was his financial dealings that first got him into trouble. He was part of a gang run by another family, with whom he would remain in close contact in later years, who were kiting cheques around the city. The scam was run by one of the Dawes family, who later based themselves in Sutton-in-Ashfield, in north Nottinghamshire, and it ran into tens of thousands of pounds. Colin, then in his late teens, received his first custodial sentence of six months. One young officer who interviewed him at the time said there was nothing in his nature to mark him out from scores of other crim-inals doing the same thing: 'He was just an average, run-of the-mill, petty criminal. He didn't seem at all bothered that he had been arrested or that he was looking at prison time for the first time in his life. If anything he was probably looking forward to it in the sense of it being a badge of honour.' At around the same age, David was arrested but no charges followed, though he was to later be convicted of other crimes including threats to kill and possession of offensive weapons.

By the early 1990s, with both in their mid-twenties, David and Colin were steadily clocking up convictions such as burglary, theft, handling stolen goods and violence. Like other fledgling criminal gangs, they built up their enterprise by banking on the people they had grown up with and who they could trust. Most were from the estate, though there were others from Sherwood and even further afield who had good drug supply connections in Leicestershire. Some were minions but would later rise to be lieutenants in the command tree of the criminal group, like Jamie Neil, who came from gypsy stock. Others were already well respected and trusted by Colin, men such as Dave 'Baz' Barrett and Kevin Warsop. All of them would play their part in helping to control various criminal activities on their patch and all would become members of the Bestwood Cartel – a name coined by the gang itself. For each person who swore loyalty to the brothers, there was an extended family in all sorts of jobs who could help them out.

'It was mad, like you could find out anything,' said one former associate. 'Somebody had a relative in the council who had access to this or that, could find out where so-and-so had been moved to if they owed a debt and they needed to be tracked down, somebody else's girlfriend worked for social services, so-and-so had a couple of mates working for British Telecom, all that kind of thing. If you wanted to find someone it was no bother, you could trace just about anybody and the beauty of it was that the people doing the favours never really knew they were ultimately doing it for a criminal enterprise. They were our friends.'

Colin and David realised that for all the brawn needed to maintain the standing of their Bestwood Cartel, they also needed information. Information was power. The growing army proved to be useful in all sorts of ways and the brothers, too, were united. 'You knew that you couldn't upset either Colin or David if you wanted a quiet life,' said another former associate. 'They looked after each other; they were pretty close in those days. David would be the only one who could get away with taking the piss out of Colin. Colin had this kind of compulsive obsessive fear thing about dirty ashtrays and fag ends and one stunt David would pull would be to fill up Colin's coat pockets in the pub with the contents of various ashtrays while he went off to the bog. When he came back in David would just sit there and watch as the touch paper was lit and Colin would go berserk until David calmed him back down. On the other hand I think it was Dave who got Colin into the coke big time and that was a big mistake.'

Colin was forging stronger links with the crime family he previously had been involved with in cheque fraud. It was run by brothers John and Rob Dawes and their friend Gary Hardy, the son of a Hell's Angel leader in north Nottinghamshire. Colin was also talking deals with people like Robert Briggs-Price and John Paul Allen, a major dealer from Woodthorpe, Nottingham. Allen was eventually jailed following a drugs bust and went on to receive life sentences for ordering the shooting of a young associate, Ian Taylor, who, Allen wrongly believed, was about to grass him up. David Gunn, meanwhile, was cementing links with other major criminals like Wayne Hardy (no relation to Gary), who supplied amphetamines and cannabis wholesale to the Cartel, and Jonathan 'Donny' Quinn, who was trying to build up a drugs and tobacco smuggling operation with criminals in the Sheffield and Doncaster areas of South Yorkshire.

The Gunn brothers stepped up their criminal activities in Bestwood, nearby Bulwell and Arnold. On leaving school, Colin worked as a doorman and soon discovered this was a good way to supply recreational drugs to those who wanted them. He gave the job up though after he was on the receiving end of a beating, losing some teeth outside one venue in a fight with somebody who had no respect for any reputation that preceded the brothers. It wasn't the only fight he lost. 'After a few incidents when Colin and David got battered, though mainly Colin, they grew to hate the city centre,' said one associate. 'Colin in particular felt vulnerable when he went into town. He expected people to respect him but of course to other players in the city he was just a nobody from Bestwood. He was a big lad and had a short fuse and attracted trouble and he was inevitably a target for bruisers who were a bit more tasty than him. You had people like [the Taxman] and the Hardy brothers who already had a massive reputation for being able to look after themselves and their domain was Carlton, Sneinton and the city centre. I think it was about this time that

Colin got sick of going into the city centre and ending the evening with a fight, and he started to get this attitude of, well fuck 'em then, I'll show them what I can do on my own patch.'

And for the most part, Colin Gunn did stick to his own patch. By the late 1990s he was running a large operation which spanned money lending, burglaries, extortion, robbery, drugs, car ringing and fraud. He enforced his leadership with extreme violence. Colin was also beginning to use police officers extensively, something some knew and others didn't. His corruption of officers had started in an innocent fashion. He would pass on information to a few well-chosen officers in return for favours. Many justified giving information back to him on the basis that they believed there were bigger fish to catch and the information he was giving them was grade A1. Some even felt that the Gunns were looking after the estate in a perverse kind of way. The brothers even had one safe house where they stored drugs in the city 'looked after' by an officer who lived nearby. He would warn them if there was ever a potential raid coming up at the property.

The relationship with police officers was self-serving: it gave Colin Gunn the means by which he could take out competitors by passing on tip-offs about drug or cigarette shipments that were coming in. It also kept the police and other law enforcement agencies away from his own activities, to an extent. There were fringe benefits as well, since the closer that the Cartel got to some officers, the more they learned of police methods. They could then pinpoint flaws which could be exploited and used as leverage if they ever needed to get themselves out of a sticky situation. Police officers were also only human. It was only a matter of time before some of the more weak-willed might be compromised by something. They came in a variety of guises: some were tired detectives from the old school, waiting to clock up their 'thirty service' for the pension and had forgotten what they joined the police force for.

Others were young men who were compromising themselves from the day they took their police oath. Their weaknesses also came in diverse forms; from greed to dependence to selfishness to naivety. The limitations of their standards meant they could easily succumb to a line of cocaine or a prostitute – at least that was the way the villains now saw it.

By 2001, such was Colin Gunn's reputation as a provider of good information that he was trailed by a police officer with a National Crime Squad background. The officer wanted him to become a registered informant, but questions were asked when the application went in. One officer said, 'With all the information that was coming in from the army of people who were effectively working for him, he must have begun to think he could become invincible. Certainly by 2001 he was approaching a better network of intelligence than the police had. There had been rule changes in the use of informants, particularly after the Eaton Green case, and at the same time as it was becoming more complicated and difficult for us to get informants on board, Gunn and his crew were recruiting like there was a war about to happen.'

By this time Colin, who had been on steroids for more than a decade, was also using cocaine regularly. The combination of the two drugs was a timebomb. Colin's propensity for violence was itself becoming like a drug. He craved seeing fear in his victim's faces and took pleasure in inflicting extreme pain upon men or women. Incidents began to filter through to the police about tortures being used on people. There was the man who Colin thought was going to grass him up. He was taken to a remote area outside Bestwood and his hand nailed to a wooden bench. Then he was saturated in petrol while Colin toyed with a flame. It was almost as if he was playing out a role in a gangster movie. While he enjoyed putting a smile on to the faces of elderly people on the Bestwood estate, who received him warmly like a regal visitor to their homes, he seemed to get a bigger kick out of seeing dread in people's eyes. And if they expected to get a beating, or worse, then who was he to disagree with the penalty?

'His favourite punishment for those that displeased him – and sometimes it was over a hundred quid or less – was to have the person kidnapped and then taken somewhere quiet out the way,' said a former associate. 'Colin would then turn up and that person would then have their hands held down while Colin got a hammer or a baseball bat out the boot of the car and start smashing the person's knuckles. Colin would smash one knuckle and then get someone to hold the other one and he would say, "Don't flinch. If you flinch you get it on the other one. Nobody rips me off, understand?" This happened on a regular basis and believe me they never displeased him ever again. Colin also used to get really paranoid about people looking at him when he went in the pubs. Some unfortunate would get a right pasting and sometimes they never knew why. As far as Colin was concerned they always looked guilty when he eyeballed them and saw how scared they were, so he took that as a sign.'

People who were on the receiving end of his almost psychopathic violence would rarely go to the police and if they did they soon got a visit from a member of the Cartel, who told them what would happen if they testified. A police officer who dealt with the Bestwood Cartel said, 'By the late nineties, they were running protection rackets all over Bestwood. The fact that shopkeepers and businessmen don't talk about that to this day is a testament to the fear that was being created. Their *modus operandi* was to visit a business and ask to see the gaffer. Colin would point out to the boss that his security was not very good and for a hundred quid or more a week, Colin pledged to make sure they were safe. Often the businessmen would just shrug off the initial visit and send them packing. The same evening something would happen to the business – it was either burgled or the windows would be shot up or it would be attacked by arsonists. Most of the businessmen paid, those that didn't received a second visit and Colin would drive up past the business, call out to the gaffer and feign a gun pointed at the boss with his hand. It usually achieved the desired effect.'

One scam that Colin masterminded was the kidnap of a criminal associate, which was to bring the Cartel more than £200,000. The associate, who dealt in a little cocaine and cannabis but mainly made his money from large-scale cigarette smuggling, owed Colin and David some money which had been lent out on a property he was buying. He was already paying them £1,000 a week protection money to allow him to trade in various criminal enterprises on their patch and call on their henchmen for any 'business problems'. Colin took the house as part payment on the debt, which was worth close to £200,000, and then, with the agreement of the associate himself, had him kidnapped by a gang of gypsies, who drugged him and obeyed the order to 'rough him up a little' with some relish. The businessman's Spanish-based father and some of his criminal associates put up the ransom money, which was then split various ways, with some of it going back to the 'kidnap victim' himself.

According to former associates, Colin Gunn also had a penchant for teenage girls. If he took a fancy to someone on a night out, and they were with their boyfriend, Gunn would go up to the young man and simply tell him he had two choices: either the girl went home with him or he had to take a beating. He was also fiercely protective of anyone who had relationship problems, relatives and those considered to be part of the Cartel. Anyone finishing a relationship with one of the junior members of the extended family would be looking over their shoulder if they chose to move on to someone new. Most learned not to incur Colin Gunn's wrath but if he found out and they were still living on the estate they would be hounded out or would get a visit threatening violence if their new relationship carried on. One woman, who fears for her life to this day, told me how she was sought out by Gunn. 'I was out with a girlfriend of one of his top men at a pub where he was and he just wouldn't let me leave when she went. And the next thing I remember is waking up the next morning. He'd obviously drugged me. So I haven't got a clue what happened to me. It could have been anything. I knew who he was and wouldn't have gone anywhere near him, so he had to drug me.' Despite this, she had a brief relationship with Gunn – she says out of fear.

One night he tried to suffocate her, so she went to the police. It would result in her eventually going into witness protection and being unable to see her young daughter for more than a year: 'They put me into police protection, saying I was in danger, but what they were obviously doing was trying to get me to give evidence against him. I wouldn't sign anything because I was too scared, then they said they'd got enough evidence so they didn't need my statement. At the same time I was getting messages passed to me saying that my family was in danger if I didn't come out of witness protection – and that I shouldn't be a naughty girl and say anything. So I had no choice. What can you do when your family's being threatened? I came out and went to stay with a friend in London, but the police tracked me down there and told me how worried they were about me.

'I know there's a bullet with my name on it. Sometimes I think I should just go back and take what's coming because I know they will find me. I know he's got people all over the country looking for me. Colin used to brag about how he had cops in his pockets and it's true. During the few weeks I spent with him, he used to tell me things that made me shudder. He even told me about this guy who'd been fed to the pigs and when he talked about the people who'd been killed by his gang it was as if he was just ticking off a things-to-do list. He'd say, "He's gone and he's gone," as casually as if they were away on holiday, but these were people he'd had killed.'

At the same time, both Colin and David were capable of grandiose acts of compassion, particularly to families on the estate who had been the victims of crime or who were struggling financially, such as the elderly. A number of people told me about regular incidents where Colin would pop cash into an envelope and card, sometimes up to £100, and post it to old people who were celebrating birthdays. One year the brothers paid for a huge firework display on Guy Fawkes Night for all the community to enjoy. One woman didn't have enough money for a cake for her five-year-old's birthday and David popped round and sorted it out. Another elderly woman who had lost her husband and was fearful of being burgled talked about the time Colin came round to put her mind at rest. He told her not to worry and that he would be looking out for her. And he did, as far as she was concerned, because as soon as he was jailed, her house was burgled for the first time. Then there was the couple who had been burgled and lost their jewellery: 'David came around to see us and he was so polite,' said the woman. 'He took his shoes off at the door and he listened intently to what had happened and the fact we would probably never see the jewellery and stuff back again and he said, "Don't worry, we'll sort it out for you. We'll get your stuff back." And he was true to his word. A few days later we had most of the stuff back. He's a good lad.'

The fact was that the Cartel's tentacles stretched so far within the criminal world that even if the burglary hadn't been done by their own people, they knew who it had been done by and could trace them quickly. The tales of returned plunder were not propagated by people who were part of the Cartel, these were genuine, law-abiding citizens who could see little wrong in the Gunn brothers and felt they were looking after the local community.

When Colin walked into his local chemists on the estate to get his regular prescriptions, the queue in the shop would part to let him to the front, such was the respect he commanded. More than that, people felt the Gunn brothers were doing the job the police should have been doing.

This had two consequences. Firstly, it made it difficult for those people to believe the stories they might have heard about the darker side of the Gunn brothers, particularly if they came from the police. Secondly, it bolstered the support that the Gunn brothers were getting so that, as every day passed, the police found it more and more difficult to get a foothold in the estate. If it was an intentional strategy then it was an act of criminal genius, because it ensured that the Bestwood Cartel was perceived by residents to be the true police force on the estate, the real authority in the community, and a significant number of people stopped ringing the police as a result. In turn that meant the crime figures were also giving a false picture of what was going on in Bestwood. 'If you had a beef about anything or with anyone you went to Colin and David before you went anywhere else – that was the rule and that included any police officers who wanted a quiet life,' one resident told me. 'Those that didn't follow the rules didn't get any help, simple as that, and quite often would be targeted under the assumption that they were grasses for the police. In return for what Colin or David did for you, they demanded total loyalty and often, though not always, would ask for the favour to be returned. God help you if you refused.'

At the same time as they were instilling some sense of community, however warped, into the area, they were branching out into areas such as money-lending, targeting poor families who needed some extra money for things like Christmas or birthdays – and if the borrower couldn't pay up then they could come to some other arrangement. Some people's houses were taken over so that drugs could be dealt from them, or hydroponic cannabis farms set up. Some were asked to commit crime. A former officer who worked at nearby Oxclose Lane Police Station, where the Gunn brothers had a relative working as a cleaner, conceded that by the time police started to realise what was happening on the estate, it was too late. 'We let the area down and then when we realised the impact that was having it was too late,' he said. 'It had almost become a no-go zone for us. No one wanted to work up there because of the intimidation so it was nigh on impossible to get a regular beat officer up there who would do the work and get in with the community. It was like going into a paramilitary area in Northern Ireland at the height of the troubles. I remember one time the bosses were getting so much grief about the lack of bobbies on the estate that they offered us double time to do patrols but there were no takers at all.'

Officers brave enough to take up the crusade against them soon learned the consequences of their actions. 'Colin and David Gunn had the means to know where we all lived, make no mistake about that,' the ex-officer said. 'One time there was a detective who had pissed them off being a bit too good at the job and not checking in with them. They sent someone up there to shoot out his windows. I mean people wanted to do their jobs properly but what was the cost going to be to them and their families?'

Colin became increasingly unstable and erratic. He would sometimes explode at the slightest thing and usually lashed out at the first person he saw, leaving others to pick up the pieces and wrap the broken bones. His psychotic alter-ego was beginning to surface more frequently than his community-spirited, Robin Hood persona, and he was starting to believe in his own myth as a type of real-life Tony Montana in *Scarface* – an all-seeing, all-powerful man who could control the lives of anybody around him. But like Tony Montana, and his fictional descent into hell, Colin was breaking the drug dealer's number one rule: never get high on your own supply. He would gather his selected inner circle to a room in one of the pubs they controlled, depending on which was the favoured venue at the time, and preside over mafia-style board-room meetings to plan various criminal enterprises and discuss any problems the Cartel was having with other criminals. His girl-friend, Victoria Garfoot, who had loyally stood by him since her teens, would regularly complain that they should go to live abroad in a nice house and get away from Bestwood. But Bestwood was everything to Colin – there he could be a big fish and everyone would look up to him with respect. The couple, who would have four children, would eventually move to a large bungalow in Revelstoke Way, in nearby Rise Park, with a high-tech security system, electric gates and a gold-plated mailbox and address plaque, but Bestwood was in Colin Gunn's blood. He loved adorning his cars with person-alised plates and had one vehicle fitted with the registration plate POWER; his favourite Porsche Carrera was fitted with the plate BIG UN, his nickname to all except his brother, who had by now taken to affectionately calling him Fats. The years of steroid abuse were beginning to manifest physical signs. Colin was overweight as well as being on a short fuse.

COLIN GUNN MADE an ill-fated trip into the centre of Nottingham on a stag night in October 1998. He was to be best man at the wedding of a member of the Cartel who collected money for them. Some of the gang, including Colin, travelled into town for drinks. The group ended up at the Astoria (later the Ocean) nightclub, near the Broadmarsh Centre, and, worse for wear from a cocktail of drugs and drink, Colin got into his usual dispute with a reveller whose crime was not to know that you didn't answer Colin Gunn back without the red mist descending.

A huge fight erupted, ending with Colin and another Cartel member beating their victim senseless. The group made their way back to the safety of Bestwood but the reveller reported the incident to police. They arrested Gunn at a property in Radley Square, Bulwell, and another man, Kevin Warsop, at a house in Raymede Drive. The duo did not come quietly, fighting fiercely with several officers as they were arrested.

This time, Gunn was in trouble. His victim was prepared to pursue GBH charges and apparently CCTV footage of the incident was held by the nightclub. Gunn skipped bail and decided to lay low in Skegness, where his mum had the family caravan, and also travelled out to Spain, where he had allies who would give him sanctuary. There he could wait out any possible prosecution, giving him time to do something about the witness statements if the worst came to the worst. He needed as much help as he could muster, as within a short space of time police had issued an arrest warrant for him. The favours included the help of another villain who had some access to the club. This man, who when he was not helping out the brothers was supplying cocaine around the city, got hold of the only CCTV tapes and ensured they were destroyed before the police could seize them. At a later date he was able to call on the aid of a doctor who provided Gunn with a statement that said he had been prescribed a number of pills for a variety of ailments and the cocktail of the drugs had such a side effect that this would explain the violence at the nightclub. It had the desired result. Colin Gunn returned back to Bestwood, faced court and was given a few hundred hours' community service instead of a potential prison sentence of five years. Then he stuck his other two fingers up at the system by getting an impostor to complete the community service.

The same year, Colin and David's sister Julie was involved in an incident which made national headlines and consolidated their reputation as a family you just didn't get into an argument with.

Julie Gunn went to Henry Whipple Junior School in Bestwood after her nine-year-old son, Sam, complained that a teacher had made him sit in front of the class for being naughty. She disputed teacher Jeanelle Brown's account of how much time Sam had been punished for and lashed out, breaking the teacher's nose. Jeanelle Brown later needed several operations to repair the damage. Julie Gunn was subsequently order to perform 240 hours' community service. The story made the *Daily Mail* in July 1998, raising a debate about violence in the classroom and the lack of discipline in parents. Gunn apologised and said she had not known what had come over her. 'I was annoyed, like any mum would be,' she said. 'I accept what I did was wrong and I know how close I came to a jail sentence.'

Meanwhile David Gunn, who was living in Leybourne Drive in Bestwood with wife Sandie, bringing up three children with a fourth on the way, was facing problems of his own. Just a month after Colin's nightclub fracas, he was about to face the courtroom himself on charges of assault and threats to kill. He had been accused of brutally attacking a man who had dared to get into a row with Sandie in a pub. In November 1997, Keith Copeland had ticked off a child in the Standard of England pub after he heard her make a racist remark. Then he started arguing with Sandie, who claimed he slapped her. David, who was drinking in the pub, exploded with rage – nobody took liberties with a Gunnie without consequences. He launched a sustained assault, knocking Copeland unconscious and kicking him repeatedly as he lay on the floor. Copeland, who lived in Bestwood, was left with a broken arm, nose and ribs and needed stitches to a head wound.

Two months later, Copeland tracked down David Gunn to the Sporting Chance At The Goose Fair pub. There he confronted him and tape-recorded him admitting the attack. David threatened to shoot him if he saw him again. When the case came to court, Gunn denied he was even in the Standard of England on the night

Copeland was beaten up. He said he had in fact been in the Sporting Chance that night and had witnesses to prove it. But by a majority verdict of 10-2, he was convicted at Nottingham Crown Court of grievous bodily harm and threats to kill.

Mr Justice Poole, presiding over the case, said there had been some provocation on Copeland's part but added, 'This kind of behaviour is quite intolerable and I have no alternative but to send you to prison.' On 27 November 1998, he jailed Gunn to four years and nine months. It was a shock to the defendant, who had not expected such a heavy sentence and was desperate to keep out of prison with a baby on the way. He was also suffering from diabetes and had no faith in the health care within the prison system. Colin was even more affected by the sentence. Now he would have to run the Cartel without the support of his brother and without the stabilising influence that some of the Cartel believed David brought to Colin's decision-making.

Nottinghamshire Police were pleased one of the Gunn brothers had been taken off the street but had been preoccupied with taking down other crime groups involved in drugs using sophisticated covert methods, which had resulted in the convictions of Wayne Hardy in September 1998 and would eventually result in the arrests and convictions of Robert Briggs-Price and Dave Francis by 2000. The jailing of Francis in particular left a gap in the East Midlands drugs market, from wholesale to street level. Colin Gunn could see this was well worth exploiting and set about recruiting middle-tier dealers who could negotiate their way through the tribal ganglands of the Meadows estate, St Ann's and Radford. The Cartel would move into heroin and cocaine in a big way, the very drugs that Francis's street dealers had been peddling in large quantities.

Having seen three members of the Gunn family convicted of criminal offences within a single year, the police were about to embark on an operation which, had it been followed through to its logical conclusion, would have halted David and Colin's growing influence in its tracks and perhaps saved lives. The operation would be called Opal and it already had in its sights the very dealers Colin Gunn was recruiting. But Colin was also working on an audacious plan that he hoped would protect the long term future of the Cartel and their associates. Its success would eventually leave a trail straight back to his door, but for a time it would help the Cartel stay a step ahead of the police. The idea came to him after visiting one of his favourite clothes stores, Limey's, in the centre of Nottingham. As one of the shop's best customers, Colin had become very friendly with two of the employees, Jason Grocock, the store manager and one of his sales assistants, Charles Fletcher. An impressionable young man, he had expensive tastes in clothes. When Charlie told Gunn, one day in the summer of 1999, that he was leaving the store for good, Colin asked what he planned to do next.

'I'm going to join the boys in blue,' Fletcher told him.

Gunn couldn't believe his ears. He already had some useful contacts in the police but, even if Fletcher never became a detective – as he planned – another lost soul in the force would be extremely beneficial. By filling the vacuum left by Dave Francis's conviction, the Cartel was taking more risks and it was imperative to stay on top of the game. Another secret source of intelligence would be very welcome. Whether Charlie Fletcher knew it or wanted it, he was about to become a clean skin for the Bestwood Cartel. To refuse would be more than impolite.

CHAPTER 6
WATCHING THE DETECTIVES

One bright day in the spring of 2001, a woman is in the kitchen of her modest home in Dale End Road in the Derbyshire village of Hilton when her doorbell rings. She is expecting the visitors. They are police officers and are well known to her. They are not visiting her on official business. One of the officers, who has recently been working as a detective inspector in the elite National Crime Squad (NCS), is the woman's lover. Two colleagues from the NCS's Nottingham branch are with him. The scene is an unusual one. Cocaine is being chopped on the kitchen work surface and in the corner of the room another man is smoking a joint of cannabis. He is a prisoner on day release from HMP Ashwell, serving six-and-a-half years for drug offences. The detective inspector talks to the prisoner as a long-standing friend; he knows him well. After all, he had personally busted him a few years earlier. The DI argues with his mistress about who should feed her cat and who should chop out the lines of cocaine.

Unknown to any of them, a covert investigation into their activities, codenamed Operation Lancelot, is underway. For six months it has been following the DI's every move, even tracking his car via the blue road camera networks across Derbyshire and

Nottinghamshire. A few months earlier, in the dead of night, officers from Merseyside Police had broken into the woman's house, in Dale End Road, and hidden a listening device with a video camera somewhere in the kitchen area. This, it had been reasoned, was where most conversations would take place. Hours of footage turned out to be useless because the household cat's favourite sleeping spot was in front of the pinhole camera lens, but now the Merseyside team were rubbing their hands in glee. They were in business.

Their target is David Redfern, a highly respected Derbyshire officer of eighteen years with a wall cabinet full of commendations, who until recently had been on secondment to the NCS. There is also likely to be collateral damage to those associating with him. Alongside him is Derbyshire colleague Detective Sergeant Mark Jennison and Nottinghamshire colleague Detective Constable Heather 'Charlie' Bossart. The other two people in the house are Redfern's thirty-six-year-old mistress, Nicola Bladen, and David Jones, the prisoner enjoying a day on release. Redfern had collected Jones earlier that day from the prison and driven him to Bladen's home. Redfern would later say in his defence that he was trying to recruit Jones as an informant.

The cocaine goes down well. Investigators hear the sniffles of the participants' nostrils as it is inhaled. The blonde-haired DC Bossart is heard saying that the last time she took it she had gone shopping and it was so good she felt like 'dancing in IKEA'. Redfern advises Mark Jennison how to avoid detection if caught with a wrap of cocaine: 'What you do is you hand in a wrap of Charlie to the exhibits desk and say you took it off an informant. Then if you happen to get pulled on something and you have a wrap on you, you can say, "This is some stuff I just took off an informant, it's not mine, I was just going to hand it in. Just check, I did the same thing a while back." Honestly, it works every time.'

Jennison is restless. His kids are waiting for him in his car outside and he has to make tracks. The group slowly dissolves. Redfern has some work to do; he needs to see a potential informant in Nottingham. He has had a run-in with his bosses already. He was sent back to his home force in Derbyshire the previous year because of something to do with his informant handling. 'Was it something to do with trying to register one of his informants in Nottingham?' he wonders. He is not sure but is sure it's not due to his coke-snorting antics, after all no one knows about that except those in the room with him and he always has an explanation if he gets caught with anything. He must have felt safe. Maybe he knew other officers who got up to no good. Who knows if a sergeant smokes a bit of cannabis now and again, or a constable sells knock-off clothing to some of his mates? Maybe everyone is at it and no one cares much if a detective turns a blind eye to the Class A drug-dealing that his informant is up to.

BY THE END of April 2001, the covert team of Merseyside officers working on Operation Lancelot had compiled enough damning evidence against the three police officers and their drug-taking friends to make their move. All the material from the covert surveillance was being overseen by a management board from the National Crime Squad. It was a situation without parallel, underlining the seriousness of the situation – the material on the bugs was only known to them and those compiling the transcripts. The sensitivity of the material discussed on the bugs would present hurdles to negotiate once the case came to court, but no matter; the team was ready.

On Saturday, 28 April, in a series of dawn raids at their homes, Redfern, Jennison and Bossart were arrested along with seven other people, including two further Derbyshire officers, for alleged drug offences. The offices of the NCS in Nottingham and Belper were in turmoil. In addition, two of the NCS's senior officers in the region, top boss Detective Chief Inspector Roger Hardy, senior manager Detective Inspector Ian Tucker and Detective Constable David Branston, were sent back to their home force, Derbyshire, in a move unconnected to the drug charges, though arising from intelligence received as a result of Operation Lancelot. It was later revealed in the High Court that they were told that the Director of the NCS, Bill Hughes, had lost confidence in the managerial abilities of the senior managers and questions had been raised about the informant handling going on in this NCS unit.

DI Tucker, who faced no disciplinary charges, later challenged the decision against him in the High Court. He had never been told what he was supposed to have done wrong, but such was the secrecy surrounding the case that even the High Court was unable to make a ruling to hear the case by judicial review. It was clear that Operation Lancelot had uncovered something more sinister than just the drug-taking, but taking it further would be a legal minefield opening up the possibility that previous convictions handled by the NCS unit in Belper could be challenged by jailed villains. This was an unprecedented moment in terms of policing at this level and a deeply embarrassing one for both Bill Hughes and the then Home Secretary, Jack Straw, who had set up the elite National Crime Squad in 1998 to replace the old regional crime squads. NCS officers were often perceived by both themselves and colleagues in more mundane police posts as the cream of the cream. Their role was to work in small teams of between six and ten officers, targeting the biggest criminals, who were often involved in large scale drug importation and organised crime.

By April 2001, some sixty-one detectives, from a total of 1,400, had been expelled from the NCS and sent back to their home forces. The scandal at the East Midlands units, however, was of another dimension: this was to be the first time that officers from one of the most elite police units in the country would be arrested and convicted. The NCS, which would later be swept under the umbrella of the newly formed Serious Organised Crime Agency, was only three years old and already some of its officers could not be trusted. By the time the case came to trial, at Northampton Crown Court in November 2002, Redfern, forty-two, and Bossart, forty, knew the game was up and pleaded guilty to possession of a Class A drug. In Redfern's case, the charges also included possession with intent to supply and perverting the course of justice. Jennison, forty-one, denied supplying and possession of drugs but was convicted. Redfern was jailed for three years and nine months and Bladen for two years; both sentences were reduced on appeal on the grounds that the judge had been 'manifestly excessive' in his sentencing. Jennison was jailed for a year. Bossart received 100 hours community service for possessing cocaine. The officers were also dismissed from the Derbyshire force.

Rogue coppers are a blight on any police force but the repercussions when those involved are supposed to be part of an elite detective squad can undermine public confidence on a national scale. As Jon Murphy, Assistant Chief Constable of Merseyside Police, pointed out to a conference of the Association of Chief Police Officers in 2007, the police force is a reflection of the people who make up the society in which we live. 'Society has changed and so have the people we recruit,' he told the packed audience. 'Many have been exposed to drug use, many have been involved in drug use – that involves purchasing substances and that involves criminal relationships. One thing we have learned is that once you cross that Rubicon there is no stepping back – even before officers and police staff join the service they can be compromised, this makes them vulnerable and this results in leakage of information and worse. It is not of course restricted to new recruits – there are vast amounts of criminal money swilling around the streets and some of it will inevitably be used to try to seduce and compromise our staff. Criminal corruption is borne out of poor culture, a culture where poor standards are tolerated.

'Almost every investigation we complete tells us the same things: opportunities to get rid of corrupt individuals have previously arisen when they have come to notice before for bad behaviour, often resulting in discipline or even court. Yet the nettle has not been grasped. People bending the rules to get the job done ... we can all produce results if we play by different rules. Abject failure in supervision at every level – often why covert investigations create collateral damage. It is tragic watching, as I have, good people getting sucked into criminal conspiracies because they are too weak to challenge poor behaviour and consequently become increasingly compromised to the point where they can't intervene without incriminating themselves. Intelligence is power and people want the power that access to our information and intelligence gives them. We rely greatly on the public to provide the information and intelligence that allows us to do the job. They provide it willingly, trusting us to protect it and use it appropriately. If we are not vigilant, our lifeblood will dry up and that hard-won trust and public confidence will be lost.'

By the late 1990s, senior police officers in Nottinghamshire suspected that there were a number of detectives involved in unhealthy relationships with criminals borne out of a less than rigorous informant system. Indeed the whole system was flawed. On paper the role of an informant and the role of the police or agency involved in it should be clear. The informant is usually an offender himself or herself and, in return for a favourable outlook on offences he or she may have committed, and sometimes a fee, they will agree to pass on information to a handler that would prevent crimes being committed by others of a greater magnitude.

But the simplicity of it also made it ripe for abuse by both sides, particularly when the informant started to control the handler. The trouble would start when the informant would begin to use the handler to get away with their own crimes, to suck information from the handler and to plant information into the system which, while looking good for the handler, would also help the informant carry on with their illegal activities.

I met a detective who had two particular informants in Nottingham who he used to great effect, at least so far as 'getting a result' was concerned. I knew the history of both informants. One was a young black man who was a prolific drug dealer; so prolific, in fact, that he was dealing large amounts of cocaine to two Premiership footballers during in the mid to late 1990s. This young man, who I shall call Norbert, was willing to do anything to take out rival dealers in the city. On one occasion, there was to be a coke bust on a dealer who was hiding his double life as a take-away owner in Nottingham city centre. Norbert had told the police about the man and dutifully agreed to go to him and see whether the gear was still there so they could carry out the raid.

'He went in as planned but he was only supposed to do a recon-naissance to see whether the target had anything there at the premises,' recounted the detective. 'He came out as planned and gave us the signal that it was a goer. Sure enough the gear was there, several thousand pounds' worth, but a bit less than there should have been. What Norbert had done was take a large amount off the bloke on tick to be paid for later and then left him to be busted. He knew that the guy was probably going straight to prison and there was no way that he was going to have to pay up. Not only that, Norbert got paid handsomely for the information he had given us. He was a winner on both counts.'

Another informant was a heroin dealer who we shall call Pamela. She was another prolific dealer who lived with a pimp and ran a number of prostitutes in the city. Time and time again she provided good information about the movement of heroin around the St Ann's estate. She got paid thousands of pounds for her information but was actually passing on details of the large-scale dealers she herself was buying from and also details of her own competitors. In one year alone she had salted away £100,000 from her trade in heroin, selling it at £1,000 per ounce. Pamela had security cameras on her door and, in effect, her own protection; the police let her deal as long as she came up with results. That carried on until she did get busted for heroin and couldn't argue her way out of it. Results of a kind were clearly achieved but this was tainted by the fact that the information was being supplied in order to make the informant's drug dealing activities profitable and eliminate her competition.

The Nottinghamshire Police department which dealt with corruption had been renamed the Professional Standards Unit (PSU) in 2001. It was headed up by Superintendent Michael Leyton, who had been one of the detectives leading the 1993 Eaton Green investigation when he was a detective inspector. He took to the task of investigating fellow officers with zeal, so much so that he sometimes attracted criticism from peers who felt his anti-corruption specialists were targeting the wrong people. Fervour was, though, the very characteristic needed to bring down corrupt officers, who, by the very nature of their work, knew how to cover their tracks – and which methods the PSU might use against them. Nevertheless, the determination of the PSU to nail a corrupt officer could often lead to blind spots and the chasing of red herrings. That was just what occurred in the early part of 2002 when a police officer, who was suspected of corruption, came under the PSU's spotlight.

This man was a respected detective constable who specialised in handling informants and in undercover and surveillance work.

He knew all the main players in Greater Nottingham and also knew the drugs trade inside out. He got excellent results, albeit by walking a fine line. That was sometimes the only way to catch the villains, he would say: you don't get results by sitting in the office behind a computer – and he was right. But by 2001, the PSU had drawn up a list of officers who they believed fulfilled the criteria likely to make them corrupt, and this officer was one they were going to take a closer look at. He ticked some of the right boxes. He was 'old school' and had been doing the same kind of job for more than a decade; he hadn't shown much inclination to rise above the rank of constable, preferring to be at the sharp end; and he had a large number of informants. He also enjoyed getting his hands dirty. He didn't like paperwork and hated being stuck in the office.

On 9 December 2000, an incident occurred which had major consequences. The detective constable had been involved in an investigation into a shooting at CJ's Bakery on Alfreton Road, Radford: a man had been shot in the groin during a black-on-black 'disrespect' argument. The suspect, Christopher 'Prince' Llewellyn, had been arrested during a police chase and a firearm believed to be linked to him was booked into the Carlton Police Station storeroom, where exhibits were securely kept until they were needed for court. But when Llewellyn's defence team asked to see the firearm, it could not be found. Llewellyn's defence team, sensing something was up, or perhaps having been tipped off, were champing at the bit. Although the case was not ready for trial, the judge was not happy about the situation and was demanding answers. The weapon had been placed in the store by the detective constable some weeks earlier and now he was frenetically trying to find out where it had gone. He spoke to everybody who could have come into contact with it. There was no doubt that it had gone into the secure store, because it was there on the log in black and white. The supervisor responsible for the storeroom also remembered the detective booking the weapon in, because it wasn't a run-of-the-mill item. Yet a series of searches at various police locations all proved fruitless. The detective constable, along with the exhibits officer responsible for logging the items, was served with a disciplinary notice for 'property issues'. But while the exhibits officer carried on his job as normal, the detective constable was told he would be put on restricted duties and moved to a police station in the sticks until the matter could be resolved.

By the time the CJ's Bakery case came up for trial in March 2002, the gun has mysteriously turned up again – in the very store cupboard which had previously been searched from top to bottom several times. The detective constable was understandably relieved but also bemused. Weeks and then months passed, during which time Christopher Llewellyn was found not guilty of attempted murder and possession of a firearm. But the officer was still under PSU suspicion. On 8 November 2002, he received a call telling him to see his boss in the office for a chat about informants. When he arrived, his boss, Detective Superintendent Michael Ward, was standing next to Superintendent Michael Leyton and another officer, Chief Inspector Vince Treece, from the PSU. They informed the detective that he was under arrest on suspicion of malfeasance in public office: in short, corruption. He was ushered to a police car by two more senior officers who had been waiting to take him to Worksop Police Station. They even tried to handcuff him before he got in the car but he refused to be humiliated in front of fellow officers and they relented.

The detective constable could not believe what was happening. He felt the PSU officers were deliberately trying to humiliate him and it soon became clear that the PSU had been running a fine-toothed comb through his life. Such was the depth of the investigation that they had accessed his bank records and tele-phone calls. He had clearly been the target of a long and protracted enquiry which had raised questions about his informant handling. As he languished in a cell for several hours, his home was searched without anyone being present. Dumbfounded, he then faced a barrage of questions, culminating in the assertion from the interviewing officers that he was a 'corrupt and dishonest officer'. With the interrogation over, he was allowed to go but not before being told that he was suspended from duty pending further enquiries, though on full pay. The detective constable knew from the line of questioning that the PSU had spent the preceding months tracing and interviewing his inform-ants. It seemed to him nothing more than a fishing expedition and, as far as he was concerned, the PSU hadn't hooked any fish at all. For a while the PSU officers had also felt that way – until they had approached one of the detective's most prolific inform-ants, whose information had led to dozens of arrests.

This informant, a heroin dealer, claimed among other things that the officer had pocketed money which should have been paid to her. That specific allegation had been the grounds for arresting the detective constable, he was to learn later. However there was no *prima facie* evidence that the allegation was true. The informant was someone who had recently been jailed for dealing large quantities of heroin; not the most credible witness, by any rule of thumb, but particularly when it was a case of the officer's word against hers. Still, despite the protestations of the detective's solicitor, it would take another year before the officer heard that the Crown Prosecution Service was not going to recommend any charges against him. Even after that, he was kept suspended from duty 'pending further investigations into possible misconduct issues'. It was not until January 2004 that he was told that not only would he face no criminal charges, he would not have to face any disciplinary charges. He was free to return to work. The PSU had spent more than two years turning his life inside out and it nearly broke him. He had colleagues pointing the finger at him and the stress of a two-year investigation had nearly ended his marriage. He was understandably angry and, after another six months in the job, still suffering from the stress and depression resulting from the investigation, he took the option of retiring on ill-health grounds. Not only had the force lost an excellent officer who had given his life to them for the past twenty-six years, the PSU had targeted the wrong man.

A few miles from the Major Crime Unit offices at Century House on Carlton Hill, where the officer had been based, another man was busy helping out the Bestwood Cartel. He was their clean skin. Shop assistant-turned-trainee detective Charles Fletcher had been in the job since autumn 2000 and was based at the busy Radford Road Police Station. In the two years the PSU had been investigating their red herring, there had been a real double agent operating under the radar. Fletcher had already been able to pass on a wealth of useful material to Colin Gunn and his associates. It would be 2003 before an operation was mounted to look at information going to Gunn via corrupt officers. Operation Salt was to be one of the most secret investigations mounted by Nottinghamshire Police. In the meantime a war was about to be unleashed on the city's streets.

BY THE BEGINNING of 2001, Colin Gunn and his associates had assembled a band of middle-tier dealers to supply the markets in St Ann's, Meadows, Radford and areas of nearby Derby. Two of these dealers, Dion Griffin and Carl Rose, were about to be targeted by Nottinghamshire Police's Major Crime Unit. Intelligence suggested that Griffin and Rose were dealing with a Derby heroin dealer named Daniel Walsh and that Colin and David Gunn – David was now out of prison – were using Griffin to supply Nottingham's estates outside of Bestwood and even to inmates within the prison system. Intelligence revealed that several prison officers from different prisons had been corrupted by the Bestwood Cartel to allow heroin inside. Operation Opal was set up specifically to target the middle-tier dealers used by the Cartel. Bugs were placed in Griffin's hire car, and at thirty-year-old Rose's home in Aspley, Nottingham, mobile phones were also bugged. The material gained from bugs in the car headrests revealed twenty-eight-year-old Griffin to have a big ego. He bragged to customers sitting in the car: 'Look, I'm the only one who can get away with dealing in St Ann's, the Meadows and Radford, no one else has got the contacts to get past the territorial problems, I can even get stuff into the prison. I'm the top man.'

During the weeks of surveillance, officers discovered that Griffin was overseeing up to ten kilos of heroin per week, as well as large amounts of cocaine and amphetamines. The heroin was coming in from the Bestwood Cartel's links to the Liverpool underworld and was high quality. The cocaine, however, at wholesale level, was less than twenty-five per cent pure. By the time it had been cut to go out on to the streets, there would be less than five per cent cocaine in the grams people were buying for £30 to £50. It was cut with all sorts of other agents, including an anaesthetic which duped the user into thinking the numbness they were feeling came from the drug. Such was the demand for cocaine, poor quality or not, that people were still buying it.

Having gathered a large amount of information on what the Bestwood Cartel was up to, in autumn 2001 police decided to arrest Griffin and Rose. They watched Griffin meeting two other men in Radford and knew drugs had arrived at the premises. On 18 October, at around 12.30pm, the Operation Opal team burst into the property on Croydon Road. Griffin and the others tried to escape through a window but were not quick enough. Police found half a kilo of cocaine and more than £10,000 in cash. At another bust in Derby, police found more than £650,000 of cocaine and heroin belonging to Griffin and another £7,000 of amphetamines. Griffin was buying his heroin at £18,000 per kilo and selling at £21,000. Police estimated that his profits in the limited time they had looked at him were in the region of £100,000. He had properties in Ruddington, Nottinghamshire and Beaumont Leys, Leicester, a Porsche, Lexus and VW Golf, and sent his two children to private school. Next they arrested Rose, who had made at least £40,000 in just a few months. They found live ammunition and a Brocock gun which had been converted to fire live rounds. Griffin was jailed for five years at Derby Crown Court in December 2002 and Rose for eight years after initially pleading not guilty. Daniel Walsh, twenty-one, from Derby, who had been supplied with heroin by both Rose and Griffin after police had disrupted his own heroin network, was jailed for eight years.

When he eventually came out of prison, Griffin, who had more ego than sense, would make more headlines after filming himself on his mobile phone camera driving one-handed at speeds in excess of 130mph in his Mini Cooper on the busy A614 into Nottingham. He planned to put the film on a website but police found the footage after he was arrested in connection with a £14 million heroin haul in Ruddington in October 2007. They were astonished by the footage and chose to prosecute him. Griffin, much to his consternation, was sent back to prison for eight months in May 2008.

The taking down of Griffin and Rose had been only the first phase of Operation Opal and the detectives on the ground were eager to begin the second phase, which would see Colin and David Gunn targeted. In autumn 2001, over beers in the Carlton Police Station bar, some of the team discussed how long it would take to get to the heart of the Gunn's operation. The general consensus was that, with the infrastructure for the investigation in place, including bugs and informants, it could be done in less than five months. It was a goer and, better still, they had the ear and the support of the head of CID, Detective Chief Superintendent Phil Davies, who had decided that the Gunn brothers were a threat that needed dealing with before they became any bigger. Some time during the mid-1990s, DCS Davies, along with the previous head of CID, Peter Coles, whom he succeeded in 1996, drew up a list of significant organised crime targets. The Major Crime Unit was the jewel in Nottinghamshire Police's crown and had a track record which was the envy of many – so successful had it been in taking down major targets that a number of police forces used it as a blue-print. The list of targets Phil Davies and Peter Coles drew up was based around the intelligence they had on which villains were the biggest threat at the time. These included Wayne and Dean Hardy, David Francis, Robert Briggs-Price, and Colin and David Gunn.

Full of expectation that Opal would carry on to its conclusion, the team had a bombshell dropped on it: the top corridor at Nottinghamshire Police had decided that it was time to wrap up the operation.

STEVE GREEN JOINED Nottinghamshire Police as Chief Constable in June 2000 from Staffordshire. He was a surprise choice for many and a departure from the old-school, detective-influenced style of his predecessor, Colin Bailey. He told his officers that there would have to be radical changes at the force – that was what the Home Office wanted and he was there to see it implemented. Green believed that Nottinghamshire Police as an institution was riddled with problems. If it was a house, it would be condemned and demolished, he thought. He was going to stamp his authority on the force and breathe twenty-first-century change into it. The Home Office was behind him; it specifically wanted him to sort out the 'volume crime' problem and changes were needed in the force to achieve that.

The Doncaster-born Yorkshireman was forty-four, an ex-officer with the Royal Signal Corps. He had joined the police in 1978 and rapidly worked his way up, become Assistant Chief Constable of Staffordshire Police in 1996. Crucially, however, he had never spent any significant period within a criminal investigation department, something his critics would later hold against him. In June 2000, he made the drive to Nottinghamshire Police head-quarters at Sherwood Lodge to take up his new appointment. He had already told the local media what he thought the priorities would be: 'I do not see my role in Notts as making the police so specialist they become totally remote from the public. Reducing crime has to be the priority, no matter how hard that may be.' He was taking over a force which had the third highest crime figures in the country and tackling this volume crime would be one of the cornerstones of his approach. 'I am aware of the high crime rates and, make no mistake, it is going to be a challenge. I need to understand why it is so high first before looking at how it can be reduced, but reducing it will be my priority. I want it known throughout the force that I am coming to the table wanting to know how our service is being delivered and what effect it is having. The public often look for words of reassurance from the police and that is fine, but the best way of reassuring and making them feel safe is to reduce crime. It is the same with crime detec-tion. I put far more priority on crime reduction than just solving crimes. Detection is just one of the many ways of reducing crime, which is what we all want.'

Green's priorities soon became apparent. Over the next few months, the drug squad was disbanded. The Major Crime Unit, perceived by many officers as the jewel in the crown, was halved in manpower and detectives were sent back to their divisions. Murder cases would now be dealt with by those divisions instead. Green spoke passionately about speed cameras during the early part of his tenure, and in 2001 Nottinghamshire became the pilot from eight police forces allowed to keep money gained from speeding fines to be used to buy hi-tech digital cameras which could catch three drivers every second. His philosophy was clear, as he stated in a regional BBC television interview looking back on his arrival in Nottinghamshire. 'The force desperately needed to modernise,' he said. 'It had got out of date in a whole range of ways. Secondly, we had to address volume crime: burglaries, car crime, robberies. They were going up; they needed to come down. It would have been impossible to say to the Home Office and indeed the public, "Just forget about that 'cause we've got something more important to do."'

But by 2002, the battle against crime in Nottinghamshire was becoming affected by poor management of resources. Scene-of-crime officers were sent out to only seven out of ten house burglaries and two out of ten car crime cases – well below the national average. It meant these crimes were now less likely to be solved and would trigger higher insurance premiums for house-holders in certain NG postcodes. A new call system, introduced by the Chief Constable, failed calamitously within a few months of going live in December 2001. For at least two months, thousands of people trying to contact the police to report crimes over the call system were greeted with a message telling them to call back later. In June 2002 alone, the county's police failed to deal with 14,000 phone calls, including 2,500 emergency calls.

'It was total chaos,' one senior officer told me. 'We had been undergoing a massive reorganisation and it just wasn't working. There were people who just didn't know what they were doing any more. There were times when two different teams of officers would be sent out to a job and then arrive to find that neither knew the other one was covering it. If you got burgled you would be lucky to get SOCO (scene-of-crime officers) out at all, let alone within forty-eight hours of the crime being committed. Added to that, lots of areas had lost their beat officers, some of whom had been there for years and knew the community, and instead you had police cars doing the beats. The message it sent to the public of Nottingham was that we were afraid to do foot patrols in difficult areas and we didn't give a toss any more, so much so that we couldn't even be bothered to answer the phone – we were only worried about targets.'

The changes meant that the Operation Opal drug investigation would not be progressing any further than the charges laid against Dion Griffin and Carl Rose. There was huge disappointment within the team at the decision. 'We couldn't understand it,' said one officer. 'We had been geared up to take on the Gunn brothers for a long time, they were definite major targets by any criteria you used to measure these things and this seemed the perfect opportunity – everything was in place at that time so we could step up a gear. There was no clear explanation other than the resources required did not merit the worth of the job, which was usually bosses speak for, "The Home Office are on our backs and we have got to spend the money in other areas so we hit our targets." We were stunned and very disappointed. It was a missed opportunity. With hindsight, of course, I'm sure the top brass would have done things differently, had they known what would happen over the next few years.'

The Major Crime Unit had just successfully wrapped up Operation Long Island, which had led to the arrest of Robert Briggs-Price, but the view from the top corridor was that Long Island was to be the last major investigation of that type for the foreseeable future, unless an emergency cropped up. The cost of such operations was cited as a major factor in the decision, backing a view now held by the Chief Constable and several others at senior command level. It chimed well with the Home Office obsession with targets and, in a climate in which league table positions meant everything, it was a decision which the new Chief Constable Steve Green had wholly endorsed when he arrived in June 2000. Within months of his arrival he had brought in a raft of new measures, many of which did not strike a chord with either the public or junior ranks in the police force.

'There was a view in the top corridor that we would be frittering away valuable resources on targeting individuals and as such taking out one or two top villains was not going to affect that many people,' said another officer involved with Operation Opal. 'They saw the major players as just one crime number, which of course it is but that was the only way they gauged it. You had to measure the impact that taking the top man out had on other crimes and the reputation you reaped from that. The feeling was that those valuable resources would be more wisely used to tackle volume crime, problems such as street robberies, burglaries and car crime. But if you look at what is causing all that volume crime, well it's the gangsters. You need to take a holistic view of things if you are going to solve the problem and that means taking out the top players. Yes they will inevitably get replaced by others once you have taken them out, but by disrupting them continually you don't give them a chance to settle and dominate the situation. We ended up going from a position of having an enviable reputation in the 1990s for taking out top criminals to a poor reputation where major league criminals from outside the city thought Nottinghamshire was a soft touch in 2001-2002.

'There were some strange decisions being made around that time which basically came about as a result of the new Chief Constable wanting to put his stamp on things, so you had the disbandment of the drugs squad, the Major Crime Unit's resources were being halved and on top of all that some of us were aware that there was a storm about to hit us in the form of gun crime – although we didn't predict it would come on two fronts and be as acute as it was, all the signs were there to be read. The problem was some of the decision makers were just not *au fait* with the challenges that were facing them. Detectives from the Major Crime Unit were being sent back to their geographical divisions and there seemed to be a view that the specialist units were elitist. Well I suppose they were in a way because they had expert knowledge, but that is the way to meet the challenges facing you – you invest in the expertise available on the problem.'

It meant when the decision was made to draw detectives from whoever was available in the divisions, instead of from a pool of experts within the Major Crime Unit, senior officers ended up with a hotch-potch of a team which was not unified in the way that they had been before. Sometimes the teams contained detectives who were not even on speaking terms. 'Sometimes we had divisional superintendents who wouldn't let people out on major jobs because they wanted to keep their own staffing levels up to optimum levels,' said a senior detective involved in Opal. 'So senior investigating officers were often left understaffed, scraping around for detectives and without the expertise they needed or knitted team they needed. As a result of the specialist units being disbanded, we were losing large rafts of our intelligence system. The disbanding of the drugs squad had a major knock-on effect – there were areas where we simply didn't know what was going on any more. The drugs squad had been very good in giving us an early warning system. It told us who was doing what and who the new players were coming through, and what the knock-on effects might be. We had seen firearms used but mainly connected with armed robberies or being discharged into cars or buildings as a scare tactic. By 2000 we started to see firearms being used regularly on the person, being used in an almost nonchalant, everyday way by very young street dealers who were shooting each other, particularly in terms of young black men shooting other young black men – all of it was connected to the illegal drugs market. That was of course where we took our eye off the ball; we were concentrating so much on dealing with the black-on-black shootings that we ignored what was going on in Bestwood and what Colin and David Gunn were up to. Until it was too late as far as some people were concerned. Had Opal been taken to its logical conclusion many of those people who were murdered would still be alive today.'

Some observers even suggested the disbanding of the drugs squad (which Steve Green reversed years later by creating a Drugs Directorate) was a misguided way of minimising the drugs problem, although this was strongly rejected by senior officers. Former CID boss Peter Coles said, 'There is a school of thought, not mine I have to say, which would say if you don't have a drugs squad – by that I mean an institution which is recording activity in the illegal drugs market – then you can almost say you don't have a drugs problem. If you don't have something dedicated to tackling a problem you can never measure it and know just how bad the problem actually is that faces you.'

As it would later prove, the decision to bring Opal to a shuddering halt was more than a missed opportunity; it was a decision that was to have tragic consequences. By the time the Gunn brothers were targeted again they had grown stronger and more powerful. A new operation would have to start from scratch and the force would have to dig far deeper to find the resources needed for a successful outcome than they would have in 2001. It would be another two years before it got underway and would be called Operation Starburst, a multi-faceted, top secret project which would be likened to a Russian doll, containing operations within operations, and which would at last attack the very core of organised crime.

In the meantime, the city's reputation would be shot, literally, to pieces.

The quiet village of Trusthorpe, on the Lincolnshire coast, was the unlikely setting for one of the most brutal murders of the new century. Joan and John Stirland (below), an innocent middle-aged couple, were gunned down in cold blood at their home by brazen killers seeking revenge for the actions of Mrs Stirland's son.

Meadows Posse leader Dave Francis worked as the manager of a drugs charity, a perfect cover for his crimes.

Wealthy drug baron Gary Hardy owned forty-four properties and a string of luxury cars.

Wayne Hardy featured in a documentary by TV reporter Donal Macintyre.

The Dawes Cartel: Family patriarch Arthur (left) was jailed for eight years for his role in the drug gang, while his son John (centre) got twenty-four years. John's cousin Gavin (right) was later sentenced to fifteen years for money laundering and drugs offences.

Colin Gunn, the archetypal tracksuit-clad thug, liked to assume the role of philanthropic Robin Hood to his neighbours, but ruled his crime empire with an iron fist.

Older brother David Gunn was described in court as the leader of an organised crime group trading in amphetamine and was jailed for eight-and-a-half years.

The Bestwood estate, with its rows of 1960s semi-detached housing, was held in the grip of fear by the Gunns. Many residents viewed them as the *de facto* law in the area.

Chief Constable Steve Green (centre) with CID boss Phil Davies (right), who pursued the Bestwood Cartel to the end. Green arrived at Nottinghamshire Police with new ideas about reducing crime levels but was quickly overtaken by events.

Father-of-two David 'Drakey' Draycott was shot dead over a drugs debt, his body riddled with bullets. No one has been convicted of his killing.

Twenty-five-year-old John Shippam was assassinated a month after Draycott, over a friend's cannabis debt, in yet another unsolved case.

John McSally, the Bestwood Cartel's number one hitman, bragged about killing five people and carrying out numerous punishment shootings.

Michael O'Brien, the son of Joan Stirland, shot dead Marvyn Bradshaw and then taunted his family in court.

The Sporting Chance At The Goose Fair pub, a haunt of the Gunns, where Marvyn Bradshaw (inset) was shot in the head and died in the arms of his best friend, Jamie Gunn, nephew of Colin and David.

Jamie Gunn (above) went into a grief-stricken decline after the death of his pal Marvyn Bradshaw and died himself soon afterwards. At his funeral (right), journalists who tried to ask questions were chased down the road with baseball bats.

John Russell claimed he was flying a kite on the seafront at the time the Stirlands were shot, but was convicted of murder.

Michael 'Tricky' McNee, a close friend of Jamie Gunn, was also jailed for life for murdering the Stirlands.

The Time Centre jewellery store, where Marian Bates was shot dead in front of her husband and daughter during a bungled armed robbery that shocked the nation.

James Brodie, the suspected shooter of Marian Bates, has not been seen since and is presumed dead.

Thief Peter Williams broke the wall of silence around the Bates murder. He was jailed for life.

Tony Tirado was Griffin's enforcer, a gangland wannabe now serving life for what a judge called a 'Wild West' shooting attack.

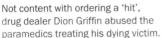

Not content with ordering a 'hit', drug dealer Dion Griffin abused the paramedics treating his dying victim.

Police cordon off the city centre scene where Bernard Langton (inset), a twenty-seven-year-old father of two, was gunned down after leaving the Paris nightclub. It was the first fatal shooting in the city for three years.

CHAPTER 7
GUN CAPITAL

Tommy Lau is philosophical, considering he knows he will never walk again. His life was wrecked one November evening in 2001 as a friend helped him out with some Spanish translation. Tommy was at a house in the quiet hamlet of East Stoke, near Newark, and was on the phone to his wife of just eight weeks, who was preparing to make her way over to England from South America. Halfway through their conversation, he heard the sharp crack of glass shattering and felt a sensation like a burning poker in his back. As he turned to look over his shoulder, he could see small wisps of smoke, as if his back was on fire. Guy Fawkes Night had been just a few days earlier, and he thought he had been hit by a firework.

'It was all a dream in slow motion,' Tommy recalled. 'When I fell to the ground I could see my friends coming up to me and saying stuff but I didn't know what was going on. At first I thought someone had thrown a firework through the window, especially when I saw the smoke coming out of my back. But then it dawned on me what it was and I was apparently screaming, though I don't remember too much of that. The gunman had fired through the living room window. I don't know whether he was aiming for me thinking I was Laurie, or whether the bullet ricocheted.' As he writhed in pain he found that he couldn't feel various parts of his body and finally realised he had been shot. He was paralysed from the waist down from that moment on.

Tommy had nothing to do with gangs, drug dealing or crime; he was in the wrong place at the wrong time. He was just twenty-three when he became a mistaken assassination target, at 5.20pm on 8 November. He was nearing the end of a degree course in fashion at Nottingham Trent University and had a new wife he was head over heels in love with. Police, who ruled out Tommy as the target early in their investigation, had some obvious leads straight away. The woman in whose home he had been shot was a mistress of a local drug baron. She was having an affair with a young man, who I shall call Laurie, who according to police was the intended target. There was clearly a motive if one accepts that the drug baron, at that time on remand in Strangeways Prison in Manchester awaiting trial for cigarette smuggling and a heroin conspiracy, had sent the gunman, and from the outset the police certainly felt that he was their prime suspect. However, as time has moved on the less likely it seems to most of those who know anything about the case that he had anything to do with it.

Laurie had done a lot of work for the Gunn brothers at one time and it is possible that Colin may have become upset about something he had done or owed them. The gunman, who made his getaway on a motor cross bike, has never been caught and the people who hired him have never been identified. That, more than anything else, occupies Tommy's thoughts every day. He mulls it all over in his mind, trying to make connections, trying to make some sense of why he ended up in a wheelchair. The police say they are still working diligently to identify the shooter, but as each year passes it looks increasingly unlikely that Tommy will get closure. In all probability he will never get to see anyone in the dock for the shooting, though he remains optimistic that someone will tell him what it was all about. There has been very little information from the public to give a clue to the mystery and Tommy's case, which followed an explosion of gun crime in the city, has been left on a shelf gathering dust. It is often the way that if a case has not been solved relatively quickly any leads start to peter out into nothing.

Tommy feels let down by the police – and with good reason. He has had to badger them on a regular basis just to try and put out an appeal about the case. It was left to him to organise an appeal on BBC's *Crimewatch* programme in 2005 and even then the programme almost disguised where the shooting had taken place, such was Nottinghamshire Police's paranoia about encouraging another gun crime tag to the city's reputation. 'I have been told lots of different names for the gunman but the trail just goes cold every time I follow it,' he said. 'There were rumours that the Bestwood lot might have had something to do with it, but no one seems to want to know. I just want to know why it happened and who was behind it, that's all, and the police really have done nothing to help in that respect. I know they are under pressure but if they can't help somebody like me, what is the point in them being there?' Tommy is getting on with his life as best he can. He had to give up his college course after spending six months in a hospital bed, and cannot work, but he goes to the gym regularly for weight-training and to burn off the steam that builds up from the frustration of being in this situation. He does still try to live life to the full. He just wishes he could put the nightmares to bed.

It is hard to believe today that in 1990 Nottingham was voted the most desirable place in the UK to live after a Gallup poll carried out for *Moneywise* magazine. That same year, the *Independent* dispatched writer William Leith to find out about the city. The comments prove interesting when read with the passage of time. Leith asked a number of new residents what they liked most. 'It is a great place to live,' said Phil, a well-dressed engineer. 'You want for nothing, things are not expensive, there's plenty of work and it is a nice size too – quite big, but not too big.' Helen, a young housewife recently moved from London, was bowled over too: 'There's no need to worry about bringing up children here. It's so much safer.' Leith himself wrote, 'The nightclubs are friendly and fight-free because each one has a rigorous door policy – you can only go in if you are dressed exactly like everyone else in the nightclub. At 2am, punters from Rock City (short hair, flares) stand chatting in a group, ignoring the heavy metal tribe streaming out of New York, New York (long hair, drain-pipes). Policemen wander about grinning. It doesn't seem quite real.'

It seemed a very different place nearly two decades later. I have lived in Nottingham since 1995 and no matter what the crime figures say, there has been a palpable change in the atmosphere of the city. In the darkness of night it has become colder, more cynical and more unfriendly in the city centre. There is a brooding, menacing air outside bars late on a Friday night, where once there was just exuberance. You certainly don't see many policemen wandering about grinning anymore. New 'community support officers' are now stationed in the centre, ostensibly to make people feel safer, but as the public and criminals alike are well aware, they have no powers of arrest. The Home Office has effectively placed these volunteers in potentially hazardous situations without the powers or authority of regular police officers, but had the audacity to place them in police style uniforms.

In 1990, the city was still seen as a quaint yet vibrant capital of middle England. If there were three legends outsiders connected to Nottingham they were Robin Hood, Brian Clough and three women to every man. Only one of the legends was true. Now the city has a fourth legend which has almost strangled it:

crime. The city has been desperately trying to shrug off the label of crime capital of the UK, or more often than not, Shottingham – gun crime capital of the UK – since 2002. It is very difficult to get away from the label. The impact that the gun crime tag has had on the city's image cannot be overstated. It has affected all walks of life, from employers struggling to get credible candidates to job interviews to the two universities: in 2002 alone, Nottingham and Trent suffered a fourteen per cent drop in applications from students. At the height of what became the troubles, in 2002-03, investors stayed away, tourists stayed away, revellers stayed away, even a crown green bowls team which had toured from Kent to Nottingham every year for more than a decade stayed away, fearing it might be caught in the firing line.

A few week earlier, the British ambassador to Saudi Arabia made a reference to the city's crime problems at a function which landed on the front page of *The Times* newspaper. Sir Sherard Cowper-Coles told an audience of several hundred people in the eastern Saudi city of Al-Khobar an anecdote about a British expatriate worker visiting Nottingham. 'The businessman was saying he felt completely ridiculous having to give British businessmen from Nottingham assurances about the security here in Saudi Arabia when Nottingham is the murder capital of the UK at the moment,' he said. 'It is far more dangerous, statistically, to be in Nottingham than to be in Al-Khobar, Dammam or Riyadh.'

The first indications of a massively negative media portrayal of Nottingham came in 2002 when the headline writers in London began their assault on the city, although the headline which probably did the most harm was 'Assassination City'. That came from the *Daily Star* in 2004, but well before then the writing was on the wall – not least because of the high-profile murders of jewellery shop owner and grandmother Marian Bates and schoolgirl Danielle Beccan (see Chapters Eight and Eleven). But it was 2002 when things really got out of control. In that year alone there were more shootings than the previous seven years put together – and many of them were connected to the Bestwood Cartel.

When the number of shootings first began to rise dramatically in late 1999, Nottinghamshire Police unveiled their response: Operation Real Estate. It began in earnest in February 2000, after a spate of gang-related shootings in St Ann's and the Meadows, and led to armed officers routinely patrolling the streets of a UK mainland city for the first time. This, in turn, led to a national debate about whether the police should be routinely armed. The then Assistant Chief Constable, Sean Price, who was in charge of the operation, was keen to play down any conclusions that the police's response was an exaggerated one: 'There is nothing exceptional in what we are doing,' he said. 'This is not a Genghis Khan approach. We're only doing what the police have always done: deploying the level of force appropriate to the threat. With the shootings that took place in February I knew at the time this was the thin end of the wedge. If we hadn't got a grip quickly, it would have got out of control.' He admitted that the violence involving the gangs in the NG Triangle had prompted the move. 'It's fair to say that it was the escalation of that rivalry that led to Operation Real Estate. We had a situation where, because of disputes between these rival groups of criminals, shootings were happening. In that one week in February we had five incidents alone. We had to protect the public.'

For two years, six armed officers carrying Walther P990 pistols on their hips worked in pairs between dusk and midnight around the St Ann's and Meadows estates. The patrols had a major impact during their first year. In the first six months, six shootings were recorded on the estates, compared with six in a fortnight just before Real Estate was launched. Police also made some 150 arrests connected to the gang violence and recovered fifteen firearms in the first year. But some community leaders felt the use of armed officers stigmatised their areas and encouraged the gangs to go underground. 'We are being used as a laboratory for a bigger experiment,' said Delroy Brown, community leader of the Afro-Caribbean National Artistic Centre in St Ann's. 'This marks the paramilitarisation of the police.'

By November 2001, Operation Real Estate had made 400 arrests and thwarted a number of assassination attempts. More than 100 firearms had been recovered and forty-seven Jamaican nationals were among those arrested for attempted murder, firearms and drug offences. Of those, the Jamaican authorities wanted to speak to forty-one in connection with serious criminal offences. Nevertheless, gun crime overall continued to escalate. In 2001, police in Nottinghamshire dealt with 685 firearms incidents; back in 1990, the year it was voted the most desirable city in the UK to live in, the figure had been just 282. By the beginning of 2002, police had decided a new approach was needed and in July 2002 set up a project which would be intelligence-led and tackle gun crime across the city. Operation Stealth would be more proactive than Real Estate. Its remit was to stamp out the black-on-black shootings by arresting offenders with firearms before they committed serious offences. But before the Stealth team had got stuck into their task, there was another brutal shooting.

At about 7pm on 19 February 2002, a young black teenager, Brendon Lawrence, was waiting in a friend's Ford Fiesta XR2 near his home in Watkins Street on the St Ann's estate. It had been pouring with rain and Brendon had accepted the offer of a lift from his friend, who had nipped inside a house on Watkins Street. Minutes later, a man in a dark blue, hooded Donnay top, wearing Nike Bohemian trainers, approached the car, pulled out a gun and told Brendon to get out. Then he shot him twice in the leg, pulled him out of the car and shot him again in the chest. The sixteen-year-old died on the street.

His mother, Janice Collins, would become a tireless campaigner for Mothers Against Guns, a group set up to try to stamp out gun crime. 'We buried him in black jeans and a black polo-neck he had just bought from Next that week,' she later told reporters. 'His friends were pallbearers, and they looked so young, so little. They were only kids. When Brendon died they kept him eight weeks in the mortuary. I couldn't bear to think of him so cold like that. I hated it that we couldn't bury him. Every week, Calvin, his twin brother, would take me down there to see him, and they would pull him out, cold, so I could see him, see he was all right. No mother should have to go through that. Someone must know something.'

Brendon was not known to be involved in criminality but intelligence came through to the police that half a kilo of cocaine had been stashed under one of the car seats, which indicated a robbery motive, as the drugs were missing. The killers, who clearly had information that there was a substantial amount of drugs in the car, had driven off in the Ford Fiesta XR2 which was later found burnt out in Westville Gardens, St Ann's. Some DNA was extracted from the partially burnt wreckage but little headway was made by the police in terms of getting witnesses to come forward. And so it dragged on year after year, despite there being a £20,000 reward for information leading to a conviction. Every February, Brendon's distraught parents, Janice Collins and Roy Lawrence, have made an annual appeal for information which they hope will lead to the identification of the killer. In the years that passed since Brendon's death, police arrested more than twenty suspects but without a breakthrough. In January 2009, two defendants went on trial for his murder and a third for assisting an offender. The jury acquitted one defendant of murder but failed to reach a verdict on the other two. A retrial was rescheduled.

A list of some of the incidents police were called out to in July

2002 showed how indiscriminate the use of firearms was becoming:

July 1: Ten-year-old Lorrell Akim Warner is shot and wounded at his grandmother's home in Wilford Crescent West, the Meadows. A seventeen-year-old youth was later arrested.

July 5: A would-be robber walks into a newsagent in Old Basford, asks for cigarettes and then fires a shot from a handgun, narrowly missing the fifty-seven-year-old store owner behind the counter.

July 9: A taxi driver who picks up two men outside the Commodore pub in Nuthall Road at 6.20am is robbed with a handgun to his head and is forced to drive the men to Brockhurst Gardens, St Ann's. The taxi driver later tells the local paper, 'I served in the Gulf War but left the Army for a quieter life. It's not really turned out how I imagined.'

July 16: A two-year-old boy is shot in the right arm with an airgun pellet as he plays in Cotmanhay Park, off Beauvale Drive, Cotmanhay, at 6pm. Surgeons remove the pellet.

July 17: Two robbers enter an unlocked house in Noel Street, Forest Fields, and hold a thirty-seven-year-old woman and her young children at gunpoint in their own living room.

July 18: A seventeen-year-old boy is shot in the leg in Fenton Road, Old Basford, as he and two friends drive down the road. A gun is pulled out among a group of youths as the car passes and three shots are fired.

July 22: Thirty-six-year-old Mohammed Yousaf Hussain is shot in the chest by a masked gunman in Berridge Road, Forest Fields.

July 22: An armed robber shoves a handgun into the faces of two staff in a raid on the Mansfield Road Spa in Sherwood at 12.20am. Witnesses then report hearing a gunshot as the raider runs from the store with the takings.

July 26: A thirty-three-year-old man is shot and wounded outside the Drum nightclub, off Ilkeston Road, Lenton.

July 26: Courtney Graham, twenty-three, is shot in the groin and stomach as he cycles along Alfreton Road, Radford, after becoming involved in an argument with the occupants of a passing white saloon car.

July 27: A man is seen brandishing a handgun and a shot is reported to have been fired in George Street, Hockley, in the city centre.

July 29: A young couple in Long Eaton are attacked by three men wielding a gun and a knife after they spot them acting suspiciously. The man, a twenty-three-year-old sales manager, has a gun pressed to his forehead and his teeth smashed in with the butt of the pistol. He is told, 'That's what you get for interfering.'

July 30: A wounded, twenty-year-old man is dumped in Wolsey Avenue, Radford, from a white van. Police say he has been shot in the thigh with a handgun. The van is soon found burned out in Johnstone's Paints car park in St Ann's.

July 31: Three masked robbers, one brandishing a gun, beat a Securicor guard to the floor and steal two cash boxes outside a Barclays Bank in Old Basford at midday.

Analysis by Operation Stealth in the central city area revealed the following: around seventy-three per cent of the shooters were black and British-born; educationally they were almost always underachievers, living in areas where there were limited employment opportunities; the majority were from single-parent families; their family, or brethren, were the gangs to which they belonged; they were territorially protective and their role models were drawn from gangsta rap, with lots of 'bling' or jewellery, designer labels on clothes, cash in pocket, firearm in one hand, doll on the other. Their career paths were firmly rooted in criminality and particularly drug dealing, progressing from street runner at the age of twelve, eleven or sometimes younger. Their job would be to deliver small amounts of drugs, sometimes on a pushbike, sometimes on foot between people or addresses. For this they would be given a few pounds, or perhaps a rock of crack or wrap of heroin to sell themselves. By the time they were thirteen or fourteen they might be babysitting a firearm for one of the brethren or a larger amount of drugs at their home, and by the time they arrived in their late teens they might be street dealing themselves or have a pack of runners working for them, just as they had done themselves.

Other black-on-black shootings demonstrated the cheapness with which life was perceived by those living in the ghetto. Two resulted in murders and both had the fingerprints of Yardie gunmen on them, though both failed to result in convictions. On 9 November 2002, thirty-three-year-old Theresa Jacobs, a female crack cocaine dealer, was shot in the back of the head outside the Drum nightclub, off Ilkeston Road. Jamaican national Aston Bola faced trial over her murder but the case collapsed when the CPS offered no evidence, though Bola was deported. Almost a year later, at 1pm on 7 November 2003, twenty-four-year-old father-of-two Omar Watson walked into his local barber shop to have his hair cut, but almost as soon as he sat in his chair a gunman walked in and shot him dead. It was believed his killers had lookouts who had phoned to say he was on his way to the hairdressers shortly before the murder. Two Jamaicans were subsequently cleared of his murder.

ON A COLD February morning, a young man waits in a telephone box on St Matthias Road on the St Ann's estate to hear from his dealer. It is a phone box well used for the purpose. The man, though, is disturbed by a youth banging on the glass partition. He is saying something. Gradually the man can make out his words.

'Hey mate, mate. What do you want, rock or brown? I can do you anything,' the youth says, nodding knowingly.

The man has not seen the youth before and is intrigued enough to abandon the wait for his dealer's call. He steps out of the kiosk to talk to the thirteen-year-old. Soon he learns what he can buy from the youngster: heroin, crack cocaine, weed. The teenager gives his street name, pointing to an emblem sewn into his jacket: 'Yeah that's me, just ask for ABC.' He gives the man a mobile phone number to call and within a few days a drug deal is arranged.

The next time the man sees the youth is to arrest him: he is an undercover police officer. When the youth is searched he has almost £1,000 of drugs on him, including ninety-four wraps of heroin, and crack cocaine. ABC's tale is a familiar one. He has been smoking cannabis from the age of twelve, buying it on his way home from school as he walked through the St Ann's estate. Pretty soon he started buying it on tick or credit. He built up a debt he could not pay off and the dealers began to threaten him. Then they told him he could settle it by selling some of their drugs. Within a few months, he was pushing crack and heroin. The courts do a deal with ABC: he is given an anti-social behaviour order which bans him from the St Ann's area. But for every

ABC there are now thousands of others doing the same on the built-up estates of the UK's cities.

OPERATION STEALTH PROVED to be hugely successful in its first two years, particularly given its limited resources. It was set up in much the same way that the better-known Operation Trident had been set up by the Metropolitan Police four years earlier to tackle black-on-black gun crime. Nottinghamshire officers had a good working understanding of Trident because by the early part of the millennium they were getting regular visits from the Trident team, looking at drugs networks that had connections with Nottingham and safe houses in the city. Stealth had a team of just thirty officers compared with around 300 at Trident, yet between July 2002 and October 2004 the Stealth team seized 306 firearms compared to 333 by Trident, and 6,100 rounds of ammunition compared to 1,200 by Trident. The Stealth team also secured 263 convictions over a two-year period compared with fewer than 200 by Trident. While the success rates were something to be proud of, the intelligence coming through was worrying. There seemed to be easy access to firearms, particularly replicas which could be bought across the counter. These replicas could, with a bit of engineering know-how, easily be converted to fire live ammunition. The team was also discovering that these firearms were going into the hands of younger and younger offenders – they were becoming fashion accessories for wannabe gangstas as young as thirteen. The Stealth team could have been helped further if the Government had been braver with new legislation. A minimum five-year prison sentence for possession of a firearm was brought in during January 2003. It would do little to curb the youngsters' taste for firearms, even after some of those close to the victims saw the impact that guns were having on lives. A minimum ten-year sentence would have been a far better deterrent, in the eyes of many police officers.

In the early hours of New Year's Day 2003, one of Colin Gunn's enforcers was involved in a reckless shooting incident which almost claimed three people's lives. He turned up at a party being held at a house in Jedburgh Walk, St Ann's, and within a short space of time had been 'dissed' by some of the partygoers, who took the mickey out of him over something. The man was known to have a short fuse but no one could have predicted what he did next. He pulled out a handgun and fired five times at a number of the party guests, leaving two writhing on the floor with injuries to their legs and groin. The man fled.

Nine days later, Darren Hayden, aged thirty-eight, was picked up by officers from Operation Stealth as he drove down Vernon Road, Highbury Vale, Basford, at 1pm on 10 January in his red Ford Mondeo. Hayden, who lived near the Gunns' mother on Raymede Drive, had convictions for armed robbery and burglary and had recently returned from Tenerife. Police searched his car and found a two-ounce bag of crack cocaine and one ounce of heroin worth £4,000, along with a 9mm semi-automatic handgun and ammunition. Hayden was charged with three counts of attempted murder at the party – a third person had been shot at but not hit – along with possession of a firearm, ammunition and controlled Class A drugs.

But as police attempted to get witness statements from those shot at the party, the message came back: 'No one wants to talk about it anymore. We just want to get on with our lives.' By June 2003, the CPS had dropped the attempted murder charges against Hayden. He then changed his plea to guilty on the firearms and drugs offences and was jailed for seven years in October 2003. An aggrieved Kate Carty, Chief Crown Prosecutor in Nottinghamshire, said, 'The CPS decided that there was sufficient evidence to proceed with the three counts of attempted murder. The matter then progressed as far as it could in the Crown Court until notification was received that key prosecution witnesses had changed their minds about giving evidence in court. Disappointingly, other witnesses gave further statements that were at odds with previously stated positions. We reviewed the case and concluded that its success was dependent on the willingness of witnesses to attend court. In these circumstances it was agreed that no further progress could be made on the three counts of attempted murder. We believe that, unless victims and witnesses are prepared to report crimes and give evidence confidently and effectively in court, the public cannot be properly protected.'

Despite this disappointment, in June 2004 the Operation Stealth team was celebrating success when nine St Ann's gang-bangers were taken off the streets for life after killing a man in Sheffield. The victim was another tragic case of mistaken identity. Some of the gang were in Sheffield's Meadowhall Shopping Centre when they were ambushed outside a takeaway and robbed of their mobile phones. On 18 December 2002, the gang returned for revenge in a convoy of four cars. They pulled up outside an Afro-Caribbean Club in the Steel City's Pitsmoor area, believing that the people who had robbed them earlier were there, and fired two shots from the lead car. An innocent bystander, Gerald Smith, aged forty-two, was fatally wounded in the head and leg.

Ezra Taylor, twenty-six, of Collison Street, Radford; Craig Brooks, twenty-six, of Lorne Walk, St Ann's; Roger Gordon, twenty-eight, of Hungerhill Road, St Ann's; Gareth Lindsey, twenty, of Perlethorpe Drive, Carlton; Richard Powell, twenty-six, of Amesbury Circus, Cinderhill; Leon Bryan, twenty, of Limmer Gardens, St Ann's; Gordon McPherson, twenty-six, of Curzon Gardens, St Ann's; Dean Pinnock, twenty, of Melville Gardens,

St Ann's; and Christopher McKenzie, twenty, of Melville Gardens, St Ann's, all received life sentences at Sheffield Crown Court in July 2004. It was the first time a group had been convicted of murder where no one except the killers knew who had fired the fatal shots. They were all, said trial judge Mr Justice Wakerley, as culpable as whoever pulled the trigger. 'This conviction gets right to the heart of all the violent drug and gun crime in St Ann's,' said Superintendent Nick Holmes, deputy commander of Nottinghamshire Police City Division. 'It smashes its infrastructure. The gang caused misery to all the people of Nottingham and have been well known to us for years. We have put a massive effort into tackling drug and gun crime in St Ann's and all over the city and are starting to see the results.'

The level of urban terrorism being visited upon the community was becoming shocking, and while Stealth concentrated on the black-on-black gun crime in the city centre, another touch paper was about to be lit. All eyes would soon be turning to the north of the city, where a ferocious white gang held sway.

CHAPTER 8
WARZONE

David Draycott was in trouble. He owed money and those he owed were running out of patience. He could feel it in the darkness as he pulled his black Mercedes into the driveway of his home in Woodlands Way, Sutton-in-Ashfield. It was 9.17pm on 7 October 2002. He had just been to his estranged wife's home a short distance away and had received two phone calls while he was there, telling him to pay up or he would be in trouble. He had had to ask his wife, Andrea, if she could help him with a banker's draft to help settle the debt. She had never seen him so worried. He had borrowed £10,000 from some unpleasant characters for a cocaine deal but had not been able to keep up the repayments and now the debt had escalated to more than £30,000, though he told his wife that he needed the money to pay off the VAT bill on the sheet metal business he was running.

'Drakey', a big bear of a man, always had a smile on his face. He could be a bit difficult to pin down – sometimes when asked what he was up to he would tell people he did 'a bit of this and a bit of that', and laugh. He had worked the doors of pubs and clubs in the Ashfield area, and had come into contact with a myriad of unsavoury people. Wanting to be his own boss, he had sunk money into a sheet metal business but found it was not easy to make an honest crust. His friends knew he had become involved with people who were selling Class A drugs in Nottinghamshire and they were heavy hitters but Drakey kept everything to himself. He never told his friends he was worried about the spot of bother he was in; he thought he could handle any trouble himself.

Two major drug gangs were interested in the debt that Drakey owed: the Dawes family, who controlled the supply of drugs across the East Midlands from their base in Sutton-in-Ashfield, north Nottinghamshire, and the Bestwood Cartel. As he steered his Mercedes into the drive, Drakey was still thinking about trying to reconcile his marriage. Though he and his wife had been estranged for six months, things were getting better. He knew his daughter, aged eight, and son, aged eleven, wanted him to go back home and he and Andrea had become closer in recent weeks, thanks to a holiday in Devon and Cornwall and a break in Skegness. He had even told his mum that he reckoned he and Andrea would be back together by Christmas. If only he could get these people off his back he could start making plans.

Drakey was tired and didn't see two men get out of the silver Peugeot 206 across the road. They had been waiting there for more than two hours. He didn't hear them walk down his drive. He only saw them as he opened his door and before he knew it they were pumping bullets into him. Even with his body riddled with ten shots, Draycott managed to crawl to a neighbour's house to raise the alarm. He was wheeled into an ambulance semi-conscious and fought hard to stay alive but ten bullets was too much even for Drakey. Four days later, he was dead at the age of forty.

Andrea, who had arrived at the scene of the shooting just as her husband was being carried away, issued an appeal that Christmas: 'No child's last memory of their father should be of him being wheeled into an ambulance riddled with bullets. They have had their childhood taken away. If anybody knows anything, but they are scared to come forward, I would just ask them to think about themselves in the same situation. How would they feel if their children had lost a father? I would ask them to be strong, because without their help David's killers won't be brought to justice.'

A month after the murder, in the early hours of Thursday, November 7, a man called John Shippam was finding it hard to sleep in his new flat in Chiltern Way, Bestwood. Like David Draycott, he was no stranger to violence. Shippam was not long out of prison, having severely beaten up a man in his home in the Sherwood area in 1998. Now he lay listening to music in his room, but he was worried. The Bestwood Cartel were chasing him over a friend's cannabis debt. His mate has done a runner and left Shippam to bear the brunt. Although it was only a couple of hundred quid, they meant business. He was still nursing the bruises from a beating he had taken outside the Anchor pub in Gunthorpe village on Guy Fawkes Night. They told him then that he would have to find the money quickly. He had asked friends to help but they were slow to come through.

As Shippam listened to his music, two men entered his flat and walked in on him. He knew them – two brothers who had worked with Colin and David Gunn, collecting money and selling drugs for them. One had something in his hand. Shippam pleaded with them but they refused to hear his explanations. A single shot rang out and John Shippam lay dead. He was twenty-five years old.

As the two men walked out of the block of flats, an associate of Shippam saw them get into their car and made a mental note. Later the same man would tell police what he had seen and would be forced to go on the run with his family because the gangsters knew he knew and threatened to murder him. Though two of Colin Gunn's associates were arrested for John Shippam's murder, the case remains unsolved. Friends of those arrested claim a rogue police officer tipped off the suspects that a bug had been placed in their sofa, throwing the investigation into chaos. Like Andrea Draycott, John Shippam's mother Josie has still to receive justice for the murder of her loved one.

IN THE SUMMER of 2003, beleaguered Chief Constable Steve Green found himself in a building he had never been in before. He had been summoned to a meeting in the Pimlico area of London to discuss how certain law enforcement agencies could help him in the battle against organised crime. Green had problems locating the building and had to ring his secretary twice to double-check the address. Having finally found it, he was ushered into a room. Senior managers from the National Crime Squad, National Criminal Intelligence Service, Customs and Excise Investigations Service and other shadowy figures who 'worked for the Government' were there to greet him.

'We gather you have a problem in Nottingham,' he was told. 'Well, we are here to help. You have our full support to make use of the resources we have. This is a problem that must be sorted out before it goes any further.'

That problem had become so acute that, in March 2003, David Blakey, one of the senior inspectors from Her Majesty's Inspectorate of Police (HMIC), refused to give Nottinghamshire Police a clean bill of health. They were, he concluded, neither effective nor efficient. 'If you lived, worked or visited Nottinghamshire in April 2002, you were more likely to have a crime committed against you than anywhere else in the country,' stated Blakey's report. He was particularly critical of the abilities of the police force to deal with drug crime. Some senior CID officers had also made clear to HMIC that the disbandment of the drug squad and the use of divisions instead had seriously hampered their ability to fight organised crime. 'There was a widely held view that the Force drugs investigation function was not robust,' wrote Blakey. 'The main response to drug investigation, at all levels, remains with divisions who respond within available resources. HMIC was advised during divisional visits that most drug investigation activity took place at local area command level, and that they were unable to respond effectively to drugs intelligence. Overall, the re-deployment of Force drug squad resources had not increased the drug investigation capacity at divisional level.'

There was also reference to the pressures that the CID was under. Green's reorganisation strategy had been forced upon the CID at the most inopportune moment, coinciding with the explo-sion of gun crime in 2002. The report stated that some of the failures to meet HMIC targets were due to 'the wider Force re-organisation and unprecedented resource demands for murder investigations'. Regardless of any leap in crime which may have put Nottinghamshire under pressure – it was dealing with twenty-one new murder investigations that year, against an average of twelve – this was either a veiled criticism of the abili-ties of frontline officers to do their jobs or an indictment of Green's reorganisation.

The Labour MP for Nottingham North, Graham Allen, had been critical of Green as early as 2001, particularly over the issue of beat bobbies being taken away and replaced with officers in cars, and in 2002 he had raised the issue in the House of Commons. 'We in the City of Nottingham division are losing bobbies on the beat,' said Allen. 'In addition, our local police stations are losing large numbers of officers to response units – in effect, those stations are being hollowed out.' Was it right, he asked the Home Secretary, that at a time when the Government were being congratulated for employing more police than ever before, people on some estates were seeing fewer of those officers?

The Chief Constable, however, had stuck to his guns. 'I would challenge anybody to undertake change of this depth and not have a few plates fall off,' he said. 'It's the inevitable consequence of trying to tackle so much change.' At the same time he admitted, 'The beat officer issue was a stumbling block that we tripped up on. Officers were unsure about their role.'

Now the table of heavyweight officials who confronted Green were talking about organised crime and the problems caused by gun-wielding gangsters, including the Bestwood Cartel. Green was stunned by the detail that the officials had. As he would later admit, the tackling of gun crime in the NG Triangle had distracted attention from the city's white gangsters. 'By 2003 it was clear to us that something else was happening,' he later told the BBC in an interview. 'There was a different dynamic, so that, if you like, we are kind of fighting the war against gun crime on that front but there is another front opening up, and that led us to sort of re-appraise the situation and take stock and conclude that something, I think, far more evil and more insidious was taking place in the white community of north Nottingham that required a completely different approach.'

A few months earlier, when approached by his own senior officers about the problem, he had approved an investigation but had told them they would have limited resources and their work would have to be completed in six months. Now he was being told by representatives of national agencies that it would have to be a bigger operation, involving them. Technology only just being field-tested by MI5 would be available. National Crime Squad officers would be used for covert surveillance and, as part of stage one of the operation, a police officer from London would be sent in under-cover to try to infiltrate the Bestwood Cartel. It would be a multi-layered investigation overseen by a clandestine caucus of operatives. Each individual sub-operation against an arm of the

Gunn brothers' empire would be given the codename of states in the USA, such as Utah and Texas. Less than a handful of officers would know what the overall operation would be about. Everything would be on a need-to-know basis only. By August 2003, Nottinghamshire's head of CID, Phil Davies, had been given the go-ahead that he had been pleading for over the previous twelve months. Operation Starburst was born.

THEY BEGAN WITH Operation Texas. An undercover police officer was brought up from London to infiltrate one side of the gang. Officers decided they would target one of Gunn's lieutenants, Jamie Neil. The plan was that the officer would pose as a drug smuggler from London who was forced out of the capital and was now lying low in Nottingham. His story was carefully constructed – and it needed to be. Once introductions had been made in Nottingham, Neil turned to Gunn to make enquiries about the bogus villain's background. Associates went down to London to check out his story and found it was true. Within a few months, the undercover officer was making significant inroads into the gang and picking up vital intelligence on drugs coming in. Then one evening, he was invited to a boxing match. Things were going well until he moved on to a nightclub where Neil and his associates had booked a VIP area, closed off from the public, and proceeded to get very drunk. At some point in the evening, one of the gang took offence to something that had been said and launched a ferocious attack on an associate. As the undercover officer intervened, he too began to take a beating from Jamie Neil, and suffered a fractured skull. The secrecy of Operation Texas meant medics could not be sent to the scene in any other manner than a normal response to prevent suspicions being aroused within the Cartel. Eventually an ambulance was sent for and the officer was taken to hospital but Operation Texas was now in tatters.

Operation Utah was then launched. Bosses decided that it was too dangerous to send in any more undercover officers and so results would have to be achieved through a total surveillance of the gang using covert methods including bugs and cameras.

Events in the underworld, however, began to move at a breathtaking pace.

IN THE EARLY hours of 29 August 2003, after a lock-in at the Sporting Chance on Hucknall Road in the Bulwell area, a group of young men were draining the last dregs of their drinks. The group included Jamie Gunn – Colin and David's nephew – and Marvyn Bradshaw, plus two other friends. It was 4am and they were finally about to go home. They had enjoyed a good evening, even though it had threatened to turn sour three hours earlier when two men tried to muscle their way into the pub and had to be forcibly ejected. Jamie knew both the men – they had dealt drugs on the Bestwood estate before and one had been going out with a Bestwood girl, which had caused some trouble with one of his uncle Colin's right-hand men. A scuffle had erupted and Jamie Gunn had smacked one of the men with an ashtray, causing a deep cut to his head. The man was Michael O'Brien, a renowned hothead. The other, Gary Salmon, told him to cool it and dragged O'Brien away. Salmon had an ongoing beef with the Bestwood Cartel and was keen not to antagonise any of them. Four weeks earlier, a white van had parked near his home in Brooklyn Road. As Salmon stood in the doorway, a gunman had jumped out of the back and fired three shots at him. He was a marked man.

Jamie Gunn's group began to disperse from the bar and make

their way to the car park. Jamie was keen for his pal Marvyn to drive his car; he was drunk and didn't want to get pulled over by the police. Marvyn, who was sober, agreed and got into the driver's seat of the silver Renault Megane, while Jamie sat in the back. Two other men occupied the rear and front passenger seats. As Marvyn turned the ignition key, the windows were still steamed up, but he began to drive off anyway. Jamie turned and rubbed the glass to clear his window. He saw a shadowy figure wearing a balaclava walking towards the car. There was a loud bang and glass from the driver's side window shattered all over the passengers. Everybody in the car ducked down except Marvyn, who groaned but continued to drive until the car slowed and finally came to a halt on a grass verge, the engine still running.

Jamie Gunn got out. He did not know what was going on. A car carrying two men in balaclavas screeched off. Through the shattered window of the driver's door, he could see his friend slumped over the wheel, groaning.

'I feel sick,' said Marvyn. 'I want to feel my head, I want to get out of the car.'

Jamie could now see a red hole in Marvyn's head and realised his friend had been shot. He took off his red T-shirt, wrapped it around his best friend's head and lifted him out of the car, comforting him.

'Just stay here with us mate, it's gonna be all right.'

But Marvyn Bradshaw was dying there on the desolate car park. Part of Jamie Gunn was dying right there too, he just didn't know it yet.

DESPITE THE BRUTALITY of Marvyn Bradshaw's murder, it was barely reported by the media other than the local papers. Outside Nottingham it was simply another gun death and warranted little more than the odd newspaper paragraph. The police were keen to stress that Marvyn was a likeable young man who had never been in trouble with the law. He worked hard as a shopfitter, sometimes six days a week, and he was well liked. Although police initially believed Jamie Gunn was the intended target, another man in the car that night had in fact been in O'Brien's sights. They were also aware that feelings would be running high. They would have to race against time to catch the people responsible before revenge was sought by the Bestwood Cartel.

Detective Chief Inspector Phil Walker, leading the investigation, told the media, 'We have not had many witnesses at all really, so far. There was an after-hours drinking session at the pub and people who had been in there have been a bit reluctant to give us a statement.' This was nothing to do with fear of being caught drinking out of hours. Those in the Sporting Chance that evening had already been told by the Bestwood Cartel that this would be sorted out their own way, not by the police or anyone from Operation Ozone – the name for the investigation into Marvyn's murder. Police had the names of O'Brien and Salmon but the Bestwood Cartel's tentacles reached deeper and further than theirs. Within twenty-four hours, Colin Gunn had put the word out within the criminal fraternity. 'We need to find these two before the police. Put the word out to everybody. If you get a bite, you will be rewarded,' he told his troops.

By 3 September, intelligence was coming in to the police that Gunn was pulling out all the stops to track the duo and that if O'Brien or Salmon could not be found then their relatives and friends would be targeted. The Cartel's soldiers got to work. On 7 September, a brick and then a firebomb were thrown through the window of a house Salmon had once shared with an ex-girlfriend, Alison Oldham, in Leybourne Drive, Bestwood. On the same day, a homemade hand grenade was thrown through the window of

Salmon's house on Brooklyn Road. Colin Gunn also learned that two associates of Salmon had helped him get away. On 8 September, as one of the two drove in a car with a friend, a motor-bike with a pillion passenger pulled up alongside and two shots were fired into the car, one hitting him in the buttock. Police attributed the shooting directly to the Bestwood Cartel.

By this time, officers had been visiting Michael O'Brien's mother, Joan Stirland, almost daily as they stepped up their efforts to track down her son. She helped them as much as she could and said her son had intimated that he had been involved in the murder in a telephone conversation, but she did not feel she could make a statement. This was also information that the Bestwood Cartel had become aware of, almost certainly through a police contact, and it incensed them that she was unwilling to make a statement. The Cartel also knew Mrs Stirland's home address and were aware that O'Brien had a sister in Boston, Lincolnshire. The police could not work out how Colin Gunn was getting so much intelligence, yet they now knew that anybody connected with the two suspects was in danger.

There was a collective sigh of relief from the Ozone team when Michael O'Brien was arrested in Leicester on 9 September, at a girlfriend's house. Mrs Stirland had been told about the shooting of Kevin White but not that she or any of her family was in danger, even though there was clear evidence that she was. Gunn himself believed that a few scare tactics were needed to concentrate Mrs Stirland's mind about giving the police a statement implicating her son. Late on the evening of 14 September, two crash-helmeted gunmen left their motorcycle and approached her house in Southview Road. They fired five times: twice from a .38 revolver and three times from a shotgun. One bullet went through the first-floor bedroom window, another through the bathroom window, a third through the front door and two through the downstairs window. John and Joan Stirland dived onto the living room floor and lay there, paralysed with fear before, until Joan was able to crawl upstairs and make a 999 call from her mobile phone. They were very lucky to be alive. That same day the Bestwood Cartel again targeted Alison Oldham's house in Leybourne Drive with an arson attack, while another former girlfriend of Salmon's reported seeing a gunman on a motorcycle pointing a shotgun towards her near her home.

The next morning, the Stirlands decided to leave Nottingham for good. They were terrified and had no faith in the police being able to protect them from the gangsters; indeed they thought that the presence of officers in their vicinity was aggravating the situation and making them less secure. They had good reason to feel that way.

IN LATE SEPTEMBER 2003, a young Scot sat in a pub being lectured by a tall, burly, shaven-headed man in a Lacoste tracksuit top. The young man quietly took in the message as the shaven-headed man explained his plan to rob a jewellery shop. He had recently lost a £70,000 cocaine shipment and needed some quick cash to pay off the suppliers. The young man had already carried out several armed robberies for him in the past few weeks, three of them over a single twelve-hour period. During one raid he had discharged the gun he was carrying to frighten the victims. The same day he had also been part of a gang of men who brutally attacked dreadlocked social worker Derrick Senior while he was enjoying a pint with a friend in the Lord Nelson pub in Bulwell.

The shaven-headed man knew the Scottish lad was a hothead and sometimes a liability, but he could groom him, he thought. He would try to buy off the Rastafarian social worker with a bribe but for now he needed this robbery carrying out. Two other men working for the gang had already reconnoitred the shop and decided which jewellery cabinet to target. The shaven-headed man stressed that he did not want anybody killed.

According to an account later given to the police by one of those involved, and outlined to a judge in legal submissions before trial, the burly man was Colin Gunn and the young man James Brodie, one of his underlings. They were planning the robbery of the Time Centre in Arnold, Nottingham, run by Victor and Marian Bates. The robbery would involve a four-man team led by Brodie. In the getaway vehicle would be Dean Betton, and driver Craig Moran. Peter Williams, the youngest member of the gang at just seventeen, would carry a crowbar and assist Brodie. A high-powered scanner would help the gang to monitor police radio messages. The robbery was set for 30 September.

Peter Williams would later tell police that Gunn continued to outline the plan, ordering Brodie to park his scooter up an alleyway and to make sure there were no customers in the shop when they entered. Brodie nodded, listening almost reverently. Gunn, said Williams, was adamant that he did not want any shooting, but Brodie was a loose cannon; who knew what he might do?

On the morning of 30 September, Victor and Marian Bates made their way into Arnold, taking the road from the village of Ravenshead. Victor was sixty-five and Marian sixty-four. Their jewellery store had a bit of early trade but by 11am only a handful of customers had come into the shop: a woman looking for a watch for her husband, a couple who browse through the engagement rings before leaving empty-handed, another man looking for a some special earrings for a girlfriend. The shop was empty when, at about 1.30pm, two young men wearing motorcycle crash helmets with the visors up and rucksacks on their backs burst in. Xanthe Bates, Victor and Marian's twenty-three-year-old daughter, was helping out in the shop and happened to be on the telephone to her husband. She was startled by the noisy entrance of the two men storming in. One of them opened his jacket, took out a crowbar out and walked towards one of the glass cabinets, which he tried to jemmy open. The other man, slightly older, looked Xanthe in the eye.

'This is an armed robbery. Put the fucking phone down now.'

It seemed unreal, like a scene from a movie. Xanthe was rooted to the spot, phone still in her hand. Marian and Victor heard the shouting from the back of the shop and rushed to the front counter. Marian saw the two young men and walked towards her daughter to take charge of the situation. One of the men levelled a gun at Xanthe, who still had the phone in her hand, and took a couple of steps forward. Marian rushed in front of Xanthe. Trying to protect her daughter, she stretched out her arms instinctively and screamed, 'No!' There was a roar of gunfire from three feet away and Marian collapsed on the ground. The shooter shouted at Marian, now slumped on the shop floor, 'You stupid cow.' All hell broke loose. Victor had managed to press a silent alarm button underneath the counter and now had an old fencing foil which he grabbed from the back of the shop. He rushed towards the gunman, later identified in court as James Brodie. Brodie aimed the gun at him and pulled the trigger but this time the weapon misfired. Then Xanthe jumped on Brodie's back, screaming and grabbing his arms so that he couldn't raise the weapon again at her father.

Peter Williams, who had been grabbing jewellery from the cabinet and throwing it into his rucksack, saw his accomplice in trouble and swung his metal bar at Victor, slamming it into the side of his face. Reeling in pain with a fractured cheekbone, Victor remained undaunted and attacked Brodie with the foil once again. Williams raised the iron bar and aimed several more blows at Victor's arm as the shopkeeper tried to stab Brodie. Finally Brodie threw Xanthe off his back, cutting her lip badly with the handle of his gun in the process. He made for the exit, quickly followed by Williams.

They headed for a nearby alleyway where they had left a scooter with the engine running, but the gunshot and commotion attracted the attention of several shoppers, who were trying to see what was going on. Brodie brandished his gun menacingly and screamed, 'Get out the fucking way.' The startled shoppers parted and the raiders make their escape. At a petrol station about a mile away, their getaway car is waiting with Craig Moran driving and Dean Betton in the passenger seat. Betton's job was be to get rid of the scooter, while Moran drove Brodie and Williams back to a safe house to check their spoils. They found two rings, three pairs of earrings and a pendant worth just £1,100 in the rucksack. It was the price of Marian Bates's life.

The death of Marian Bates again trained the eyes of the nation on Nottingham. The fears of the white Middle Englander were concentrated in that one brutal murder: the Bates were grandparents, middle class, owned their own small business and lived in a village. Chief Constable Steve Green wondered what he had done to deserve such pressures. It was a far cry from the blueprint for success that he had devised and envisaged for Nottinghamshire some three years earlier, when he had taken over the force of 2,500 officers and a budget of some £170 million per year. Now it was attracting a reputation for being the worst policed county in England and Wales, despite the setting up a 'reputation unit', costing council taxpayers more than £400,000 a year, to tackle the media portrayal of the city. By then it was too late: the adverse headlines had sunk into the public consciousness.

BY 23 SEPTEMBER 2003 John and Joan Stirland had moved to a council flat in Goole on the Humberside coast. The place was not the dream home by the seaside that they had hoped for; in fact it was barely big enough for the two of them. They had received some help from the police in getting the tenancy of a one-bedroom flat but they felt increasingly isolated. Both were taking sleeping pills and anti-depressants and Joan was suffering from severe depression. Her son had been charged with a brutal murder and now they were living in a tiny flat in a place they hated, constantly looking over their shoulders. As the months ticked by the depression got worse. By November 2003 Joan had had enough. She wrote in her diary:

Tuesday the 2nd of Sept 03 police came to our house said they wanted to speak to my son JJ about a murder. After that they came every day for over a week. Then he was caught. Then the next Sunday at 10pm two men on a motorbike came to our house and fired six shots. They tried to kill me and John, my husband. The next day police told us to leave Nottingham. We didn't know where to go so we just drove. We ended up in Bridlington, we went to the council there and the manager Karen Jordan said why land on our doorstep why Bridlington. We were in such a state we didn't know what to do or who to turn to. She told us to come back Monday which we did. She took us to a single person's flat in a house with a man living upstairs. We were told to sign a tenancy, we were told we had no choice, so, desperate, we did it. We are on anti-depressants plus sleeping pills. The GP Dr Moran wrote us a letter to get us moved, so did the psychiatrist, but the CID in Nottingham put a stop to it. They said it is dangerous for us to go back. We have done nothing wrong. We are decent innocent people we have worked all our lives and now we have nothing. We are desperate to get out of Goole. So desperate that, if we are

not out by Xmas you will be taking us out in a box. We just
need you to know we want to be buried in Nottingham,
Wilford cemetery. This is just because the police in
Nottingham can't control the Gunn family who run the
Bestwood estate and everyone in it. It is disgraceful the
police can't do anything about them they used me three
times and now they don't want to know. Our lives are non
existent. We haven't been out of this bedsit since the day we
moved in on September 22 2003. We are at the end now, all
we wanted was to come back home.

During a phone call to her daughter Rosie in early November
2003, Joan said both she and John had talked about taking an
overdose of sleeping pills and ending it all. Rosie tried to cheer up
her mum and told her to get the police to do something. A few days
later, Rosie rang her mum back and told her she had looked
through a newspaper and seen some adverts for retirement
bungalows on the Lincolnshire coast. She gave Joan the phone
number and a few days later got a call back from her mum, who
was ecstatic. 'Rosie, it's fantastic!' she gushed. 'This place in
Trusthorpe is right next to the beach and it's quiet but there is
plenty to do. It's the perfect place for us, it's out of the way. We are
going to take it. Everything is going to be all right.'

ON 11 DECEMBER 2003, police officers were watching Colin
Gunn. Operation Starburst had made him and his brother
David its number one target. Colin had driven over to
Lincolnshire from Bestwood and was at a caravan site on Sutton
Road, on the way to Trusthorpe. He was having a dispute with
one of his crew who had displeased him. The man had fled
Bestwood for the East Coast after bodging a kidnapping for

Colin in Calverton village. Instead of taking the man away from the house in Calverton and giving him a hiding, the man had been persuaded to let his victim go free for the £200 he had in his pocket. Colin was furious when he found out and demanded that the kidnappers be dealt with using the most severe tactics. One of them had also bodged a previous shooting, almost killing a child. He had been warned at the time that any more failures to carry out Colin's orders would have fatal consequences for him.

Colin called John McSally, his favoured enforcer, over to Sutton to brief him on the job. He made it clear he wanted the man dead with no mistakes or messy leftovers. McSally was staying nearby in a caravan owned by Colin's mum while he planned the job. McSally approached his target but ended up shooting him through the shoulder instead of the head. Shocked and badly injured the man lived and made his way to safety. McSally was later arrested for the shooting but walked straight back out of the police station without being charged.

On 14 December, Joan and John Stirland gathered up their small bundle of belongings and made the journey down to Radio St Peter's, their new street (its distinctive name derived from its role as a wartime RAF station) in Trusthorpe. They were looking forward to life again, a new start, and could put some of the past behind them. Joan thought she would phone the police, just to let them know where they were. They had done little for her, but she felt she ought to call in case the Gunns were up to anything she needed to know about.

On 15 December, she rang her contact at Nottinghamshire Police to tell him about their move to Trusthorpe. He warned her about the Gunns' connections with the area but she was adamant that this was where they were going to start a new life. The officer would later be asked in a courtroom whether police had subse-

quently examined the security issues surrounding the Stirlands'
move to Trusthorpe. 'I had satisfied myself that they were not
vulnerable at that location, yes,' he replied.

CHAPTER 9
FRIENDS OF OURS

The Bestwood cartel now exercised control over a number of pubs in the Bestwood and Bulwell area, extorting protection money and laundering cash through its books. Colin and David Gunn were now masters at creating fear to suit their ends. Both played football for their favourite pub, the Scots Grey, and during one Sunday league match in March 2003, at Bulwell Hall Farm, the visiting team received a reminder of the Gunn brothers' intimidation skills. The Jolly Farmers football team walked into their dressing room ahead of the match to find a severed pig's head in a plastic bag with a message scrawled in blood: 'Welcome to Hell.' Someone had acquired it from a local butcher. The opposition team lost their spark, suffering a 3-2 defeat after extra time. Jolly Farmers team secretary Geoff Best was urged to make an official complaint to the FA but was less than enthusiastic. 'We have got nothing to say,' was his only comment after the match.

The Scots Grey pub had been frequently used by the Gunn brothers. Any trouble which flared up on the premises was rarely dealt with by the police. In February 1999, a thirty-five-year-old man was stabbed several times outside the pub in a Friday night fracas. When police went to see him, he told them from his hospital bed that he had no idea who his attacker was and he did not want them to take it any further. He was, as he pointed out, already in poor shape and talking would be bad for his health.

The rundown pubs they operated, which would otherwise have been boarded up and shut down, were given at least some lease of life with the Bestwood Cartel behind them. The Cartel was also branching out. Colin had renewed his association with a family-run gang in north Nottinghamshire who were equally brutal in their methods, and with Jonathan Quinn, another Nottingham criminal from the Bilborough area, who had branched out significantly from cigarette and cannabis smuggling into Class A drugs importation and firearms to service the north of England.

John and Rob Dawes were the generals of the Dawes Cartel, based in the Mansfield and Sutton-in-Ashfield areas of Nottinghamshire. By 2001, they had come under investigation by law enforcement agencies, who were surprised by the magnitude of their operation. They ran a multi-million-pound drugs empire from a small house in Tudor Street, Sutton-in-Ashfield. Their *modus operandi* was almost a blueprint of the Bestwood Cartel, with whom they enjoyed extensive links, not least through John Dawes, who had worked with Colin Gunn some years earlier. The Dawes Cartel would recruit young street dealers, who usually had addictions of their own, to act as runners for them and enforce their rule of law. Their number one rule was that fear brought great loyalty: if you could grab them by the balls, their hearts and minds would follow.

Like his pal Colin Gunn, John Dawes eschewed life within the legitimate working world and preferred the black economy where no taxes were paid, other than to those higher up the drugs business ladder who could 'tax' you. From 1991 until his arrest in 2005, there is no evidence that John Dawes did a single day's legitimate work. He lived almost exclusively, according to his own accounts, as a jobless man claiming benefits. His hot-headed brother Rob, who had a penchant for ordering the shootings of anyone who displeased him, was operating from Spain from 2002 onwards, organising shipments of cannabis resin and cocaine, while the rest of the gang organised wholesale deliveries of amphetamines and heroin, mainly from Liverpool and Runcorn. Until 2001, they operated almost undetected by any meaningful probe by law enforcement.

Police in Nottinghamshire launched Operation Normality in 2001 with the help of the National Crime Squad and customs investigators. By 2003, it would receive additional resources with the sanctioning of Operation Starburst by law enforcement agencies in London. It found that the Dawes Cartel was made up of three generals: John and Rob Dawes and Gary Hardy, another Mansfield man whose father had been the high up the command chain of a Midlands Hell's Angels chapter. These three leaders would take a three-way split on each shipment, with Rob organising the smuggling of cocaine and cannabis from Spain and John organising its distribution across the Midlands, as well as the wholesale importation of amphetamines from Holland and heroin from within Britain. In addition, the Dawes Cartel was operating with Anthony Handley and Keith Harrison over cannabis shipments into the UK; these were handled by John and Rob's father, Arthur. By 2001, this close-knit group was importing so many drugs into Nottinghamshire that they had a backlog, so they began to bury large amounts underground in coded locations in woodland in Sutton-in-Ashfield, at Sutton Lawn, Mapplewells Recreation Park and in woodland near Pleasley. Police would eventually find £500,000 buried in woodland hides near Sutton Parkway train station, together with a sawn-off shotgun and ammunition. Other burial grounds for the drugs remain hidden to this day.

On 1 June 2001, investigators made their first major inroad into the gang. Officers lay in wait as two Dawes Cartel lieutenants drove to Colwick industrial estate, on the outskirts of Nottingham. Police were staggered by the scale of drug-running they discovered. Inside the industrial unit was around 100 kilos of amphetamine, six kilos of cannabis resin and eleven kilos of paracetamol cutting agents – enough to make thirty kilos of heroin ready for sale on the street. Jonathan Guest, Ian Butler and Martin Smith were all taken out by police within a few days. All were linked to the production unit at Colwick, which was used to cut cocaine, heroin and amphetamines as well as manufacture ecstasy pills and store cannabis.

John Dawes decided it was time for a holiday. A break on the Costa del Crime would enable him to rethink strategies as well as link up with his brother Rob, who spent regular breaks in Spain and was laundering their money in two bars and a restaurant supply business near Fuengirola. He would be able to decide whether new recruits were needed and whether to put a scare into those arrested. Fear was needed to ensure that those who had been lifted by the police did not lead to his door. John and Rob Dawes flew out to Malaga with some haste in June 2001. John rented a villa for nine months, hoping the police interest would eventually dissipate. He flew back to the UK in September 2001 to test the water. Police just kept watching, knowing that if they bided their time more would be revealed. They had taken out a middle tier of the Dawes pyramid and the gang's generals were running scared. Now John Dawes was relying on a twenty-three-year-old to be one of his lieutenants. Ryan Smith would take on the role. On the legal front, the arrested Guest, Butler and Martin Smith were all beyond help, thought John Dawes. He just hoped the fear that he and Rob instilled in them would be enough to prevent them grassing for favourable sentences.

When their case eventually reached Nottingham Crown Court, in January 2002, Guest admitted conspiracy to supply amphetamines and cannabis and possessing £150,000 of heroin, and was imprisoned for fourteen years. Butler, who admitted possession of heroin with intent to supply, received eight years. Smith, whose fingerprints were all over the Colwick industrial unit and who was caught with a carrier bag stained with heroin and with £22,000 hidden in his pantry, received a four years.

At the same time as National Crime Squad officers were tackling this lower end of the Dawes Cartel, they had come across links with another gang smuggling large amounts of cannabis from Holland and Belgium via the North Sea. Keith 'Red' Harrison and Anthony 'Nottingham Tone' Handley, had come to the attention of Dutch police investigating the perplexing murder of a middle-aged schoolteacher. On 24 November 2002, fifty-two-year-old Gerard Meesters answered his front door in a quiet area of Groningen. He was surprised to find five men outside. One handed him a phone number on a torn-off packet of red Rizla cigarette papers. They spoke with English accents and the message was this: 'You are Gerard Meesters. Your sister Janet [sic] has done something bad, she has stolen something from us. You must ring this number in Spain and tell the man who answers the phone where your sister is. Be aware that if you do not do this we will come back and if we have to come back it will not be for a chat.'

Gerard was shaking with fear. He had never been involved in crime. He knew his sister had gone off the rails but he had no more idea where she was than the hoods who had visited him. Gerard contacted the Dutch Police and told them what had happened. They told him he should take the threat seriously and consider moving out of his home temporarily. Overnight Gerard moved himself, his wife and their two children. Police kept watch on the property for a couple of days, but were not there when, four days later, Gerard decided he needed to use his computer and returned home alone to Uransstraat, a sleepy suburban street. As he opened his front door to leave at 7.22pm on 28 November 2002, he was approached by a man who pulled out a handgun and shot him eight times.

Dutch investigators were baffled by the murder. Here was a man who had no criminal background and who had been living a quiet life. But as their attentions turned towards his sister, Janette, they slowly began to unravel a criminal network which centred on the Dawes Cartel. They placed telephone intercepts on the phones of certain Dutch criminals which soon threw up the names of Nottingham Tony and Red Harrison, as well as Rob and John Dawes. Through a massive total of 20,000 phone calls analysed, ninety-five per cent of which were in basic drugs code, they had stumbled upon another huge syndicate sending drugs from Holland and Belgium to the UK. What they learned from the bugs was that Janette Meesters had become embroiled in the criminal network while living in Spain and had been working as a courier for the Dawes Cartel.

In autumn 2002, Janette and her friend, Madeline Brussen, had been given the job of driving a van from Spain to Holland carrying a large amount of cannabis. The couple were pulled over by Dutch police on suspicion of drink-driving after they were alerted to the erratic behaviour of the van. Inside police discovered more than 350 kilos of cannabis. When Rob Dawes found out about the drug bust, he exploded with rage; it was a shipment intended for Nottingham Tony and was supposed to be around 1.5 tonnes of cannabis. According to evidence later given in court, Dawes made the assumption that the rest of the drugs must have been stolen by the two women. He set about trying to locate them and sent a message to Daniel Sowerby, a forty-seven-year-old heroin addict who had been working for the gang since absconding from open prison in 2000. The message was clear: 'Put the frighteners on relatives and family of these two and we will smoke them out. If the women don't do anything, we'll take it to the next stage.'

Sowerby recruited a man called Steven Barnes as his driver and the two of them started to trace relatives of Meesters and Brussen. First they paid a visit to Meesters' older brother, Gerard. Sowerby and Barnes returned to Groningen on 28 November. Barnes later said he was not told the reason for the visit to the city, and claimed he thought it was for a drugs run. At around 7.15pm that night, Sowerby, who was living under an assumed name with a false passport in Breda, a city in southern Holland, took a handgun from a bag and left the car, while Barnes waited for him. A few minutes later Sowerby returned and shouted at Barnes, 'Go go go, let's get out of here.'

'What the fuck's going on?' Barnes asked.

Sowerby replied: 'I've been told to kill somebody, which I have, and that is all you need to know.'

The duo stopped on the way back to their safe house in Breda and Sowerby dumped the murder weapon. Their victim was Gerard Meesters.

A week later, Madeleine Brussen's mother, ex-husband and boyfriend received a note telling them to contact the same Spanish phone number given to Gerard Meesters. Along with the note were cuttings from a newspaper which detailed Meesters' murder. The implications for the family should they not call the phone number were clear. Dutch police set up surveillance on the family's properties. In the summer of 2003, the relatives received another note warning them to tell them where Madeline was or their lives would be in danger. Police set about forensically testing the material which had been sent in the post. Incredibly Sowerby had failed to check the material he posted to the Brussen family was clean and Barnes, who was known to Dutch police, had left his fingerprint on one of the newspaper clippings.

Investigations revealed that Barnes had since been arrested and was serving a sixteen-month prison term for a fatal road accident in Rotterdam after driving while drunk and high on cocaine. Sowerby had also been locked up for drug offences. Police visited Barnes first and he confessed to driving Sowerby to the scene of the assassination. Barnes said he had initially been sent to Amsterdam by the Dawes Cartel because he had stolen forty-two grams of heroin from them. He was told he would have to pay off his drug debt by doing errands for them in Holland and was ordered to become a runaround for Sowerby. After he ferried Sowerby to the scene of Gerard Meesters' murder, he fled to Spain, where Rob Dawes had ordered him for a 'debriefing'. The debriefing session ended with him being severely beaten with an iron bar; he suffered several broken limbs. Barnes was told he would be killed if he ever mentioned the murder.

A Dutch court gave Barnes, described as a 'victim of a criminal organisation', an eight-year sentence for his involvement in Meesters' murder. He had known the Dawes brothers from school and made a number of visits to Amsterdam with Rob Dawes, acting as a drugs tester before being 'exiled' to Holland to repay his heroin debts. His lawyer pointed out that once he became a soldier for the gang he could not just leave. His life and the lives of his family would be in grave danger. If he was arrested or tried to flee, the gang would assume he was a risk and could compromise their operation. Sowerby, who was described by the Dutch judge as a 'very dangerous man', was sentenced to life imprisonment. He had already spent much of his life behind bars, having previously been serving a life sentence in the UK for the brutal murder of sixty-six-year-old Harold Burdall, who was beaten to death during a burglary in Lincolnshire in December 1977. Sowerby had fled North Sea Camp open prison in 2001 before initially going on the run in France and then Holland, where he was recruited by the Dawes Cartel. Both men refused to give any details of the people they were working for.

'I have to think of my family and relatives,' said Sowerby. 'If I confess the murder, I have no life any more. Then I fear for the lives of my brothers, nephews and nieces. I will never confess.'

Barnes said, 'What happened to Gerard Meesters is not unusual. These people know how to deliver pain in your life.'

Throughout the investigation, Dutch police were only able to speak to Janette Meesters once, while she was in Spain, before they lost contact. 'We have no idea where the two women are,' one investigator said. 'The trail ended in Spain. We don't know whether they are alive or dead.'

The spin-off for National Crime Squad investigators in the UK was that, as a result of the Dutch phone taps, they now knew that the Dawes Cartel was a ruthless, calculating gang willing to murder on the same scale as the Bestwood Cartel, and they were dealing in much larger quantities and with wider networks than had previously been thought. The telephone taps had also thrown up a link between large-scale drugs shipments flowing from Spain, Holland and Belgium and the cartels runs by the Dawes family, Keith Harrison and Anthony Handley, and the Bestwood Cartel. All roads were leading back to Nottinghamshire and southern Spain, where Rob Dawes was still holed up near the town of Fuengirola.

OPERATION NORMALITY, THE probe into the Dawes Cartel, was in full swing. After bringing down some of the Dawes lieutenants and realising that the Cartel was bigger than they thought, officers began to take a closer look at the financial transactions of the gang. They found more than £8.5 million going through their hands between November 2002 and June 2003. In addition, members of the gang were logged on more than forty flights coming in and out of Malaga and Amsterdam over a two-and-a-half year period. In the midst of Operation Normality, Nottinghamshire Police had to deal with the murder of David Draycott, shot dead outside his home in Sutton-in-Ashfield in October 2002 over a £30,000 debt to the Bestwood and Dawes gangs. John Dawes was given a police liaison officer on the basis that he might be at risk because people believed he was linked to the murder. Dawes even had the cheek to offer the detective constable a job. In October 2002, he telephoned the officer.

'When are you due to hang up your truncheon?' he said. 'You know we are always on the lookout for lads like yourself – you know, due for retirements. With the kind of stuff you could help us with, you would shoot up the promotional ladder in our organisation.'

As officers listened in to calls between the group, they heard the coded names of mystery figures the Cartel was dealing with: The Fisherman, High Tower, Special Bill and Carlos. As arrests began to take place in 2003, police also managed to turn some of the Cartel's drug runners, despite the threats of violence which were being levelled against them. Crucially it led to four runners – Richard Carrington, Marc Simpson, Lee Blackmore and Kristian Barsby – giving detailed accounts of how the Cartel operated. Marc Simpson told police how he had been recruited by John Dawes after coming out of prison in January 2002. Two months later, he and a friend agreed to sell heroin for John Dawes. Anything they made above £750 per ounce would be profit. A meeting took place at which Dawes and Gary Hardy were present and outlined the areas where the runners could sell. Dawes told Simpson he would let him sell heroin in Sutton and that another man would handle Kirkby-in-Ashfield. Simpson always took the money to Dawes, usually at his house in Tudor Street but once at a public house. On two occasions he picked up ten kilos of amphetamine and Dawes told him where to drop them, but some of the speed went missing and Dawes exploded with rage. 'Ten minutes later John Dawes came round and battered me round the head with a cosh, then they got my hands and smashed them,' said Simpson. 'I was absolutely terrified, I soiled myself.' He said Dawes had beaten him senseless with a baseball bat on another two occasions. 'If you lied to John, he hit you. He was an absolute psychopath.'

Richard Carrington told police how he worked as a courier for Rob Dawes from 2000 until early 2002. Carrington was also involved with John Dawes and saw him operating an electric money-counting machine at his house, putting notes into bundles of £1,000. In 2001, Carrington went to the Colwick unit, used for making ecstasy tablets and cutting cocaine and amphetamine, to pick up some drugs. He told police how he would usually pack the drugs under a spare wheel on John Dawes's Shogun 4x4. Among the other tasks carried out by Carrington were shipping drugs to Rugby and Manchester and moving money to Holland and Spain for Rob. Carrington would fly from Heathrow, East Midlands and Gatwick airports to Amsterdam and Malaga with wads of cash secreted in shoes or the false lining of suitcases.

Lee Blackmore was released from prison in June 2000 and began selling heroin for himself before John Dawes told him he would have to work for the Cartel 'or suffer the consequences'. Blackmore told police how Dawes used a myriad of burial sites, safe houses and runners to keep his own fingerprints off the drug shipments. Marc Simpson would collect heroin from Matlock and bring Blackmore seven ounces a week, which he divided into half-gram bags. He paid Simpson. After a while Barsby replaced Simpson and supplied Blackmore. Both Barsby and Blackmore became stressed after a load of heroin went missing and first Barsby went on the run, eventually walking into a police station to confess all, closely followed by Blackmore. Barsby's role was to take heroin to Blackmore and then divide it into ounces. They were supplying two or three people every day with an ounce of heroin, selling it at £900 a time. It would be collected from a Tesco car park in Nottingham once a month. Barsby would make a profit of £75 per ounce. He also collected amphetamines from the same place in Nottingham, the smallest quantity being two to four kilos and the largest twenty kilos. Like Marc Simpson, he suffered from the gang leader's uncontrollable rages: Barsby told police how John Dawes beat him up badly because he did not like the girl that Barsby was going out with.

The Dawes brothers' fifty-nine-year-old father, Arthur 'Eddie' Dawes, posed as an antiques dealer, even allowing another Essex-based cocaine gang with close links to the Dawes Cartel to use his addresses for bogus businesses. Between 1997 and his arrest in 2003, Arthur claimed thousands of pounds in disability benefit, but appeared to be quite capable of helping his son transport drugs from place to place. He lived in Ingoldmells, on the Lincolnshire coast, in a modest house in Central Avenue with his partner, Rebecca Bridge. When police eventually raided the property they found £10,000 in cash, two bank note counting machines and a Dutch mobile phone in a bedside cabinet. In another room was a holdall with two maps, one of Barcelona and one of Santander, with hotels marked in rings. In a sideboard cupboard in the living room was a 2003 diary with the entries 'in' and 'out' for the period from February to 12 June and references to names, places and flights. Also in the lounge were a large number of receipts for mobile phone cards, ten phone chargers and a number of other items. Among the items in Bridge's handbag was a book containing a number of phone numbers in a mixture of her and Arthur's handwriting and the names of middle-tier suppliers, which had come from Anthony Handley. Arthur Dawes had also been observed at Newport Pagnell service station on the M1 motorway handing over a Tesco coolbag to the driver of a black London cab. The cab was pulled over as it left the service station and police found £100,000 in the bag. Dawes said the money was for Anthony Handley.

By late spring, with a number of arrests having already broken the gang down, the Dawes Cartel began to unravel, first as a result of an accident. On 29 April 2003, one its couriers crashed his car containing two kilos of heroin. Analysis of a mobile phone in the car showed a link with the major drugs dealer Donny Quinn. Then John Dawes himself was arrested. Having lost many of his troops, he had been forced to get hands-on. On 23 May 2003, the police saw his fellow boss Gary Hardy driving a black Porsche near Sutton-in-Ashfield. It paused at a junction long enough to give the impression that it was waiting there, before pulling round the corner. The police then saw John Dawes at the passenger door. He got into the vehicle. Police saw body movement in the Porsche, as if something was being handed over, and moved in as Dawes stood on the pavement with a carrier bag and the Porsche drove off, arresting Dawes as he got into his car. The carrier bag contained £14,000. Other members of the gang were also rounded up, including Arthur Dawes, Rebecca Bridge and Ryan Smith, who had been acting as one of John Dawes's lieutenants.

TONY HANDLEY AND Red Harrison were the next to trip up. Thirty-three-year-old Handley, who was also known as 'Spunky', worked with Harrison as the kingpin in charge of distributing drugs, including ecstasy, amphetamines, cocaine and cannabis, to the west of the UK after they had been imported from Holland and Belgium. When their Dutch counterparts informed them that Handley and Harrison's names had turned up on bugs connected with the murder of Gerard Meesters, National Crime Squad officers from the Midlands launched Operation Shearson against them in March 2003.

Handley and Harrison had got to know one another while serving time in HMP North Sea Camp in Lincolnshire, Handley for an armed robbery and Harrison for manslaughter. Handley was an unlikely villain. His father was heavily involved with a Hucknall church and Handley had been trained as an accountant. When he partnered the opening of a sport shop in March 1995, there was little sign of him becoming heavily involved in organised crime – he even gave away its first £100 to help Glaisdale School in Bilborough help replace sports equipment destroyed in a fire. But the business went under, leaving Handley to consider crime as an option to attain the wealth he sought. His first major brush with the law came in February 2000 when he was convicted of armed robbery along with two others: Dale Wright, who he would later recruit for the drug business, and Keith Staniland, a thirty-year-old, from Huthwaite. The trio jumped Robert Bolam in his Ford Transit and relieved him at gunpoint of 160,000 cigarettes on the A610 near Giltbrook on 2 November 1999. It was while serving some of his sentence at HMP North Sea Camp that Handley hooked up with Harrison.

After absconding from the open prison, Harrison, using the false identity of 'Graham Harley', managed to get a fake passport and driving licence and disappear into obscurity in Amsterdam. He had been involved with ecstasy shipments before and clearly felt he could make even greater profits by being in Holland. His name first cropped up in Dutch investigations into Franciscus Peiter Beikmans, a wholesale supplier of drugs in Holland. When the name of an Englishmen called 'Red' turned upon the tapes, they discovered Harrison's real identity and a link was subsequently made to the Gerard Meesters murder.

Harrison was shipping drugs to Handley after buying them from Beikmans, who was based in the city of Tilburg. Harrison had looked up other friends from HMP North Sea Camp to assist in the UK distribution and these included a number from Nottinghamshire. Handley would arrange for the drugs to be transported by lorry. Harrison only had to secure a space in a lorry driven by someone who innocently thought they were carrying a legitimate load. Millions of pounds worth of drugs would be shipped over to Felixstowe on a ferry from Rotterdam in taped-up cardboard boxes. Harrison was also shipping drugs for other gangs, including the Bestwood Cartel and Jonathan 'Donny' Quinn. It was easy to then use Handley for some of that distribution. He would meet the loads and arrange distribution throughout the East Midlands, West Midlands and London. The pair soon enjoyed a lavish lifestyle. Harrison had swanky apartments in Amsterdam and Breda and both men drove around in Mercedes and Audi TTs.

Handley would talk on his mobile while sipping a latte in an Internet café in Hucknall on the edge of Nottingham, listening to Harrison complain how bored he was in Holland and reveal how he spent up to £11,000 a time on raucous nights in the red light districts, picking up expensive hookers while his wife was back home in the UK. Much of their talk – monitored by the National Crime Squad – was drug shipments. The duo used basic code words in their phone conversations. Cannabis was referred to as 'a bit of green', speed or amphetamines were 'them fast things', ecstasy tablets were 'the little ones' and cocaine 'the expensive stuff'. However, Harrison, who became rash when things went wrong, would sometimes fail to stick to the agreement on code words, particularly when a shipment was intercepted, and would talk explicitly about 'coke' and 'speed'.

One officer said, 'Harrison was a Billy no-mates who only got friends by paying for high-class hookers. His phone became his best friend. That was his undoing. Even when he couldn't get through he left a trail, he just couldn't resist ringing up people who we could then link the trade to through the mapping of the phones. When he did get through he was often saying things that played right into our hands.' Handley sensed danger and halted calls with Harrison. With his main contact suddenly unobtainable, Harrison turned for help to his old friend Donald James, an associate from his West Midlands days of petty crime and now an underworld figure in Birmingham. He agreed to arrange the next shipment and approached Michael Saward, a boat skipper with two previous convictions for drug importation. James paid around £5,000 towards the hire of Saward's twenty-one-foot speedboat, *Sundancer*, which set off from Ramsgate in Kent in August 2003 to make a pick-up at the Military Yacht Club in Nieuwpoort, on the Belgian coast. Also on board was Steven Bower, an old acquaintance of Harrison, whose job was to keep an eye on the skipper and the drugs.

At the same time, Harrison drove from his home in Breda with a Ford Focus filled with drugs, accompanied by his Dutch supplier Beikmans, Beikmans' brother-in-law and another unnamed Dutchman in a separate vehicle. He met Saward and Bowers with *Sundancer*, while the three Dutchmen headed back to Holland. The National Crime Squad and their Dutch and Belgian colleagues knew all about it: not only did they have phone taps in place but they had infiltrated the gang. Belgian police arrested Harrison and his English accomplices, who were later extradited to the UK, while the Dutchmen were arrested back in Holland. In England, the National Crime Squad picked up Donald James. Beikmans, known as 'the Tillerman', would later receive a six-and-a-half year sentence and his brother-in-law three years for his involvement.

After being spooked, a feeling which was proved correct by the arrest of his pal in Belgium, Handley went on the run, holing up in a £30,000 caravan in on a remote park in Scarborough, Yorkshire. For six months he watched and waited, with the National Crime Squad having little idea where he was. On phone taps, they then heard that Handley was about to get married, so detectives began ringing round register offices across the country. Nothing turned up locally so one officer joked that he was probably going to get married in Gretna Green, the Scottish border town famous for its quickie marriages. As Detective Inspector John Cudlipp, who led the investigation, recalled, 'We had tried more obvious locations in Sutton-in-Ashfield and Nottingham. It was a process of elimination. Then someone had the inspiration of checking the most obvious location, Gretna Green, and lo and behold, they were right.'

On the morning of 1 December 2003, at the Mill Hotel on the outskirts of Gretna Green, a party of eight gathered ready for a noon wedding ceremony in a chapel on the grounds. A few minutes before the start Handley, still nursing a bruiser of a hangover and feeling uncomfortably paranoid, was getting ready with his best man, who joked about any last requests. His bride was in another room alone, looking forward to a future with a man she felt could keep her in the material manner to which she had become accustomed over the past few years. But when officers moved in to make the arrest, it was all over within the space of minutes. Handley did not resist. The thirty-three-year-old later told police, 'I knew the game was up when I looked out through the window and saw a broad-shouldered man go past.'

A delighted DI Cuddlip said, 'He was surprised to see us. He didn't say very much. He was trying to keep his dad at bay.'

The gang was dealt with at Birmingham Crown Court in April 2005. Keith Winston Eugene Harrison, originally from Coventry, was sentenced to eight years in prison, while Handley was jailed for five-and-a-half years. Other members of the Hucknall trafficking ring were jailed for a combined total of more than twenty years. These foot soldiers, all employed by Handley, included Mark Ford, a thirty-two-year-old from Bulwell, who was known as 'Joe 90' or 'Goggles' because he wore spectacles. Ford was jailed for three years. He had been arrested with two other defendants in July 2003 with a consignment of drugs on the M1 near Northampton. Ford also received an extra six months for producing cannabis at a property he owned in Nottingham. Alan 'Ostrich Man' Walker, a sixty-two-year-old from Cotgrave, near Nottingham, received an eighteen-month sentence. He had been involved in a huge ostrich farm fraud in Nottinghamshire which had made more than £20 million in less than seventeen months by duping people into buying shares. He became involved in the gang as a result of his time at North Sea Camp prison and agreed to fly over to Britain from his home in Nice, France, in 2003 to transport drugs for Handley. He was arrested in Newmarket driving a van containing eighty-five kilos of cannabis.

Adrian Haywood, a thirty-six-year-old from Underwood, got six years for supplying mobile phones and transport for the traffickers. He was a motor trader with a workshop in Somercotes, Derbyshire. Officers found 37,500 ecstasy tablets in a search of the premises. Dale Wright, thirty-one, of Skegby, who was the security man for batches of drugs held in various locations, received three years, while Michael 'The Geezer' Saward, fifty-seven, who lived on a houseboat in Kent, got six years after being hired to take his speedboat to Belgium to collect drugs from Harrison. Steven 'Little Baz' Bower, thirty-five, of Grantham, received four years. He acted as a runner and a security man, holding drugs and going on trips to Belgium with Bower and, after becoming seasick, had unwittingly ensured the entire group decided to prolong their stay at

Nieuwpoort until he recovered. They were there when police swooped the next morning. Subsequent drug seizures included £1.9 million of cannabis in Felixstowe and 1.2 million ecstasy tablets, worth £4.8 million, in Holland.

By the end of the Operation Shearson, police had dealt another big blow to the drug shipments being managed from Nottinghamshire. Large amounts of Class A drugs were seized in Holland, Germany, Ghent, Brussels, Antwerp and Birmingham. With the help of Customs and Excise, the operation seized 870 kilos of cannabis, worth over £1.9 million, and sixteen kilos of cocaine with a street value of £848,000. Officers were ecstatic with the results. 'Dismantling this well-established network is a major achievement and is down to the hard work and dedication of all the officers involved,' said DI John Cudlipp afterwards. 'Harrison and his cohorts have paid the heavy price of their freedom for thinking they could make easy money through drugs-trafficking and we hope this sends out a strong message to others who are tempted to do the same.'

ANOTHER OF THE Gunns' associates, Donny Quinn, had been building up a massive drugs operation of his own. Quinn was no stranger to police and customs, having been lifted several times in large-scale cigarette and cannabis smuggling busts, but nothing had stuck. He had based himself in the Bilborough area of Nottingham, where in Cockington Road he had a large house which had been pimped up to make him the laird of the council estate. Such was the cheek of the man that he even had several former police officers from Nottinghamshire, who had branched out into gardening services on their retirement, willing to tend his expansive garden for him. He had already managed to wriggle out of a major bust in October 1999, when 120 kilos of cannabis was found in a lorry in Huthwaite. One of the gang's main men was a thirty-one-year-old tetraplegic called Nathan Graham who had suffered his massive disability as a result of a diving accident. Graham would later die of a fatal asthma attack six days after being remanded to Nottingham Prison; an inquest into his death recommended health care for disabled prisoners be improved. The cannabis case had been dealt with by National Crime Squad officers from Derby and Nottingham, some of whom were later embroiled in the cocaine-snorting scandal of 2001 (see Chapter Six). When it came to court in September 2000, legal submissions were heard in chambers by the judge and the trial was abandoned, though no reason was given publicly.

Quinn still faced a trial over a spectacular bust by Customs and Excise at a warehouse on the banks of the River Trent in August 1999. Investigators kept watch on the disused warehouse for several months as cigarettes were shipped in in their millions. Then, as a consignment worth more than £2 million came in, they swooped, some in high-powered rubber dinghy boats. By the end of a four-week trial at Nottingham Crown Court in March 2001, the jury was unable to reach a verdict. A retrial was sought but never materialised.

Quinn, perhaps becoming over-confident, launched himself into large-scale Class A drug shipments and firearms. Using connections he had built up over the years, he began assembling a formidable gang with some twenty trusted lieutenants spanning Nottinghamshire and South Yorkshire. Operation Myope was started in response by the National Crime Squad's Rugby branch in October 2003 and focused initially on the drug-trafficking activities of Quinn, two of his lieutenants – Michael McDonald, then aged thirty-five, from Aspley, and Jason Wesley, thirty-five, from Beeston – and the network of couriers working in Nottinghamshire. It soon became apparent that the gang was involved in the supply and distribution of drugs between London, Nottingham and West Yorkshire and had international links, with Quinn regularly visiting Malaga in Spain. Initial surveillance showed that Quinn was in regular contact over supplies with the Dawes Cartel as well as the Gunns. He also had strong links with underworld armourers across the country and had access to large caches of firearms, something he would later attempt to use to his advantage.

Among his gang was a real-life Robin Hood. Actor Mark Dickinson, who played the famous outlaw at the city's Tales of Robin Hood attraction during the early 1990s and would later appear in a film version of *Macbeth* with Jason Connery and Brian Blessed, had fallen on hard times. After getting to know Quinn – Dickinson also lived in Bilborough – he was offered a job doing runs for him and soon became one of his most trusted cocaine couriers. The thirty-nine-year-old was one of the first to be arrested during the three-year operation. Officers swooped on Dickinson after watching him drive into the Broad Oak pub in the village of Strelley on 2 July 2004, where he met a lorry driver. As he left, they pulled him over and discovered a kilo of cocaine in his car. He would later be jailed for three years and nine months. Another gang member was a Gulf War veteran from the Meadows who had served with the First Battalion Grenadier Guards in 1991. Dean Cumberpatch, thirty-four, was arrested after being caught driving a lorry with 150 kilos of cannabis resin for Quinn, and would later receive a two-year sentence.

By May 2004, Quinn had also become adept at money laundering. He entered into a deal with a group of Liverpool businessmen who ripped off the NatWest bank to the tune of £15 million in an elaborate fraud. Quinn became their banker. The idea for the sophisticated get-rich-quick scheme came from a genuine letter sent to all customers in the wake of NatWest's takeover of the Royal Bank of Scotland. It was a warning that while cheque funds would be shown as cleared on the third working day after being paid in, they could still end up bouncing if the cheque was bad. This was a signpost to the Merseyside villains that it was possible to take money that didn't actually exist from accounts. On the Wednesday before the May Bank Holiday, one of the Merseyside group went into a St Helens branch of the NatWest and placed £20 million in bogus cheques into an account. On the surface it was a legitimate deal for 38,000 Nokia mobile phones. By the Friday, well before the cheques would show up as having bounced, the funds were weaving their way through a number of other companies to disguise the origins and make it look like a legitimate financial transaction, before arriving in a bank account in Riga, Latvia. It was an account Quinn had opened in the name of Alverton Finance Ltd. Fortunately for NatWest, Latvia had just joined the European Union and been warned to be on the lookout for money laundering activities. Realising what was going on, the banking authorities in Latvia informed the City of London Police. The account was then frozen, preventing the conspirators transferring much of the cash to Dubai, though altogether £14 million of funds were cleared in Latvia before the game was up. Quinn would later receive a three-year prison sentence at Southwark Crown Court for fraud, to be added to his drug crimes.

Meanwhile his drug smuggling operations were being dealt a severe blow as police took out the middle tier of his gang, leaving Quinn exposed. Although the gang was surveillance savvy, regularly changing phones and using phone boxes, it did not bank on the National Crime Squad bugging its hire cars when they went in for a valet service. Every order Quinn gave was picked up by the surveillance team. Throughout 2004 the main players in his gang were relentlessly targeted until Quinn himself was eventually arrested. Once he was presented with all the bugged material, he threw in the towel and pleaded guilty. Altogether twenty-one members of the gang received combined prison sentences totalling 117 years. In 2006, Quinn himself received an eighteen-year stretch for conspiracy to supply cocaine, cannabis and amphetamines and a twelve-and-a-half year sentence, to run concurrently, for supply of ecstasy. More than £2 million of drugs had been discovered during Operation Myope, including six kilos of cocaine, six kilos of ecstasy, 160 kilos of cannabis and twenty-five kilos of amphetamines.

Quinn was not happy about his sentence, particularly as he had given National Crime Squad officers information about three arms caches he had knowledge of. He appealed on that basis but the judges pointed out that although the arms and ammunition had been discovered, and they had been important finds in the battle against organised crime, no one had been arrested. 'It is significant that having been in custody for eighteen months, the defendant still retained the ability to locate these weapons,' the Appeal Court judges said. The implication was clear: they were either his firearms or he was involved in their movement. Quinn was stuck with his eighteen-year sentence.

With Donny Quinn locked up and the Dawes Cartel taken down, Colin and David Gunn were running out of friends.

CHAPTER 10

STARBURST

One of the first targets of Operation Starburst was not the Gunns but a group of cocaine smugglers operating between Jamaica and the St Ann's estate. The gang was led by Lindford Shepherd and Karl Guthrie, who used female mules to bring cocaine into the city in bulk from the West Indies. Guthrie, who was jobless and lived on the St Ann's estate, and Shepherd had extensive links to Jamaica, were pouring millions of pounds worth of cocaine into the region. Operation Conduit was set up to target them and within a few months dealers working for them were being taken out – the base of the business pyramid was being chipped away. By the time the team got to Guthrie and Shepherd, they had taken out sixty-two of their foot soldiers and seized more than £3 million of coke. One twenty-nine-year-old smuggler, Sandra Cooke, who lived in Sneinton and worked as a cleaner at the *Nottingham Evening Post*, had made a number of mule runs to and from Jamaica, but was also ripping off local dealers. In February 2004, she made another trip, under the guise of visiting her 'sick mother' in Montego Bay. She was met off the plane, driven to a sugar cane field and executed with one shot to the back of the head.

Eventually Shepherd and Guthrie, having run out of workers, were forced to get hands-on. Shepherd, the senior of the two, used his son Jonathan Levine to ferry coke into the UK. He was caught and jailed for ten years. On 11 January 2005, Pamela Fogo, a fifty-one-year-old mother-of-three from the St Ann's estate, was met by Guthrie at Gatwick Airport. She had already been searched once after sniffer dogs marked her out but Customs officers had failed to find the coolbag stitched into the lining of her rucksack, containing uncut cocaine worth £320,000 on the street. Officers from Operation Conduit, who knew she was carrying cocaine some-where, followed the two as they took a taxi back to Nottingham, stopping the car on the A453 coming into the city. Fogo received a six-and-half year prison sentence for her mule work and Guthrie received ten years for conspiracy to supply Class A drugs. Shepherd, who had by now amassed substantial wealth including properties all over Jamaica, received a five-year sentence.

It was a successful operation by any standards. Now the Starburst team was ready to take on the white gangs – starting first with the Dawes family.

IN JANUARY 2004, Nottinghamshire Police arrested a young man on suspicion of burglary. Detective Sergeant Darren Mee began interviewing him at Oxclose Lane Police Station over a suspected break-in, but soon the youth, Peter Williams, stopped the interview and said he wanted to talk to a senior officer. He said he had some information about a murder which would interest them. The senior officer on duty, Detective Inspector Tony Webster, was called out to handle the matter. Gradually a story began to emerge.

'I know something about the Marian Bates murder,' Williams told him. 'Those involved were Craig Moran, a lad called Betton or

Bretton, and another lad I don't know. Craig had the car, which was a dinger, to use on the job. There was also a scooter. I think they bought that. The lad – I don't know his name – was the rider of the scooter and it's him that did the shooting.'

'So how do you know all this, Peter?' Webster asked the young man.

'I was there,' the teenager told him. 'I went into the jewellers with the other lad and I forced the lock off the cupboard with a crowbar and the next thing I heard was a shot. I didn't know he was going to shoot anybody. And another thing...I also know who set the job up and where the gun came from – it was all Gunnie's job, Colin Gunn. He said nobody should be shot.'

Peter Williams was charged with the robbery at the Time Centre and the murder of Marian Bates, but crucially DI Webster working under a heavy load at the time, neglected to write up notes in his pocket book until two days after the event. A judge would later cite this as one reason for ruling Williams's confession inadmissible in a court of law. DI Webster was also apparently unaware at the time of the arrest of police intelligence logs which stated that Williams was 'strongly suspected' of involvement in Marian Bates's murder. .

It was later also discovered that Williams had been on an electronic tag and, on the day of the killing, should have been being monitored by a private security company, Premier, but had removed his tag a week before after being released on licence from Olney Young Offender Institution three weeks earlier. He also missed seven out of eleven scheduled meetings with Nottingham Youth Offending Team. This breach of bail conditions was not picked up by the company, which should have checked that Williams was at his home address under curfew.

Later, at the trial of Williams, Dean Betton and Craig Moran, DI Webster revealed his failings in an emotionally charged moment at Wolverhampton Crown Court. 'I don't think I have been good enough in my job,' he admitted. 'I don't expect any sympathy from anyone. I have let the Bates family down, the CPS down and the barristers,' he said. 'Williams did make those admissions. He did say that, but how I have recorded it wasn't correct. The gist of what he's saying was correct, but having considered it for months, I believe it was a vast error of judgment on my part in going anywhere near him that night. In the last probably five or six years I have suffered ill health. It's not an excuse for this but I don't think my judgment has been correct. I came here today very agitated and it's because I don't think I have done the right thing. And I don't want to drag the force into any further disrepute by trying to defend a position that I've looked at for a long time now and think I cannot defend in court properly.'

Discussions took place before the trial commenced, including applications from the defence that could have scuppered any trial had they been accepted. However, the Judge Mr Justice Goldring ruled that the trial should go ahead. Williams was convicted and received a life sentence with a twenty-two-year tariff; Dean Betton, twenty-four, and Craig Moran, twenty-three, both received fourteen years.

DI Webster broke down completely shortly after his admissions and left the witness box in tears, with the judge declaring him unfit to give evidence. He subsequently suffered a breakdown and was off work for nine months, though he later returned to duty. An Independent Police Complaints Commission enquiry into the police investigation of the Marian Bates murder found that there was no evidence of any misconduct by Webster or any other officers involved, though it did say there were 'lessons for Nottinghamshire force to learn in relation to best practice with regard to the timely completion of pocket notebooks'. Inspector

Sam Wilson, vice chairman of Nottinghamshire Police Federation, pointed out that Webster had been commended five times for his work and had an exemplary record: 'Tony is highly respected by his colleagues and has never lost his focus on what this job is about: catching criminals and protecting the public,' he said. 'We are heartened he has been completely exonerated by the totally independent IPCC.'

Police had intelligence at the time that the car linked to the Bates robbery, a maroon Peugeot, had been pulled over three months before the raid, when it was driven by Colin Gunn's common-law wife, Victoria Garfoot, and by February 2004 they had information about Gunn sponsoring the raid. But it took until January 2005 for him to be arrested. Officers were rewarded with a few nuggets when they went to Gunn's mother's home in Raymede Drive on 7 January 2005. Gunn was not there (though his solicitor later made arrangements for him to attend the police station). As police carried out searches at the property, they discovered various pieces of torn paper which were clearly the remnants of faxed documents. The bundle of evidence was bagged up and then the relevant pieces removed by one of the senior officers, who realised its significance and the need to ensure the corruption investigation, Operation Salt, remained hidden from rank and file officers. Forensic examination of the paper found that it had been sent by fax from Radford Road Police Station to Limey's clothes store in Bridlesmith Gate, Nottingham. The piece of paper had the fingerprints of Jason Grocock, manager of Limey's, on it, and the fingerprints of Colin Gunn. The connection between the two was trainee detective Charles Fletcher, based at Radford Road Police Station.

*

IN DECEMBER 2003, one of Colin Gunn's runners went on an unsanctioned cocaine run into Lincolnshire. Gunn found out about it, and began to suspect the runner might be a weak link in the organisation. A bullet was fired through the letterbox of his home. Patrick Marshall, known as 'Celtic Pat' because of his passion for the Scottish football team, had become a loose canon as far as Gunn was concerned and needed sorting. Gunn also heard Marshall was trying to get a gun to settle a dispute with another man called 'Scotch Al', and decided to intervene. He sought out his deadliest gunman, John McSally, to deal with it. A junior member of the Cartel organised a car, while McSally told Marshall he would be able to provide him with a gun. A meeting was arranged in the car park of the Park Tavern, Basford, for 8pm on 8 February 2004. McSally was late and Marshall was on the point of giving up and going home when the pony-tailed enforcer turned up. As the father-of-one walked with McSally to where he said the gun was stored, McSally shot him in the head. He then made his escape in the getaway car, careering through a bollard as he made his way out of the pub car park. Patrick Marshall, forty-six, lay dying with a bullet wound to his head.

John McSally was born in Nottingham in 1956. His criminal career began when he was eleven and his first spell in custody came in September 1971, when he went to borstal for burglary. In 2002, he was jailed after visiting Nottingham pubs with a shotgun searching for a person he wanted to kill. He received a ludicrously short sentence of two-and-a-half years for making threats to kill, possession of a firearm with intent to endanger life and breaching a suspended sentence. A wild-looking man with tattoos on his neck and a greying goatee, his weakness was his penchant for getting drunk and letting his loose tongue wag. During boozy late-night chats, he even told the landlady of his local pub in Basford about some of the shootings he had carried out done, saying he got sexually aroused by it. 'Yeah, I did the Mansfield one [David Draycott] and Patrick Marshall and the black guy from the Heathfield Estate. It's just business,' he said.

The black guy from the Heathfield Estate was Derrick Senior, a social worker. In September 2003, he and a friend arranged to meet a colleague in a pub. They went to the wrong one and ended up in the Lord Nelson in Bulwell by mistake. Dreadlocked Mr Senior was chatting to his friend Esther Robinson when one of five young white men playing pool kicked her on the buttock as he walked past the table. Derrick asked them to apologise but instead they grabbed him by his dreadlocks and dragged him into the corner of the pub, where they began to kick, punch and beat him with their pool cues. He suffered a fractured eye socket and rib and Esther suffered bruises after being attacked when she went to his aid. His attackers even danced around the pub laughing and joking, holding his dreadlocks in the air. The incident, just after 10pm, was caught on CCTV.

The five men were all members of the Bestwood Cartel. They had been celebrating a birthday and also the arrest of Michael O'Brien for the murder of Marvyn Bradshaw. The men were twenty-year-old James Brodie, a young man who had just carried out a series of robberies; John McNee, twenty-four, who had a history of violence in virtually every pub he had been into; Joseph Graham, twenty-three; Lee Marshall, twenty-four, and Robert Watson, twenty-five, whose birthday it was. By the time the case came to court in May 2004, Brodie had disappeared; he was wanted in connection with the shooting of Marian Bates.

One of the Bestwood Cartel contacted a drugs worker they knew and asked him if he would approach Mr Senior and offer him some money to withdraw his complaint, but the fifty-year-old had already given police a witness statement. Colin Gunn wasn't happy that his crew would have to face court, particularly as the incident would spark more questions about what had happened to James Brodie. Mr Senior, who had started growing his dreadlocks thirty-three years earlier, told the police, 'It was the greatest insult I could suffer. I am a Rastafarian. It encompasses my life and religion. I have been more deeply affected than I can possibly imagine. The physical scars and injuries have healed, but the mental scars are never likely to heal.'

His attackers received sentences of between six-and-a-half years and two-and-a-half years at Nottingham Crown Court on 14 May 2004. Three days later, Derrick Senior was feeling more vulnerable than ever. He knew how these people might react, having gone to court to see them sentenced. He had taken to driving his car to the shops even though it was just down the road. As he got into his car that evening, he didn't take much notice of the motorcycle revving up nearby. It looked like a pizza delivery man – he had a cardboard box in his hand. He didn't see another man with a motorcycle helmet get off the bike and approach his car. John McSally thrust his handgun through the car window and pumped three bullets into Senior, shouting, 'You grassing bastard.' Senior sat in his car, his hands still on the steering wheel, trying to play dead as he battled to stay calm with bullet wounds in both legs and his armpit. He later told a courtroom, 'I was trying to play possum, play dead as it were. [Then] I got up and hit the horn and screamed, "I've been shot."'

Derrick Senior survived but was forced to enter the witness protection programme. He has not been back to Nottingham since.

CHAPTER 11
FAMILY MATTERS

J amie Gunn took his best mate Marvyn Bradshaw's death very badly. He just wanted to get out of his head at every opportunity. He drank heavily and snorted lines of cocaine. His uncle Colin found out and had given him a beating, telling him to stay off the stuff – something other members of the family were not happy about. Colin had even been 'sent to Coventry' for a few weeks. Meanwhile Jamie continued on his mission to get as wasted as he could: nothing his mother Julie or stepfather Dave Shefford did seemed to have any effect.

In July 2004, Michael O'Brien went on trial for Bradshaw's murder. The Gunn family wondered how Jamie would cope with it all. He couldn't bring himself to go to court and see O'Brien in the dock. Instead other relatives would go. Colin especially wanted to stare O'Brien in the face, the face of the man who had dared to try to kill his nephew. Gary Salmon, the other man police wanted in connection with the murder, was still missing. Colin was happy to hear rumours circulating that he had disposed of not only Gary Salmon but also James Brodie, the young man who had shot Marian Bates and had not been seen since thirty-six hours after the murder. It all added to his reputation, as far as he was concerned.

On 7 July, tensions began to spill over within the courtroom at Nottingham Crown Court. During a break in proceedings, Colin approached the dock and O'Brien squared up to him, intimating to Gunn that there was a bullet waiting for him. 'Hey Colin, I've got something for you,' said O'Brien as Gunn walked away from the dock. 'Tell fat Colin I've got something for him or perhaps something is coming his way.' Gunn had to be restrained and ushered from the courtroom. He was advised not to return while the case was on.

Six days later, the courtroom again descended into chaos. O'Brien had been found guilty and was being sentenced to a minimum of twenty-four years in jail when he launched a tirade of abuse at the family of Marvyn Bradshaw. He threw a tumbler of water over them and shouted as he received a twenty-four-year sentence, 'Hey you, your son's head looked like a doughnut. It had a big hole with red in the middle. I'm not bothered you know, I'm a bad boy. It means nothing to me. I can do that standing on my head. I know where you live as well.'

Colin Gunn was incensed by the comments. Attempts had been made already to get to O'Brien while in prison but had come to nothing. Police had become aware that the Bestwood Cartel had even corrupted prison officers and they had taken precautions to ensure O'Brien was safe. Gunn began thinking about revenge from another angle. He was sure that they could track down O'Brien's mother, Joan Stirland. He knew they were in Lincolnshire some-where because he had traced a phone number for them. Word began to reach Joan's daughter Rosie that the family could be in danger again as a result of O'Brien's comments. After several months of quiet, just when they thought they were getting back to normal, the nightmare was back.

On 13 July, shortly after her son was jailed for life, Mrs Stirland rang Rosie and told her she was really upset about what Michael had said. Crying, she said, 'I can't believe he said that to the family. I want to go and see them and apologise. He should never have said that to them.'

'Mum, I really don't think that's a good idea,' Rosie told her. 'We are all at risk because of what he has said. Just leave it and stay away. Maybe you should ring the police and ask them what sort of risk there is after this.'

Joan had last contacted Nottinghamshire Police on 19 April 2004 and spoken to a senior officer. She was keen to know how far police had got investigating the shooting at their home in September 2003. The answer was they had got almost nothing. Joan told the officer she had been worried because a few weeks earlier she had spotted one of the Gunn brothers, along with other members of the Bestwood Cartel, in Skegness. Following her son's courtroom outburst, she rang the police the next day and told them she thought the Bestwood Cartel might be trying to get to the family after what her son had said. They told her not to worry; they were keeping an eye on things and would let the family know if anything happened. According to Phil Davies, Nottinghamshire Police also held a meeting and decided for the first time that they should inform their counterparts in Lincolnshire that Joan and John Stirland were living in their area.

Six days later, officers monitoring the Bestwood Cartel became aware that a firearm was being moved into the Boston area of Lincolnshire so that a shooting could be carried out. They sat and waited, keeping tabs on the movements of Colin Gunn in particular. The Utah team had been busy making huge inroads into the Bestwood Cartel's drug operations – bugs had been placed during the autumn of 2003 and they were now achieving the desired results. The biggest bust took place on the A52 just outside Nottingham in April 2005. Darren Kirby, one of the low-level runners for the gang, was on his way back from Liverpool, having picked up a huge consignment of drugs, when he was pulled over by police. They claimed he had a faulty light on his car but in fact electronic surveillance had indicated exactly who Kirby was, what he was carrying and where he was going well before he left Liverpool – the faulty light story was concocted to lay a false trail so as not to compromise the surveillance methods.

When officers asked to search the thirty-one-year old's van, they found six holdalls crammed full of ecstasy – around 600,000 tablets. Tests later revealed the tablets, embossed with the Heineken and Playstation logos, had a very high active MDMA content of around 70 per cent. They had probably originated in the Netherlands. It was the second largest ecstasy haul by police in the UK, with a street value of some £3 million. Kirby said he had been paid just £500 for the driving job and needed the money to pay off gambling debts. He would receive a fifteen-year jail term, reduced to thirteen years on appeal, after admitting his guilt.

Before that, in June 2004, police had intercepted a huge shipment of amphetamines and ecstasy near Runcorn which was on its way back to the Bestwood Cartel. The Cartel put pressure on one of the couriers involved: someone must have been talking to the police, they said. The courier wrongly assumed his girlfriend had stitched him up – in fact the information had come from police surveillance – and told the Cartel. Two men wearing boiler suits went to her home in Bestwood, claiming they had to deliver a pizza. She refused to answer the door. Two days later, the same two men in boiler suits strode up to the house and fired a number of shots through the window. The twenty-one-year-old was carrying her thirteen-month-old baby boy in her arms as the shots shattered the window. She was hit by two bullets, which narrowly missed her baby, but lived to tell the tale.

Police intelligence indicated that one of the shooters was a twenty-six-year-old junior member of the Cartel who was himself shot for botching a kidnap job on behalf of the Cartel. He allowed the kidnap victim, who had been abducted because of a £200 debt, to go free, and in retribution Colin Gunn sent the terrifying John McSally to shoot him for his mistake. McSally was supposed to kill him but was only able to wound him in the shoulder. The twenty-six-year-old was charged with the attempted murder of Katrina Hancock and two counts of possession of a firearm but the charges were later dropped on advice that there was 'insufficient evidence' against him.

On 11 June, police busted forty-one-year-old Andrew Gascoine and thirty-three-year-old Jason Carroll, two Cartel foot soldiers. Both had large quantities of drugs in their houses and cars which were going to be cut up and distributed to smaller dealers. They searched Gascoine's Rover car and found nearly a kilo of cocaine, worth £95,700, in the passenger foot well and a bag of cocaine worth £19,400 in the glove compartment, as well as sheets of paper with names and phone numbers. At Gascoine's house they found £149,100 of cocaine in his washing machine, bringing his total stash to £264,200.

The police then went to Carroll's house in Gainsford Crescent, searched him and found he was carrying a few grams of cocaine and £1,440 in cash. He also had some paper with a list of names, phone numbers and amounts of money. Police found £74,100 of cocaine in a cupboard under the sink. There was £7,260 of amphetamines in his freezer, 181 ecstasy tablets worth £905 in a vase and a coffee tin with some cocaine and broken up ecstasy tablets. He had £800 stuffed into a jacket in a wardrobe, electronic scales and a chemical used to cut drugs. His total stash of drugs was worth £83,065. Both men pleaded guilty and were given ten-year sentences in December 2004.

More members of the Bestwood Cartel were arrested after a bungled armed raid on a city centre casino on 11 November 2004. The gunman, Martin Hogan, was jailed for twelve years and his accomplice David Martin got ten years for the hold-up at the Victoria Club in Victoria Street. In passing the sentences, Judge

Andrew Hamilton referred to the branding of Nottingham as the most dangerous city in England. 'I visit a number of institutions to talk to students and one of the first questions they ask is, "Am I going to be safe in Nottingham?" and, "Am I going to be shot in Nottingham?" I can assure the public that judges will do everything to ensure that those who commit crime will be given corresponding sentences.' Hogan, forty-nine, formerly of Birchfield Road, Arnold, was found guilty of robbery and possession of an imitation firearm after a trial at Nottingham Crown Court in April 2006. Martin, twenty-seven, of Kneeton Vale, Sherwood, admitted robbery, possession of an imitation firearm and a separate offence of affray. He received an extra eighteen months for that offence, to be served after the longer sentence.

The robbers had distinguished themselves by committing a catalogue of errors. Hogan, a convicted thief and burglar, allowed a scarf covering his face to slip during the raid. He pointed a gun at the receptionist before ushering her and other members of staff into a corner of the casino while Martin, armed with a claw hammer, emptied cash into a sports bag. The men tried to make their escape through a fire door but found it locked. It meant they had to turn back and leave through the main entrance, the court had heard. Another of the gang, Vincent Hawkins made a poor job of setting light to the getaway vehicle. He burnt himself so severely he had to call an ambulance and spent five days in a hospital's burns unit. Hawkins, twenty-two, received an eighteen-month prison sentence after admitting arson. Detectives used mobile phone records to trace all three's movements.

BACK IN BESTWOOD, the Gunn family was getting worried about the impact that Michael O'Brien's trial was having on Jamie. He was going on drug-fuelled benders on a nightly basis with some members of the Cartel, including Michael 'Tricky' McNee. Jamie's mum, Julie, tried to keep him in but he would say he was nipping out for a bit and then disappear for days on end. Jamie couldn't get the vision of Marvyn dying from his head, he couldn't even look at pictures of his best friend – every time the newspaper ran stories about O'Brien's trial, it brought everything back. Jamie was in self-destruct mode; he didn't care what happened to him.

On 2 August 2004, twenty-one-year-old Jamie Gunn was found lying on his bed at home in South Glade Road. His family couldn't wake him. His body had given up – the official cause of death was pneumonia – and his five-and-a-half month old son Rhiece would grow up without even knowing him. The outpouring of grief from the members of the Bestwood Cartel was overwhelming. Colin was down near Hampton Lodge, near Warwick, when David Gunn finally reached him just after 9.30am that day. Colin phoned Jamie's friend Michael 'Tricky' McNee immediately; maybe he knew something. Then Colin phoned another of Jamie's friends, 'John John' Russell, to tell him about Jamie's death. Tricky McNee hadn't seen Jamie since Sunday. Colin was crying uncontrollably; Jamie was like a son to him. There was also some guilt: perhaps he shouldn't have given Jamie such a hard time about the drug-taking, Colin thought, but no, he wasn't to blame for Jamie's death. It was someone else and that someone else would have to pay. An eye for an eye. Two must die. One for Marv and one for Jamie.

The day after Jamie's body was found Tricky McNee told his brother, John, what had happened. John McNee was locked up at Ranby Prison, near Retford, and the phone calls were being routinely bugged. Tricky revealed to his older brother that he had been drowning his sorrows with senior members of the Bestwood Cartel in the Royal Hunt pub. 'I can't believe it's happened,' he said. 'I only saw Jamie on Sunday. I had the big man [Colin Gunn] with me, he was in tears. I've had Baz on the phone as well in tears. It's hit Colin and Baz [David Barrett] really, really badly. I'm fucking off to Scotland for a week. It's going to take two weeks for anything to happen anyway.'

Colin had already made it clear that there would be revenge after holding an army council-style summit at the pub the day after Jamie's death. No point going for Michael O'Brien; this was personal now and his cold heart was dreaming up the cruellest revenge he could think of, something that would leave O'Brien and his sisters, Rosie and Tonette, in more pain than could ever be achieved by taking his own life away. Colin didn't need his lines of cocaine to make him feel confident. He felt supreme already. He had been implicated in no less than four murders and more than fifty shootings and he hadn't been charged with a single crime since 1998. He was invincible.

Nevertheless precautions would need to be taken, including buying some new pay-as-you-go phones for the job. They already had access to a couple of clean guns, Beretta 9000s – a gangster's best friend, reliable and deadly. Tricky would not be going to Scotland after all. A flurry of phone calls were already being made to try to trace Gunn's targets and the contacts the gang had in British Telecom were working their magic. Joan and John Stirland were effectively walking dead.

Just a few days after Jamie's death, Joan received a call from Nottinghamshire Police.

'Emotions are running high, Joan,' the officer said. 'Just watch your back.'

Joan phoned her daughter Rosie late that night: 'Rosie, I'm really scared. I think the Gunns are going all out to try and get us and you and Tonette. I want you to get out the house now.'

'Mum, I'm not getting the kids up, it's past midnight. Ring the police and ask them what you should do.'

A few minutes later, an officer from Nottinghamshire Police, rang through to Rosie.

'Your mum has asked me to call you because she's upset,' he said. 'She's heard some more stuff about the people from Bestwood.'

Rosie was angry. 'Well I'm not being funny but you're the police officer. We've been hearing we are in danger for months now but you would have moved us if we were. You're the ones who know what's going on – what do you think?'

'Well, Rosie, I think your mum is overreacting,' the officer told her, according to Rosie's account. 'To be honest I think it's all a load of pie in the sky.'

THE DAY AFTER Jamie Gunn's death, Colin Gunn began planning the most audacious and brutal crime of his career. He would use weapons smuggled into the country from Latvia by a Polish lorry driver. They were clean Beretta 9000S pistols. No history, no comeback. Colin contacted a man from the Carlton area of Nottingham called Kevin Holm, whose father, Raymond, was best friends with John Stirland and had visited the couple in April that year. Colin knew this because Kevin Holm's sister, Holly, lived with thirty-eight-year-old Shane Bird, a long-time associate of the Gunns. Bird had served a jail term for his involvement in large-scale cigarette smuggling with Robert Briggs-Price.

During 3 August, there was frantic activity on Colin Gunn's phone. He was calling Holm and Bird, trying to get information about where Joan and John Stirland lived. By that afternoon he had their phone number and postcode but no full address. He asked Bird to find out more through his contacts. One of them was a former British Telecom worker called Stephen Poundall. Bird told Poundall he needed to know the address of a J. Stirland in Lincolnshire. Poundall phoned his mate Anthony Kelly, who worked for British Telecom in Nottingham. Kelly couldn't access records for Lincolnshire so he phoned another friend, Andrew Pickering. By 8am on 5 August, after a series of exhaustive checks carried out by his former work colleagues, Poundall had the address of Joan and John Stirland. And by 8.43am that day, he had phoned Bird to let him know.

Bird spent the next hour trying to get through to Colin Gunn, until Gunn eventually answered his phone at 9.47am.

'It's not Sutton on Sea. It's Trusthorpe.'

The call lasted just a few seconds but it was all he needed. Gunn phoned Michael 'Tricky' McNee at 10.14am.

'Tricky? Put Scotland on the backburner. The job's on so get yourself sorted.'

McNee had been chosen as one of the shooters. He was itching to exact revenge for Jamie's death. The identity of the other shooter had not yet been decided – it might be John Russell, who Colin phoned a few minutes after speaking to McNee, but Colin was also pumping himself up to do it himself, such was his guilt and rage over Jamie's death.

At 10.37am, after speaking to Gunn, Bird rang Stephen Poundall. 'Thanks for all your help, mate,' said Bird. 'There will be a drink in it for you so don't worry.'

Poundall, Pickering and Kelly had all unwittingly been used in a grand conspiracy. As with many others, they will have to live with their actions for the rest of their lives. Bird, from Carlton Hill, Nottingham, would later claim in court that the phone calls between him and Poundall were in order to do a favour for another man, who had asked him for the phone number of his aunt, Joan Stirland. The day the gang got confirmation of Joan and John Stirland's address, they began to work out the logistics of the operation and travelled over to Lincolnshire to case the house at Radio St Peter's. Colin Gunn drove over with nineteen-year-old Tricky McNee in the car.

The classified section of the *Nottingham Evening Post* would be filled with obituaries for Jamie Gunn for the next two weeks, in an unprecedented outpouring of grief for a nineteen-year-old who had achieved little of note in his short life. Nevertheless, there were many people who had had dealings with the Gunn brothers who knew it was in their own interests to show some respect; there was even a notice from Godfrey Hibbert, who had looked after drugs for the Cartel to his own cost. The funeral was set for Friday, 13 August, at St Mary's Church near Bulwell town centre. Notice went out to the people of Bestwood and Bulwell that they would be expected to show their respects by attending. Jamie would be buried near his best friend Marvyn Bradshaw at Wilford Cemetery.

John John Russell and Tricky McNee sent their own death notice to the *Nottingham Evening Post*. It read:

GUNN Jamie. Bro, we still don't believe it, you are still with us. If not by our side, then in our hearts and souls. Don't for one minute think we will ever forget you. You are in our thoughts every minute of the day. Just can't believe you're gone Bro. Love you to bits always. Deepest sympathy to Julie, Sheff and family. From Tricky and John John

ON 4 AUGUST, Colin and David Gunn, Michael McNee, John Russell and others who have never been identified met at the Kingfisher caravan site, where David had a caravan. David stayed there for a few days while Colin drove back and forth from Nottingham. David was back in Nottingham by 8 August, while

McNee and Russell took his place at the caravan. At 6.45pm that day, Colin went into a Woolworths store in Skegness and bought a T-mobile Sagem pay-as-you-go phone to contact other members of the gang. All the gang would be using pay-as-you-go mobiles with no history. For years the Cartel had used this method of communication, often buying their phones from a shop called Dr Unlock in Bulwell. A clean mobile was an absolute necessity in their line of business.

David Gunn texted his brother.

'What time are you here Fats? The bits are ready. Three of them. I've got them built and bought some menthol.'

David knew about firearms, how to acquire them and put them together. His police record said as much. The Italian-made 9mm 9000S came in three parts and menthol was often used to clean the semi-automatic handguns so they had a smooth action. However, David would later give an entirely different explanation for his text message to Colin. 'I'm texting him to tell him I have got some spliffs rolled,' he claimed. 'Colin couldn't roll a spliff to save his life so I would do it for him. The menthol referred to menthol-flavoured cigarettes that I put into the joints, giving them a minty cool flavour that he liked. At the end of it, apart from you putting me in a few places using my phone, you haven't really got me doing anything. I am shocked that you have got me here.'

JOHN RUSSELL WAS busy smoking himself stupid while Tricky McNee drank and fidgeted. A takeway meal had been delivered to the caravan. It was 7 August. Colin, John John and Tricky had been reconnoitring at Radio St Peters and Colin had driven over to Trusthorpe three times that day. It was obsessive last-minute planning to make sure that nothing could go wrong. A black Volkswagen Passat, stolen a few weeks earlier from a house in

Nottingham, would be used to drive two gunmen to and from the target house, then afterwards would be ditched and burned. They had already found an isolated spot about two miles away in Crawcroft Lane to dispose of the car – it was perfect, no houses nearby. The shooters would then be transported by another car back to the caravan at Ingoldmells or Nottingham, if necessary.

Russell and McNee made another trip to the Stirlands' house late on the Saturday evening to satisfy themselves about the layout of the property and to ease any niggling, last-minute doubts – though Russell was nearly caught when one of the neighbours spotted him leaping over the Stirlands' garden fence. When the morning of 8 August broke, it held all the promise of optimism that sunny mornings have – and so it was for Joan and John Stirland when they woke to the sun streaming into their chalet.

They had barely had breakfast when their neighbour called round. 'I just thought you ought to know that I saw a prowler jump over your fence last night,' she told Joan. 'I think we might have disturbed them because they just ran off.'

The sunshine went from Joan Stirland's face. She didn't hide her worries well.

'Oh, right. I had better tell John about it.'

Joan went back inside to phone Nottinghamshire Police. She felt apprehensive.

Five miles away, at the caravan park, Russell and McNee were awaiting their orders from Colin Gunn. They wouldn't have to wait long. By 1pm they were acting the fools on the promenade of Trusthorpe. Colin had told them to blend in like holidaymakers and so Russell bought a kite, which they attempted to fly. They chatted up a couple of girls on the promenade, regaling the young women with stories about Nottingham and how they should meet up for a drink later. Then, at about 2pm, Colin rang and gave the order to strike. Perhaps he was close to Radio St Peter's – if he was then he would have seen the Stirlands' neighbour leave her house with relatives to go for a walk. She would not be returning until after 4pm. It was a good time to commit a murder, with few witnesses in the vicinity to hear the gunshots.

The VW Passat drove up onto the kerb next to the chalet and the hazard lights came on. The two gunmen moved swiftly out of the car, carrying a holdall which hid the Berettas. The blue overalls and caps and silver gloves they wore gave Joan and John Stirland the impression they were there on official business. Perhaps it was something to do with the call they had made to the police? Either way, the assassins walked straight into the house and carried out their deed with swift precision. Bullet casings lay strewn all over the floor. Joan and John Stirland had been murdered in cold blood by 2.20pm.

As the assassins left the house a taxi driver spotted them getting into the car. They screeched off towards Crawcroft Lane, tailgating a car as they tried to overtake on the narrow lanes. Whoever was at the wheel of the VW Passat drove like a madman and the two gunmen were seen arguing as their car sped down the road. Before setting the vehicle alight, Tricky McNee dumped a load of bullet casings into the car – it would all help to burn the car to a cinder and destroy any forensic evidence. By 3pm the two assassins were back at the Kingfisher Caravan Park in Ingoldmells. By the evening they would be laughing, having a few pints and even texting the girls they had met on the promenade earlier. Colin Gunn had planned the assassination meticulously.

WITHIN TWENTY-FOUR HOURS of the murders, journalists had made the link between Mr and Mrs Stirland's brutal slaying and the jailing of her son Michael O'Brien at Nottingham Crown

Court a few weeks earlier. The story was all over the national papers by the Tuesday morning.

WERE SEASIDE COUPLE SHOT IN REVENGE?

Daily Mail

COUPLE SHOT DEAD IN GANG REVENGE AT THE SEASIDE: MIDDLE AGED VICTIMS LINKED TO PUB KILLER

Daily Telegraph

MYSTERY KILLERS GUN DOWN TWO PERFECT GRAND-PARENTS IN THEIR SEASIDE HOME; REVENGE OF THE HITMEN

The Express

COUPLE'S NEW LIFE ENDS IN MURDER: POLICE FIND BODIES AFTER TIP OFF

The Guardian

EXECUTION: GANGLAND MURDER OF SNEERING KILLER'S FAMILY

The Mirror

2 EXECUTED IN 'MURDER FEUD'

The Sun

COUPLE'S MURDER IS LINKED TO PUB SHOOTING CASE

The Times

All focus shifted towards Jamie Gunn's funeral, which was held the following Friday. Jamie's mother, Julie, gave a tearful interview to the newspapers but journalists who tried to speak to other members of the family, such as Colin Gunn, were chased down the road with baseball bats. Julie described how Jamie had lost the will to live after seeing his best mate murdered. She said she had heard the rumours about the Stirlands but it was 'nowt to do with us'.

'Jamie couldn't look at a picture of Marvyn for ages – he just used to break down,' said Julie. 'It took nine months for him to say Marvyn's name again. No adult should have to see what he had seen. The estate is eerie at the moment. It's in shock. The support we have had has been amazing. Some people have to deal with it on their own but we have had an army.' But the army was crumbling. Everyone knew Colin Gunn was behind the Stirlands' murders and Jamie's funeral would be the last show of any significant support for the Bestwood Cartel. One former member said, 'Yeah there were the attacks on this person or that but most of that was business, keeping people in line and off their patch. When the Stirlands got done, that was it. People started seeing what was happening. Colin was out of control. You can't go off shooting someone's grandmother just to get at someone else. That was Colin's downfall. There will still be people who try and say he's a good 'un and he got stitched up by the cops but he did a truly evil thing that day and people started seeing him in a different light. That was the day he lost the support of the estate.'

More than 1,000 people turned out for Jamie's funeral. A black, horse-drawn carriage took the coffin through the streets of Bulwell and up to Wilford Hill Crematorium after the service. The streets were not only lined with hundreds of locals but also Mercedes and BMWs. It was a depressing day, full of menacing darkness and teeming rain and men in black suits, wearing dark shades as if they had just walked off the set of *Reservoir Dogs* – only this was for real. It was a gangster's funeral and Jamie Gunn was buried in a brand new Lacoste tracksuit specially bought by the family. After the service the local vicar, Reverend Christopher Gale, said: 'I did think about calling for there to be no revenge, but it's a difficult time and you have to be sensitive. You have to remember that people are grieving the loss of their nineteen-year-old son.'

A few weeks later, the family of Joan Stirland attended her funeral at Wilford Hill Crematorium. It was a much quieter affair. The imprisoned Michael O'Brien did not attend either his mother's funeral or John Stirland's the previous week. The family could not even bury their dead in peace. Helicopters swarmed overhead and men in dark uniforms patrolled the perimeter of the graveyard with semi-automatic guns. It took police more than twenty-four hours to go and see Joan's daughter Rosie, to inform her of her mother's and stepfather's murder. They didn't even realise she was at risk. A dedicated witness protection team didn't exist until 2005 in Nottinghamshire and several officers who worked witness protection had breakdowns – they had never been properly trained for the task. Rosie Stirland was scathing about the way the matter was handled.

'They turned up at 4.30 in the morning, two police officers,' she said. 'They said, "We've got some news for you, you might want to sit down. There's been an incident in Lincolnshire, two people are deceased." I said, "Who?" They said, "We believe it's John and Joan Stirland and they've been shot and they are dead," basically. I said, "You know who's done it, you'd better go and arrest the Gunnies, hadn't you?" They said, "Well, can you notify the rest of the family now and we'll leave you to it," and they walked out. They weren't even there five minutes. I didn't know what to do next. I said to my partner, "I can't believe they've left us."

'Lincolnshire Police rang me the next afternoon and asked if the Notts Police had been to see me yet. They said, "We've got your sister Tonette but who's looking after you?" They said I should complain about Notts Police. They sent someone down from Lincolnshire Police who spoke to me and then asked me if I would identify my mum. From that minute, we were put in a hotel with my sister and our mobile phones taken off us and we were told we couldn't go back to Nottingham. We were kept under armed guard and couldn't even be allowed out of the hotel room and if anyone saw us we had to be moved. I spoke to Lincs Police and said, "You knew she was in danger and so why didn't you go straight round to my mum's house?" They said, "Oh, she didn't want flashing lights." I said, "She meant she didn't want people drawing attention to her, not that she didn't want them to hurry up. She didn't want panda cars, not that she didn't want them to come round." She was frightened to death.

'For my mum's funeral, we couldn't even grieve properly. I gave instructions for her to be buried in her own clothes. I found out afterwards from the funeral parlour that she was buried in a hospital gown. The funeral itself was appalling. I had to sign a document that if I went it could result in my injury or death. I went, obviously. The whole road was closed off specially for it. I sat and told the officer in charge we had wanted the horse and carriage and he said, "We would have accommodated that, we told Lincs we would do whatever you wanted." He said, "I'm not very happy about that." It really upset us at the time. I don't understand what was going on with these two forces. To be honest, I've not been back to the cemetery since that day. I've asked them if they could arrange it and they said no. It's like they've got rid of us now, after everything that happened with my mum, we've now been told we don't fall under the criteria for witness protection because we weren't actually witnesses. I said, "Well what do we fall under?" And they said, "We don't know." I changed my surname and I did that myself, they wouldn't do it for me.

'The police kept us in Lincolnshire for at least two weeks. We were in a hotel overlooking a lake for about the first four days, then we were moved to a disused agricultural college in Lincs. It was in a right state, all the firearms police were downstairs and we were upstairs, me and my partner and my kids, my sister and her partner and her kids. We had a room each. It was appalling, there were no carpets on the floor, the kitchenette was dirty and if we wanted any shopping they had to bring it to us. The kids weren't allowed to play in the field at the back. The firearms guys didn't want to sit outside with them.

'My partner at the time needed to go home to sort a few things out. They said they would take him home and bring him back the same day. I got a phone call at night time saying, "He doesn't want to be a part of this, he wants to finish with you and he isn't coming back." I was like, *what*? I had a mobile phone I hadn't given to the police and spoke to my partner and he said, "Are you all right? What's going on? They said they would come back and get me tomorrow. But they've rung me up and said you don't want me to come back." I said, "No, they've told me you don't want to come back." He said, "No, no," and he was going mad. I went mental and walked out. I told them they were just trying to save money, the way I saw it. I walked six miles to the nearest village being followed by them. I phoned my partner and asked him to come and pick me up. The witness protection people said they would drive me to my partner and come and collect us in a few days.

'I just want a normal life now. Everything was cleared out of our homes and put into storage. We were in a privately rented house for eighteen months and that was furnished. When I actually got my own home they said they will bring the stuff down. But everything was green with mould. All the clothes had been chewed by mice, half of it was destroyed. They didn't even empty the fridge, there was food in there that had been in there for eighteen months. Even the cooker had oil in the tray. My mum's things were delivered to me and had just been thrown into boxes, all the stuff was chewed by mice.

'The only time I'd been to the house in Trusthorpe was in February 2004 before mum died and this shows you how frightened she was. She met me at the station and when we got off the train we sat at the station for thirty minutes, waiting to see if we knew anyone who got off the train to see if I'd been followed. She wouldn't leave, her and John. That's how scared she was. So for them to say she didn't want the police to come round is bullshit. My mum was terrified, she was frightened for her life and for them to make out that she was blase about it but she was not at all. If she was she would have gone back to Nottingham.'

In the days that followed, there were a lot of drawn faces at Nottinghamshire Police headquarters. The murders had not only shaken the most hardened of officers but they now realised they were in the middle of a huge mess. Senior officers wondered why nothing had been picked up on the bugs – the National Crime Squad officers carrying out surveillance had not alerted them to any specific information that indicated a double slaying was about to take place, and all the main members of the Cartel were being watched and listened to round the clock. But the clues were already there, particularly after Michael O'Brien's trial and the death of Jamie Gunn. It seems incredible that no one realised the extreme danger the couple were in. For their part, Lincolnshire Police were angry. They soon discovered that they had not been briefed fully of threats towards the Stirlands and if they had been given a comprehensive history about the couple, as Nottinghamshire claimed, they had no evidence to show for it.

No love was lost between the two forces. An employment tribunal back in 1996, in which a young female detective from Lincolnshire sued her force for sex discrimination, had soured relations for years with Nottinghamshire. Initial inquiries into the matter – which led to the detective, Cydena Fleming, receiving a substantial payout after suffering a vendetta at the hands of

senior male colleagues – were conducted by Nottinghamshire officers and this led to bad blood with some of their Lincolnshire
counterparts. Nevertheless, Detective Superintendent Graham
White, who headed the Lincolnshire Police investigation into the
Stirlands' murder, was determined to bring the culprits to justice.

Everyone knew who had carried out the killings; it was as plain
as day. Evidence would be needed, however, and that evidence was
in the technology which had given birth to the mobile phone.
Analysis began on phone numbers used on the day of the murder
in the Trusthorpe area; computer programmes analysed and
matched those numbers with any known to be used by members of
the Bestwood Cartel or which had been later used in Nottingham.
Gradually the numbers were whittled down. The use of pay-as-
you-go phones made the checking more protracted but eventually
officers isolated numbers which they could carry out some meaningful checks on. One was a phone which had been bought in a
Woolworths store in Skegness at 6.30pm on 4 August. It was a T-
Mobile Sagem. When officers scanned CCTV footage of the High
Street from around that time, they saw the unmistakably burly,
shaven-headed figure of Colin Gunn walking near the traffic
lights. From that phone they derived other numbers that had been
called. Most had gone dead the day of the murder but a few were
still active. By early September, police began to reel in members of
the gang.

AS IF THE murders of Marian Bates and the Stirlands were not
enough, the tragic killing of a fourteen-year-old girl was to bring
the capricious violence of the city's gangs into even starker relief.
Danielle Beccan was gunned down while walking home from the
annual Goose Fair, held every October in Forest Fields. It was had
become an event often used by the rival gangs from the NG

Triangle to settle long-standing disputes. Police were often tipped off about impending trouble but in October 2004 there were no such warnings.

In the early hours of 9 October, Danielle was with a large group of friends as they entered the Chase area of St Ann's. Danielle was no angel. She had probably smoked cannabis that night, according to what was later found in her bloodstream, and had a lot more money in her pocket than her mum could account for. She mixed with many families who were dealing drugs on the estate, but was about as innocent as she could be given that St Ann's life was running through her veins. She had grown up with crime all around her and had recently been living with her father, Dale, in Derby, who was holding large amounts of cannabis at the time. Just five days before Danielle's death, Dale, who had moved away from St Ann's in 1995, was at Derby Crown Court pleading guilty to possessing and growing highly potent skunk cannabis. In a subsequent court case less than a year later, he was convicted of possessing skunk and was again given a rehabilitation order. Danielle, or 'Baby D' as she was known on the street, had decided to move back to Nottingham where her mum Paula and many of the friends she had grown up with lived. It was a decision with fatal consequences.

At about 12.30am, as the youngsters walked from Valley Road, a gold Citroen Xsara saloon appeared and drove towards them. The car appeared to stall, then its engine revved and one of the tinted windows on the passenger side opened. Three shots were fired, popping like firecrackers. The youngsters scattered, screaming – all except Danielle, who fell to the ground. The others saw a gloved hand came out through the car window making the sign of a W, signifying the Waterfront Gang, as the car drove off. Danielle was just yards from the safety of her home and her mother rushed out to tend to her. But it was too late. Danielle's last words to her mother were, 'I'm not going to make it ... I'm dying.' She lost consciousness and, despite attempts at the Queens Medical Centre to save her, died soon after she arrived at casualty.

Meadows gang members Junior 'Prentice' Andrews and Mark 'Yardie' Kelly were arrested among twenty others during Operation Holly, after Kelly's car was traced following the shooting. Andrews had come out of prison just a few months earlier after being sentenced to four years for a brutal robbery. He was a small-time heroin dealer on the Meadows estate, but was heavily into gang culture and rap music. Sometimes he carried a small handgun in a Prada bag around his neck. Andrews had a number of tattoos on his body suggesting gang membership, including 'NG2', signifying the Meadows estate, a smoking gun, the initials 'WFG', signifying Waterfront Gang, and 'TRU', meaning The Real Untouchables. Crucially police seized a mobile phone belonging to him that contained a long rap message. It was footage of him walking through St Ann's in the early hours on his own. On the footage, recorded just a few days before Danielle's murder, Andrews was heard talking into the phone as he recorded road signs in St Ann's. He rapped into the phone with a patois lilt:

I'm here, Prentice, on my own like a real 'G',
Waterfront's most wanted. I'm on the creep.
I haven't even got no gun. I go anywhere on my own.
I'm a real killer, you can't see any Waterfront man come this
    way.
I robbed nuff man down here.
Which Waterfront man can say they've been down here at
    two o'clock in the morning? Look I'm here on my own.
Now you get me, look at that Prentice on his own rolling
    around the Ville [St Ann's] like it's the Meadows.
I don't really know anybody like me who's a real killer. I

come up here, I haven't even got my bullet-proof vest. I've
got one at home.
Prentice walking about the St Ann's Ville this time of year
   with no gun, no vest, all I got is one broomstick.
Waterfront, I've been, I've sawn and I've conquered.

On another recording, Andrews was heard rapping, 'When we shoot to kill we shoot the Ville [St Ann's] for real...how many niggers are going to get popped before you realise it's ride or die. That means I'm a ride you're going to die.'

Andrews and Kelly were convicted and sentenced to life, with a minimum tariff of thirty-two years each in prison. Kelly's tariff was reduced to twenty-nine years on appeal. He had been born in Jamaica, hence his 'Yardie Mark' nickname, but had strong gang connections to Birmingham and eventually became a member of the Raiders gang from Smethwick. This gang had strong links with the infamous Johnson Crew, whose war with the Burger Bar Crew in Birmingham culminated in the 2001 New Year's Day murders of Letisha Shakespeare and Charlene Ellis outside a hair salon. The Raiders helped supply drugs to the Meadows gangs. For all the bravado that he showed, Andrews had not killed before and it was highly unlikely that he intended to shoot Danielle Beccan that night. The bullet that killed her was almost certainly a ricochet off either the pavement or a building before hitting Danielle in the abdomen. Kelly and Andrews had gone to Clifton that night after drinking with a group of young men in the Toll Bridge; they even got into a chat with professional footballer who was in the pub. Bolstered by some cocaine they had snorted in the toilets of the Toll Bridge, Andrews and Kelly then went on to burgle a property in Clifton. They had been looking for someone who owed them money, and their mission then took them to St Ann's, but they had been unable to locate the person they were after. When they saw the crowd walking through St Ann's, someone in the car decided to let off a few rounds to tell them that the Meadows had been there. There were at least two, probably three others, in the car when Danielle was shot dead and fingerprints taken from the murder car were matched to three individuals known to police: all were young men who had links to the killers and the Meadows but all had alibis for the time of the murder. Of course they could have innocently been in the car on a previous occasion, but it helped not one bit in terms of closure on the case for Danielle Beccan's family, who were left with the feeling that not all those responsible had been caught.

CHAPTER 12
A PINCH OF SALT

On the afternoon of 8 November, three months after the Stirland murders, a probe planted inside Radford Road Police Station as part of Operation Salt picked up a conversation between DC Charles Fletcher and Jason Grocock, Fletcher's former boss at Limey's clothes store. Colin Gunn was trying to find out what the police had on him. Fletcher explained to Grocock the difficulties he would have in finding out about the murder inquiry and other operations against Gunn because of the secrecy surrounding the investigating units.

'It wouldn't be common knowledge to anybody except those who knew they were going to get him,' said Fletcher. 'There's those different squads, murder teams who are looking into various things. You've got Stealth as well, which is out of Oxclose Lane, and they're like their own unit with their own DI's , DS's and DC's. We just fucking deal with the shit on the streets. So as with something like that, it would be quite specialised, it would be kept in-house with a specialised team... Bobby wouldn't necessarily hear about it because he's got no fucking need to hear about it. Um, and what Stealth do... they do as a separate entity as a section CID. So we don't know anything that they do unless we hear about it when we see them in custody or go into the office for a cup of tea or something. But Stealth, I mean Stealth and those operations like that, keep everything dead secret because they don't like any fucker to know... So, for me, for me to hear that would be, would be rare and it would be an off-chance of me just wandering by and speaking to someone in that team but, but the chance of that are fucking approaching zilch.'

As Fletcher pointed out, 'For me to find out anything I would have to ring Lincoln and they'd think, who the fuck are you? You'd have to go through the right channels.'

On 25 January, at 5.22pm, another call was made by DC Fletcher to Grocock. Colin Gunn was now worried that he was a wanted man. Their chat was deliberately vague as they tried to skirt around the subject of their call without saying anything too incriminating.

Grocock: 'But you know me other mate, he can't work out why that bloke has said to him at the weekend that he's definitely now wanted and it's coming up that he isn't and...'

Fletcher: 'Right'

Grocock: 'He was wondering whether or not like, you know if NCIS [the National Criminal Intelligence Service] and things like that are up, would he not put it on the PNC as not to frighten him off.'

Fletcher: 'Yeah, that's always that possibility that's a tactic.'

Grocock: 'Yeah, just leave it, just leave it, that's a tactic.'

Fletcher: 'It's a tactic that you could do.'

Grocock: 'Will you check them two out then for me?'

Fletcher: 'Yeah.'

Grocock: 'The big fella [Colin Gunn] and, er, the Baz [David Barrett].'

Fletcher: 'Yeah.'

Grocock: 'And just give us a tinkle on, um...'
Fletcher: 'Will do...'

On 4 March 2005, at 14.05pm, video surveillance picked up footage of DC Fletcher putting pieces of paper into his pocket at Radford Road Police Station. Then he made a phone call to Jason Grocock.

Fletcher: 'I've just done a few things, nothing new on er, [Darren] Peters, er, [Jamie] Neil, there's a couple of bits on, er and there's a few bits on the, the fella, so I've printed that off so'

Grocock: 'Right.'

Fletcher: 'So what are you doing tomorrow?'

Grocock: 'Er, what day is tomorrow, Saturday?'

Fletcher: 'Mmm, are you working?'

Grocock: 'We're in the shop all day.'

Fletcher: 'Right I'll probably pop in and come, come and say hello. I'm working an eight, four.'

Grocock: 'Alright, and what's that, you've got one, one on Neil and, and the big lad's not, he's back on is he?'

Fletcher: 'Yeah, there's a few bits on there now, nothing fucking remarkable.'

Grocock: 'And Peters is zero, yeah?'

Fletcher: 'Yeah I suppose he is, he's just erm, the last one that was talked about erm, what was the last one that you talked to me about.'

Grocock: Inaudible.

Fletcher: 'Oh there is more, there's more, there is a couple on there, sorry.'

Grocock: 'Right, okay, well that's cool then, that's, that's brilliant then, well I'll...'

Fletcher: 'Yeah there is, I think there's one it's on about him fucking in hospital or summit and buggering off back to Spain or something.'

Grocock: 'He what, in hospital then went to Spain?'

Fletcher: 'Yeah I think that was the one.'

Grocock: 'Right okay.'

Operation Salt had by then been underway for a year and DC Fletcher's computer at Radford Road Police Station had been cloned so that all the keystrokes used by the officer on his keyboard could be replicated, showing what he had written and searches he had made or attempted to make on the Force's intelligence database. From December 2003, Operation Salt logged searches Fletcher made on the Police National Computer for the names Dean Betton and later Craig Moran. Fletcher also searched for Colin Gunn's name on a regular basis to see whether it was coming up on the Marian Bates murder investigation and on other shootings, including the attempted murder of Joan and John Stirland in September 2003.

Between December 2002 and September 2004, DC Fletcher searched for Gunn's name on the computer thirty times. He printed out sheets of intelligence at least twenty-five times between those dates. In the wake of Marvyn Bradshaw's murder and the arrest of Michael O'Brien, Fletcher passed on information on the home of Joan and John Stirland at South View Road, Carlton. Information provided by Fletcher to Colin Gunn included a report about a man who had gone to police saying he had been threatened by Gunn over his domestic situation. Gunn had allegedly told the man, 'You are a dead man if anything happens to this woman.' Another report given to Gunn mentioned how he had threatened a police officer with 'I know where you live' when he was being questioned. Fletcher also gathered intelligence on Gunn's connection to a dark-coloured BMW, about houses he owned or was linked to, and details of the pubs police believed that he had financial interests in. There was a report about Gunn smashing a man's hands with a hammer after the man had lied to him.

Fletcher was also able to tell Gunn the extent of police knowledge about security at Gunn's home in Revelstoke Way, Rise Park. Fletcher told him that officers were aware of CCTV coverage in the house and that it was relayed to a utility room. Slowly but surely, Fletcher began compromising police investigations into members of the Bestwood Cartel. One prosecution against Darren Peters, a racehorse-owning associate of Colin Gunn, involving a road rage incident in Netherfield, collapsed after Fletcher gave out the name and address of a witness, who was subsequently visited and threatened, leading to him withdrawing his statement. 'I want to know how the fuck they got my address,' complained the witness. One of Colin Gunn's more sociopathic henchmen, who seemed incapable of going out of his home for more than a few minutes without attacking someone, assaulted a man on the estate in 2005. So severe was the beating the man received that it was almost classed as attempted murder: he suffered broken legs and arms. DC Fletcher carried out 'MOT' checks on the status of the investigation and the man was able to breathe a sigh of relief. Fletcher told Grocock that no one would be charged unless they could get a statement off the victim; the victim was saying nothing.

DESPITE THE ENORMOUS police pressure on the Bestwood Cartel that winter, they continued to wreak mayhem. It was as though they were untouchable. On the afternoon of 18 December, a gunman walked into the family-run Aspley Pawnbrokers in Aspley Lane in search of thirty-four-year-old Lawrence Aitken.

'This man wearing a balaclava just came into the shop with a shotgun and shot straight at my leg,' related Aitken. 'I fell to the floor in complete agony. I don't have any idea who may have done this.' In fact Aitken knew who had ordered the shooting but was so scared he dare not even utter the name of Colin Gunn. His crime was to owe a small debt to Gunn and the shooting was a warning to settle it. His father, Reg, who ran the shop, said they didn't know whether his son would be able to walk again: 'Lawrence just said he was off when this bloke came into the shop with a double-barrelled sawn-off shotgun. He pointed it at his ankle and then there was just a bang. It was all over in a few seconds. He was a stocky chap and had a balaclava and dark clothing.' Aitken underwent seven-and-a-half hours of surgery and two blood transfusions to save the lower half of his right leg.

The gunman was John McSally. After accomplishing his mission, he jumped into a white Vauxhall Astra with two other men inside and drove off. Within a few days, DC Fletcher was passing on details of the police investigation to Gunn via the usual intermediary. 'Tell your big mate not to worry,' he told Jason Grocock. 'The bloke knows who did it but he's not talking.' It was another vital tip-off for Gunn. Fletcher was also compromising informants. He gave away details on one file about a woman who Gunn had been with briefly and who said Gunn had told her he was involved in the shootings of Joan and John Stirland. DC Fletcher put Gunn's mind at rest, texting Grocock that there could never be a prosecution as the evidence was 'purely circumstantial'.

He passed on more information in January 2005 about a sickening assault involving the Bestwood Cartel in the Lizard Lounge nightclub, when a man had lost part of his ear. Fletcher was on holiday at the time but when texted that 'the Big Man' needed to know about it, went straight into Radford Road Police Station and gathered all the intelligence on the attack. He also made checks on behalf of Gunn about an assault on a man in a pub in Nottingham in March 2005 and on a near-fatal assault on another man carried out by one of his henchmen. Fletcher even falsified records in a road traffic accident to prevent the prosecution of two other members of the Cartel who had been pulled over without insurance.

On one occasion Fletcher's own mistakes on the computer backfired on Colin Gunn's girlfriend. Victoria Garfoot had received a parking ticket and Gunn rang through to try to get Fletcher to get it cancelled. He went into the computer and punched in the name but he misspelled it and came up with an entry of another woman who had a conviction for prostitution. Fletcher passed on the information to Gunn, with disastrous consequences. 'Gunn went absolutely ballistic and confronted Victoria, accusing her of being a whore,' said one officer. 'Then he gave her a severe beating.' Victoria would remain loyal to Colin despite numerous police attempts to turn her and described her man in relatively glowing terms to the *Nottingham Evening Post*: 'No one says Colin has been an angel. He sells a few bent cars and that sort of thing. He's being blamed but where is the evidence? The police just don't like him. But everyone round here likes him. We're not scum like everyone makes out.'

Two things emerged from the probe into Charles Fletcher. One was positive and the other negative. Several officers were caught in the dragnet that had been set up to catch him. One was a constable called Phil Parr, who worked in the vice section. Parr had a passion for scooters and was friendly with Javade Rashid, who worked at Icon Scooters, which was owned by one of Colin Gunn's lieutenants, David Barrett. After Fletcher came up with the false information about Gunn's girlfriend being involved in prostitution, Gunn had become increasingly obsessed with checking out the information. He got Barrett to ask Rashid to ask

DC Parr about it because he worked in vice and would probably know. In November 2004 DC Parr received a text on his mobile from Rashid. Parr made the check and then went to the scooter shop to tell Rashid about it. Barrett was there and Gunn was waiting parked up in his BMW nearby, unknown to DC Parr. National Crime Squad officers had the shop under surveillance, something that Barrett later became aware of after being tipped off by someone within the police. PC Parr had no idea Gunn was the final recipient of the information and a promising career was ended as a result, all for 'doing a favour for a mate'. He admits he failed the highest standards set by the police force by doing the check but he was in no way linked to the criminal gang operated by Gunn, as DC Fletcher had been. 'I can't deny I did something that was wrong but I was tarnished with the same brush as Fletcher and there is no way I am a corrupt officer,' Parr later told me. 'I did something that I shouldn't have done but it was a favour for someone I thought was a mate.' Parr would be jailed for twelve months at Birmingham Crown Court after pleading guilty to misconduct in public office. As he has pointed out, he will have to come to terms with the shame of what he did, but some paedophiles and violent offenders have received lesser jail terms. His career was over and he lost much of any pension he could claim from an otherwise unblemished ten-year career.

A number of other officers were even more hard done by in the fallout that came from the surveillance of Fletcher. Detective Constable John Thorley, a highly respected officer, worked at Radford Road Police Station, near Fletcher's desk. The probes that had been in place for Fletcher caught him talking in colourful terms about some Yardies who planned to murder an officer outside Oxclose Lane Police Station. Thorley explained what happened to him and another colleague who had been caught on the bugs chatting inappropriately:

'On June 21, 2005, the phone rang at my home. Charles Fletcher had been arrested. Fletcher was a young trainee detective I'd worked with for several months. He was brash, overconfident and had a tendency to engage mouth before brain. I sighed. An hour or so later my colleagues and I sat and listened to a horror story. We were told Fletcher was a criminal, in league with some of the most violent criminals in the city; he was selling information to criminals who operated extortion rackets and ran Class A drugs. We all knew them well and had seen their handiwork. I'd stood at the foot of a bed in the Queen's Medical Centre while a man who had had most of a foot removed by a shotgun at point blank range refused to speak. We knew it was a punishment shooting for a debt. The chances of anyone talking to us were nil and so it proved. Through Fletcher, these people had access to everything about us: where we lived, where we socialised, even where my daughter goes to school. How safe were we? He'd betrayed us. That afternoon, two of us were summoned to HQ. Naively, I imagined we were going to be offered support and help in coming to terms with these devastating revelations.

'To my astonishment, I was served with notices stating I was to be the subject of a disciplinary investigation. For eight months our office had been bugged. Unconnected to any criminal investigation and out of hundreds of hours of recordings, I had been overheard on four occasions making "inappropriate and unprofessional comments". More seriously and with tedious predictability, the allegation of using racist language also appeared. I'm the first to admit that the language in a CID office can be, at best, irreverent. We've attended the post mortems of gunshot victims, cut hanged bodies down from coat hooks and sat across tables from paedophiles that have raped four-year-olds and had to pretend to be sympathetic. Gallows humour is and has always been necessary to remain sane, but always in private.

'To all intents and purposes my career ended at that moment. I was placed on restricted duties. I was to sit behind a desk doing nothing of value. I was never to do any meaningful work again. Neither I, nor my colleagues, are racist or homophobic. One of us is openly gay. From that moment I was airbrushed from history. It was as if my thirty years had never happened. When one comes near the service's obsession with racism, an unblemished twenty-nine-year service counts for nothing. I always thought that if ever I was faced with difficulties, I would receive help and guidance. Wrong! Most senior officers were almost behind barricades if I went too close.

'My despicable crimes by the way – behind closed doors and in private – were nasty remarks about, firstly, a Jamaican who was trying to recruit a 'shooter' to have one of us murdered outside Oxclose Lane Police Station as we left work, and secondly, about a woman who had invented a rape allegation that led to two innocent students being incarcerated for hours. I admit, on both occasions, it was quite likely I did make derogatory comments. To refer to a group of people as "Jamaican pond life" as I did could be considered rude. The group I referred to as this were killers and drug dealers. If I had said "Broxtowe pond life" or "St Ann's pond life", that is not a problem. What utter nonsense.

'I retired a year later but was connected with corruption and tainted with racism. I always suspected, but it took me most of my thirty years to discover, that this organisation does not value any individual. Careers and reputations are ruined on a whim. We were treated like a newly-discovered coven of the Ku Klux Klan. Fletcher's legacy wasn't only to destroy himself.'

On a positive note, though the fervour associated with the anti-corruption probe ended some unblemished careers, the force tightened up on their procedures for dealing with applications to join the police. Detective Superintendent Russ Foster ensured future applications to work for Nottinghamshire Police were thoroughly vetted in the wake of the Fletcher probe. In August 2007, Foster announced that a six-month investigation had discovered that at least six people, so-called 'clean skins' working on behalf of organised crime gangs, had applied for jobs in the force. 'They were identified and groomed to infiltrate this force with the aim of providing intelligence to city organised crime leaders,' he said. 'There was nothing obvious on their applications to suggest who they were. It was only after exhaustive work by me and my team that we identified their associates and their links with some of the biggest crime groups in Nottingham.'

ON 26 JANUARY 2005, Operation Utah, which had been investigating the Bestwood Cartel's drug-dealing activities, suffered a serious breach of security which sent shockwaves through the team. Two detectives – a constable and a sergeant – from the National Crime Squad were taking tapes for examination to the Forensic Science Service in Birmingham. It was a routine job but given the sensitive nature of the material, only a handful of people knew about it. One part of the tapes had a police interview with Colin Gunn. The other was recorded material from the bugs which had been put in place by the Utah team. The detectives' job was to process the tapes and, using voice recognition technology, see if the voices matched. On the way back from the job, the two detectives decided to stop off in the Crewe and Harpur pub in Swarkestone, Derbyshire, for a pint. They left all the material in the car, along with their notebooks and other material relating to Operation Utah. This material identified senior officers involved in the job, including Detective Chief Superintendent Phil Davies, the head of Nottinghamshire CID. It also identified a house in Bestwood where police were listening in on conversations between members of the Cartel and a building at Epperstone which was being used as the secret headquarters of Starburst and Utah. The officers were in the pub less than an hour, but in that short time the locks on their car were sprung and all the material stolen. Within two hours, telephone intercepts picked up a call from Newark. A young man was calling Colin Gunn and telling him what was on the material he had stolen. Gunn told him to destroy it.

The ramifications were huge. Once the theft was known, security at Epperstone was stepped up, with twenty-four-hour patrols around the perimeter. The house used for eavesdropping eventually had to be bought by Nottinghamshire Police at a cost of more than £100,000 and the people living in it had to be moved to a safe house and put under witness protection. Then, on 10 February, police received an anonymous letter. It said that there would be an attempt to assassinate two senior Nottinghamshire officers, including DCS Phil Davies. Threats had already been made against Detective Superintendent Ian Waterfield, then head of Operation Stealth, and the Chief Constable himself, Steve Green. The information resulted in Phil Davies having to move out of his house while security was upgraded and the threat diminished. It also led to a briefing for senior officers on how to exit their homes if there was an imminent threat to their life or their families. Two days after the threat was received, John McSally was arrested with five bullets in his pocket. Evidence suggested that McSally was on his way to a job, with a boiler suit in his car and a pair of wellington boots.

To this day there has never been any public acknowledgement of any detailed investigation into the theft of the confidential material by the Serious Organised Crime Agency (SOCA), which later replaced the National Crime Squad, or by any other body. The thief, who has never been named, was quietly dealt with at court in Derby, where he asked for more than 100 other offences, mainly thefts and burglaries, to be taken into consideration. Derbyshire Police, who dealt with the matter, refused to release any information about him on the orders of its Chief Constable Mick Creedon, saying the offender's life could be at risk.

A senior Nottinghamshire detective involved in Operation Utah told me, 'When we heard about the material going missing it was like a "Jesus Christ" moment. We thought, what the hell are we dealing with here? Very few people knew what that car was carrying that day. The fact that the theft took place in the car park of a pub in Derbyshire, the fact that someone from Nottingham was the thief and had been in a pub twenty miles away, the fact that that person knew Colin Gunn's mobile phone number, the fact that Colin Gunn was contacted within a couple of hours of the theft, it was like, well, you have got more chance of winning the lottery than of this being pure coincidence. Someone, somewhere, had told Colin Gunn that that vehicle contained important information and the vehicle was targeted as a result. Something was wrong and we passed on our grave concerns to the relevant people. I'm extremely surprised that SOCA say they didn't even conduct an inquiry because the National Crime Squad were certainly aware of it and once SOCA took over the National Crime Squad's responsibilities it would have been passed over to them.'

DAVID GUNN WAS arrested by Nottinghamshire Police involved in Operation Utah that February. The bugs they had placed in the headrest of his BMW had nailed him and he had been caught talking too loosely on the phone. After a few drug shipments were intercepted, Gunn told his associates, 'They've got another load, hope it's not the whole lot. It's just a poxy bust really. They are trying to take out the little sergeants, but they can't get to us, the colonels or captains.' Gunn was also caught talking to associates on the phone about where he could launder some of his money in South Africa. Police moved in and arrested his forty-one-year-old right-hand man, Terry Witts, who had recently married a school-teacher. They also moved in on Gunn and arrested him. The pair, along with their friend Kevin Warsop, were linked to small shipment of more than £20,000. Gunn had been watched seeing off a taxi carrying some of the drugs. The Bestwood Cartel was even ripping off its own customers by recutting large amounts of vacuum-packed drugs and then resealing them as if the stuff had come in wholesale. It was just another way to keep profits high, even if the customers were not going to get as high as they were led to believe.

But if there was any relief at the arrest of David Gunn, and the impending arrest of Colin, it would be blown away the following month when I was to personally experience how Chief Constable Steve Green handled the media. I suggested an article for the *Sunday Telegraph* on the troubles facing Nottinghamshire Police after a number of officers from both the front line and a senior level approached me to voice their concerns about the state of the force. Many claimed it was on the brink of collapse. I had also been told of some of the details of Operation Starburst and I knew there was an Independent Police Complaints Commission (IPCC) investigation underway into the shooting of the Stirlands which was indicating there had been serious failings on the part of the force. Nottinghamshire Police were also refusing to give investigators any access to material from the bugging of the Bestwood Cartel, citing legal complications over the ownership of the material. After raising the issue with Daniel Foggo, who worked as a reporter at the *Sunday Telegraph*, we decided we would first try to contact the person we assumed was head of Operation Starburst. We approached Detective Chief Superintendent Phil Davies and he initially agreed to meet and have a chat about it the following week, but then Davies told me he had spoken to his boss, Steve Green, about our approach and had told him we seemed very well briefed about the challenges facing the force. He said Green had decided he would talk to us if we approached him. Daniel then rang Green, told him what we knew about Starburst and said we were considering running a story about the issues being investigated by the IPCC. Green was clearly unhappy about this, claiming we might compromise covert operations, a dubious claim to make when we were approaching the subject in a responsible manner and would be under legal constraints about what we could print anyway. On Friday, 10 March 2005, Green agreed to an interview over the phone but Operation Starburst was off the agenda.

Daniel Foggo is an experienced reporter and someone who does not pull any punches, so he began to question the Chief Constable about various problems facing the force, based on what we knew. We were both staggered as he began to admit all the failings and pressures the force was under. The interview was completed before the end of Friday afternoon and was tape recorded. When the story emerged on Sunday morning, neither of myself nor Daniel realised the impact it would have. The story made the front page lead of the *Sunday Telegraph* on 13 March.

POLICE CHIEF: WE CANNOT COPE WITH VIOLENT CRIME

One of Britain's most senior police officers has admitted that his force is being overwhelmed by violent crime and cannot cope.

Steve Green, the Chief Constable of Nottinghamshire, said that among the principal causes of the crisis were Government reforms that compelled him to use officers for clerical tasks instead of front-line duties.

Steve Green: 'We are in a crisis situation.'

The situation was so bad that he was preparing to 'farm out' murder investigations to other police forces because his own detectives did not have time to tackle them.

Nottingham has been one of the worst affected areas for gun crime which hit record levels across England and Wales last year.

Mr Green said ministers had a 'fixation' with keeping officer numbers up – but had, in fact, been responsible for policies that had taken police away from front-line duties to do jobs that should be carried out by civilian staff, such as writing Home Office reports.

'We are reeling with the murders,' he said. 'We are in a long-standing crisis situation with major crime and it won't go away overnight. Having police doing back-office jobs is one of the factors [hampering us]. I want to increase the number of operational cops by reducing the numbers doing back-office jobs. It's frustrating to know that I could make better use of the money I've got, but I'm constrained from doing it because officer numbers is a political football. All the parties have the same fixation.'

Mr Green said he was prevented from putting more police into front-line duties because if he reduced the number of officers doing clerical work he would lose a large amount of his funding from the Crime Fighting Fund, a Labour measure that gives extra money to forces that keep officer numbers high.

'Our accountant has said that if there was a way out of it, he would tell me,' he said.

Mr Green, whose comments will increase pressure on the Government over its law-and-order policies, said his force was heavily in debt. He regularly had to borrow detectives from other constabularies to tackle a spate of largely drugs-related murders.

'We are now routinely going out to "foreign" forces to get additional officers.' One option they were on the verge of adopting was to farm an entire murder inquiry to another force. 'I'm not aware of any other force ever having done such a thing,' he said.

Nottingham's crisis has been prompted by a sharp rise in the number of murders and other violent crimes. Since 2001, the force has had to investigate 21 Category A murders – those classed as being high-profile with no immediate suspect. Before 2000, it was dealing with one Category A murder every 12 to 18 months on average. Its officers are currently running 30 murder investigations.

Nottinghamshire residents are also three times more likely than the national average to have their car broken into, four times as likely to be burgled, almost five times as likely to be robbed, and twice as likely to suffer sexual attack. Nottinghamshire was also among the bottom four of under-performing forces in official figures last year.

Mr Green's decision to speak out follows another fatal shooting last week. Paul Thomas, 34, had left a pub in Radford, Nottingham, when he was gunned down just after 4.30pm on Thursday.

Firearms offences in England and Wales rose to a high of 24,094 last year with levels in Nottingham the fifth highest per head of population after London, Manchester, Liverpool and the West Midlands.

The Association of Chief Police Officers said other forces were experiencing similar pressures to Nottinghamshire because of the need for officers to carry out bureaucratic tasks that should be done by civilians. 'We've been raising it with the Government for some months,' said a spokesman. 'There is a fixation with police numbers, and an inflexibility over budgets, which is not producing effective policing. We can recruit officers, but not necessarily civilian staff.'

David Davis, the shadow Home Secretary, said Mr Green's predicament was an example of the Government's ring-fencing of money, together with forces being swamped with bureaucracy. He said: 'We will do away with the national policing plan that creates these targets so those police they have can be properly used.'

The story broke as a General Election campaign was about to get underway and crime was top of the agenda. Shadow Home Secretary David Davis wasted no time in wading into the debate. Privately he was critical of Green but publicly he said the comments showed how Chief Constables' hands were being tied up by red tape across the country by a Home Office which was not funding them adequately. The daily newspapers were champing at the bit to follow up the *Sunday Telegraph*'s story. For a Chief Constable to be so clearly unable to cope and speak about it publicly was almost unheard of. Green was in the soup as far as the Home Office was concerned, but he would find support from the media and fellow Chief Constables over his stance rather than criticism. Only those who knew what was really going on inside the force knew that many of the problems were linked to his handling of the resources at his disposal.

Nevertheless he realised his job could be under threat and his press officer, Margaret Kirk, began to brief journalists that Green had been 'blackmailed' into agreeing to the interview. It was an extraordinary claim to make, effectively alleging we had forced him to tell the truth by committing a criminal offence. We weren't the only ones who were angry. Her Majesty's Inspectorate of Police was fuming. The comments from the Chief Constable about his force being in crisis had come only a few weeks after Denis O'Connor, a senior HMIC inspector, had given the force a clean bill of health. Sir Ronnie Flanagan, Chief Inspector for HMIC, soon had Home Secretary Charles Clarke knocking on his door demanding answers. Downing Street entered the fray too, with Tony Blair's official spokesman making a veiled criticism of Green's leadership. 'Everyone recognises there are problems in Nottinghamshire but there are different views about the cause of these problems,' the spokesman told reporters. Home Secretary Clarke demanded an urgent investigation into Green's claims, which would be carried out by HMIC and, within a couple of days, HMIC investigators contacted the *Sunday Telegraph*'s editor, Dominic Lawson, to see whether they could get access to the tape recorded interview. He was happy to oblige but said HMIC would have to make a formal request by letter; otherwise, Lawson argued, it could set a precedent for the handing over of privileged material to a third party. In the end HMIC did not follow up its informal request with a letter.

Meanwhile, MP Graham Allen lodged a complaint against Green to the IPCC. 'I believe he has been guilty of serious misjudgment, not just in giving the interview but in his original decision to take beat officers off the streets of Nottingham,' Allen told the *Observer* newspaper. Green, perhaps sensing his job was in jeopardy, told reporters, who by this time were hoping for an all-out war between a Chief Constable and the Home Office, that the interview was a big mistake. 'For whatever reasons I gave the interview I must concede that the interview itself was not my finest hour,' he said. 'With hindsight I was wrong to accept the word crisis during the interview but nevertheless investigating murders is a major challenge to us.'

Marian Bates's widower, Victor, pulled no punches: 'Nottingham has never been as lawless as it has been under this Chief Constable. The man is a menace to law and order,' he told reporters. 'The way the criminals in Nottingham have been allowed to flourish under his regime is ridiculous. It is frightening. There are less police officers on the street and we now have community wardens who have no powers. It must have cost the lives of over fifteen people over the last two years, including my wife. The criminals have been encouraged by the system that prevails. Crime is now a lively occupation because the chances of being caught are so little.'

Later Green, who would eventually leave Nottinghamshire Police in June 2008, was critical of Victor Bates's stance, claiming he was being led by others with an agenda of their own. 'I have listened to what Victor Bates has said and he is perfectly entitled to his opinion,' he told the *Nottingham Evening Post*. 'I have no problem with Victor. I respect what he's been through too much. It's the people who have been advising him that are beneath contempt. Their actions have meant that the opportunity Mr Bates had to exercise the power he had to do good was wasted.' Steve Green also claimed he had fallen into a trap because his mind was preoccupied with the arrest of Colin Gunn. 'I tried to give the journalist honest answers, as I always do, but I get paid not to fall into elephant traps. I recognise I fell into that one. All I can say is my attention was focused on operational matters and I just didn't see it coming. On the day I did the interview, Colin Gunn was arrested for the Stirlands' murder. We should have been in celebration mode; instead, we were fighting that off as best we could.'

Green's memory was faulty: in fact Colin Gunn was not arrested until Thursday, 17 March 2005, almost a week after the interview was carried out. Nottinghamshire officers picked him up and when they started driving out on the A52 and passed into Lincolnshire, Gunn was surprised.

'Where are we going?' he asked.

'Just a trip to the seaside, Colin,' replied an officer. 'Why, are you missing Nottingham already?'

Colin was interviewed at Skegness Police Station by Lincolnshire detectives. 'I had no direct or indirect involvement with the murders,' he claimed. 'John Stirland was known to me as he used to drink with me and my friends. I have never had any bad feelings towards John and Joan Stirland.' It was, of course, a blatant lie.

By now the drains at his bungalow in Revelstoke Way were severely blocked with phones and SIM cards and other evidential debris. A plumber would be called out some two-and-a-half years later because of damp patches inside the three-bedroom property. He just built over the blocked drain to solve the problem. Who knows what secrets are held on the phones but, to my knowledge, they remain where they are to this day.

CHAPTER 13
DOWNFALL

A huge armed presence ringed the courtroom at Nottingham in March 2005 for the trial of the drug-smuggling Dawes Cartel. Police spent more than £500,000 on the security operation not because they feared John Dawes would try to escape but for his protection because they thought he might turn and offer information on his brother Rob, who was still at large in Spain, his partner Gary Hardy and, not least, the Bestwood Cartel. 'We believed there was a genuine risk to Dawes,' said Detective Inspector Peter Jones. 'Our thinking was that when convicted, he may want to mitigate and give his side of the story. If he is willing to give evidence on the others he is working alongside, he becomes valuable.'

Over nine weeks, a jury heard details of how John and Rob Dawes headed a ruthless organisation making more than £1 million a month from the illegal drugs trade. At the end of it all, John Dawes, his father Arthur, Rebecca Bridge and Ryan Smith were all convicted for their parts in the operation. John Dawes was jailed for twenty-four-years, Smith for fourteen years, Arthur Dawes for eight and Bridge for four. Operation Normality had been a huge success and while Rob Dawes and Gary Hardy remained at large, police felt sure it would only be a matter of time before they tripped up. The case had shown just how much power an organised crime group could achieve. In a short space of time the Dawes Cartel had managed to corrupt officials in various organisations and rule through fear.

DI Jones pointed out the similarities between the Dawes Cartel and that run by the Bestwood mob. 'John Dawes thought he was untouchable. But no one is untouchable, no matter how violent and intimidating they are. There was information that suggested this organisation was able to penetrate the police, social services, the local authority and other organisations through intimidation or other means.'

WHEN THE TRUSTHORPE murder trial got underway, in March 2006 at Birmingham Crown Court, David Gunn sat in the dock alongside his brother Colin, with the jury unaware David had already pleaded guilty the previous year to conspiracy to supply amphetamine, a crime for which he would eventually be jailed for eight-and-a-half years and for which Terry Witts and Kevin Worsop were also jailed. Eight defendants now faced the jury. Colin and David Gunn, John Russell and Michael McNee were joined by Shane Bird, aged thirty-nine, of Carlton Hill, Nottingham, Kevin Holm, thirty-eight, of Cliff Road, Carlton, Andrew McKinnon, twenty-one, of no fixed address, and Lanelle Douglas, twenty, of no fixed address. All denied conspiracy to commit murder. In the public gallery was Victor Bates, who had decided to attend the trial to see the face of the Colin Gunn, who he knew had been implicated in his own wife's death.

Opening for the prosecution, Timothy Spencer QC said the killers were 'calculated, ruthless and merciless'. The murders 'were carried out with clinical efficiency. No disturbance, no sign of haste; the targets were located quickly and shot just as quickly ...

in other words, as part of a well organised, well planned gang operation.' There was, he said, evidence of a 'command structure' in the way the couple's murders had been organised. However, there was very little direct evidence. In fact the case was one of the most difficult ever handled by Lincolnshire Crown Prosecution Service. Eyewitnesses and forensics were distinctly lacking. It would take a jigsaw of circumstantial evidence to build up a picture of those responsible; in particular, the detailed mobile phone records that the prosecution claimed placed the defendants at the heart of the crime. The prosecution sought to show how each of the accused was implicated through the use of phones they had bought for the sole purpose of planning and organising the murders and had then thrown away afterwards. Specifically these included eleven 'murder phones' used over hundreds of miles in a ten-day period. Over 7,000 calls had been analysed and more than 100 statements about phone usage disclosed.

'With all the benefit of hindsight,' Mr Spencer went on, 'it could be said that if the police had acted more quickly to the prowler report then this killing could have been prevented. But they didn't. It's as simple as that.' He admitted, 'There are unanswered questions in this case and there will be unanswered questions at the end of it. The prosecution suggest that we have the greater part of this gang. We don't suggest we have all of it.'

John Russell's defence was to claim that he was half-drunk, flying a kite and chatting to girls when the Stirlands were shot dead. Andrew Hall QC, defending Russell, also disputed prosecution claims that his client had taken bloodstained clothing to a launderette the day after the murders. The court heard that Russell had more than 80 previous convictions for drug dealing, burglary and stealing cars, but no record of violence. He claimed that he was on the east coast with Michael McNee to look after a caravan full of amphetamines and to supply local drug dealers. 'He is a professional criminal and no doubt a considerable menace to the people of Nottingham,' said Mr Hall. 'But that's not the issue. The issue is: is he a killer?'

He continued, 'On that Lincolnshire coast, it was high season, it was the summer and the pubs and clubs were full of young people. This was a busy time for those who wanted to sell drugs. It is perhaps unsurprising to find the two of them by the coast in August. If it wasn't for the seriousness of the case, the notion of John Russell half-drunk and trying to get some girls back to the caravan while acting as a lookout would be comical.' Mr Hall told the jury that the prosecution was 'grasping at straws' and had a 'weak, circumstantial case'.

Defendant Shane Bird admitted he had used a contact to illegally access information on the couple before they were killed but denied knowing anything about the murders until he heard about them in the news two days later. In a transcript read out, and tapes played to the courtroom, the jury heard Bird make a tearful denial to police that he was involved. 'What you are trying to suggest is that I knew about it before and that is not on,' he told officers. 'It's come out all over the news. Things go through your mind, like was that anything to do with the number I got? And it made me feel physically sick.' In the same interview, Bird could not explain frequent calls made a few days before the shootings to David Gunn. The records showed the calls to Gunn were made back to back with calls made to Bird's British Telecom contact. It was suggested to Bird that the calls were about the Stirlands' address and Bird's progress in obtaining it. He denied the suggestion from police.

When he came to take the stand Shane Bird was more in control of his emotions than he had been in the police station. He told the courtroom, 'I was proper upset thinking the number might have something to do with the murders. It actually broke my heart.' Bird, who owned two scooter shops in Ingoldmells,

Lincolnshire, had made no fewer than 1,600 calls on his mobile phone in the first eight days of August 2004. His phone was tracked to the Trusthorpe area in the days leading up to the murder but he argued that his businesses in Ingoldmells required his attention and his presence in the area was nothing unusual. On the day of the killings, Bird went to Leicester racecourse to watch a horse that he owned compete in a seven-furlong race.

By the time David Gunn decided to take the stand, the case against him was looking increasingly flawed. During cross-examination, Timothy Spencer suggested to Gunn that he decided to stay in Nottingham on the day of the murder so that Colin could oversee things on the east coast, ensuring that at least one of them had a watertight alibi. 'There had to be a show and you and your brother decided that you could not both be on the coast when the Stirlands were shot,' said Mr Spencer. 'You are an intelligent man. You realise the value of being in Nottingham on the Sunday and being with your partner all day. Your role was to be the organiser, the setter-up, and that is why you did not go to the caravan on the coast. It needed one of you to be on the spot, hands-on, making sure things went to plan, and that was his role.'

David Gunn had previously told police in interviews they had no evidence against him. 'At the end of it, apart from you putting me in a few places using my phone, you haven't really got me doing anything. I am shocked that you have got me here,' he had said after being arrested. Now he was even more emphatic in his denials. Trevor Burke, his defence barrister, asked him about the suggestion that messages he sent concerned two Beretta handguns. 'That is complete nonsense,' Gunn told the court. 'I've never even seen a Beretta firearm.' He also said neither text message had been received in any case. He had spoken to his brother later on another number and told him he was on his way to Lincolnshire with cannabis joints on August 5.

'It's suggested you handled one or two firearms in anticipation of a murder,' said Mr Burke.

'No, that is not true,' replied Gunn.

The jury would believe David Gunn's explanation about the 'menthol' text message and ultimately his alibi. With David Gunn in the clear, the calls that Shane Bird had made to him became an irrelevancy as well.

The jury deliberated for more than twenty-six hours. On 29 June, they returned and delivered guilty verdicts against Colin Gunn, Michael McNee and John Russell. The other five men, including David Gunn, were acquitted. At least twelve security guards packed the dock, with police stationed at the door. The judge pronounced sentence the following day. He jailed all three for life and ordered that Colin Gunn face a 35 year sentence before parole would even be considered – it meant that in all probability Colin Gunn would be spending the rest of his life in prison. Colin could not yet be named in the press because he still faced a corruption trial involving DC Charles Fletcher, but it did not stop him launching in a tirade of abuse against the jury and the judge, Mr Justice Treacy. Colin was the first to hear the jury's verdict. He turned to them menacingly and snarled, 'Thank you, you scum bags. I hope you die of cancer.' As he was led away he called the female foreman of the jury a 'slag and a whore'. He then directed his anger at the judge, calling him a paedophile.

The judge, undeterred, continued making his statement about Colin Gunn. 'This was a murder which shocked the nation. You are a crook, a villain and a large-scale drug dealer. You were the leader of this criminal gang. To your gang your word was law. The utterly evil nature of what you did shows that you, as a criminal man, are prepared to commit the ultimate act of criminal violence as and when it suits your purpose. You are prepared to do that due to a perverted desire for revenge. You are a man who would not let anything stand in your way. You would, I believe, do the same thing again.'

John Russell gave the judge the middle finger as he was sentenced.

DAVID GUNN SUBSEQUENTLY issued a statement which read, 'Since my arrest I protested my innocence and yesterday the jury, thank God, believed me. The last eighteen months have been the worst in my life, being incarcerated and not being able to see my partner and children has broken me. I hope now to rebuild my life with my family and close friends and finally I am truly sorry for the Stirland family's loss.'

His estranged wife Sandie told the *Nottingham Evening Post*, 'Colin had asked David and I if he and a few friends could use the caravan in Ingoldmells for a break, as it had been a really tough time for all the family after Jamie died. When we heard about what happened to the Stirlands we were both shocked. I always knew David had nothing to do with their deaths. He did drive down to join Colin and the others for a drink but he didn't stay long.'

But a few weeks after being cleared of conspiracy to murder, David Gunn faced sentencing for the amphetamine seizure. When he was sentenced at Derby Crown Court, prosecutor Andrew Easteal described Gunn as the leader of an 'organised crime group' who was at the heart of a massive trade in amphetamine – the self-confessed 'Colonel – alongside second-in-command Terence Witts. Through covert surveillance, the court heard, police tailed the two men as they arranged the collection and distribution of thousands of pounds worth of the class B drug on a weekly basis. David also talked about his connections in South Africa, which were set up to help the jobless gang launder their money abroad as they strove to avoid detection. He was convicted by his own words by reams of damning evidence from the electronic devices placed in his car and in houses Gunn was using throughout 2004 and 2005, allowing the police to discover more about their business than they thought possible. Mr Easteal told the court, 'Any doubt about David Gunn's role and authority in the operation was taken away by the listening device in the car.' The bugs had recorded him regularly talking about a new 'load' or 'delivery'.

Gunn's barrister, Craig Ferguson, used his client's association with his notorious younger sibling as mitigation. 'By virtue of his name and association with his brother Colin, it is plain that he has achieved a certain level of notoriety. Many judges in Nottingham will know of the Gunn family by virtue of their day-to day jobs. The issue arises as to whether there is any prejudice, whether he can receive a fair sentence.' Mr Ferguson said there was a 'distinction in character' between Colin and David Gunn, an argument, he said, that was proven by David Gunn's acquittal for the Stirland murders.

But Nottinghamshire Chief Constable Steve Green held a very different view of David Gunn's role in his brother's gang. 'We dealt with it as a single kind of business,' Mr Green said later. 'We acknowledged the centrality of Colin Gunn to it, but as far as we were concerned David was part of the inner sanctum. He may well spend less time in prison than his brother, but he will never leave our radar screen. For the rest of his natural life he needs to look over his shoulder.'

The amphetamine convictions meant that it would be some time before Gunn would be free to walk the streets of Bestwood again. By 2008, however, he had already enjoyed a couple of home visits in preparation for his release in April 2009.

IT WAS OVER for the Bestwood Cartel. Yet two days after Colin Gunn and his underlings were sentenced, Bestwood erupted in riots. Thirty youths overturned, smashed up and set alight cars, ripped down fences, knocked down walls and built barricades across Raymede Drive during a three-hour standoff with police. They also waved placards demanding the release of the jailed men. It was a hollow gesture. 'This is the last hurrah of the remnants of people who know that their time has gone,' said Nottingham North MP Graham Allen. 'Their leader has been given nearly forty years in prison and is not likely to see the light of day so they are now feeling the squeeze. These people have realised that their days are numbered and they can no longer rule the roost in Bestwood.'

Pat Chambers, one of the community leaders in Bestwood, said the estate needed to leave the memory of the Gunns behind. 'The Godfather – that was Colin Gunn. He was the boss and everybody was frightened of him. If you had a problem, you didn't go to the police. You went to Colin and Colin sorted it. But there was tenderness as well – and he had very good PR in the fact that he helped people. He gave them money for fireworks displays for the kids. People loved him. He was a Robin Hood because if you was in trouble financially he would help you out. At any given time he could call on you. It took a long time for this culture to turn itself around and now it's turned round and we are on the way up.'

Detective Chief Superintendent Phil Davies, the man to whom a lot of the credit must go in pursuing the Bestwood Cartel to the end and who spent many a night sleeping on the floor of the operation room as the investigations gained in intensity, described the ninety-odd operations against the family as akin to fighting a form of terrorism. 'The difficulty in getting to the Mr Bigs is similar to that of trying to take on the IRA leaders in Northern Ireland in the early 1970s. There was no evidence behind their alleged IRA activity. Some criminal networks in Nottinghamshire were organised like the IRA hierarchy, using the cell system. Anyone who tried to deal drugs or commit other crimes inside their patches would get at least a good beating.'

One of those cells – what might be termed an 'intelligence unit' – was the next to be dealt with. Jason Grocock, David Barrett, Darren Peters and Kevin Warsop all pleaded guilty in 2006 at Birmingham Crown Court to conspiring to commit misconduct in public office in connection with the corrupt detective Charles Fletcher. Grocock and Peters were jailed for four years, Barrett and Warsop for three years. The police also finally caught up with Jamie Neil. Though the thirty-nine-year-old was a wanted man for his role in the corrupting of police officers and for questioning about an attack on an undercover officer, he had been flying in and out of the country numerous times from Portugal or Spain for more than twelve months. He was working the doors of nightclubs in Portugal when police finally lifted him and brought him back. He promptly pleaded guilty to conspiracy to pervert the course of justice and commit misconduct in public office at Nottingham Crown Court and received a three-year sentence.

Fletcher himself pleaded guilty to one count of conspiracy to commit misconduct in a public office and two counts of conspiracy to pervert the course of justice. He was jailed for seven years in October 2006. In return for his services, he had received discounts on designer clothes at Limey's store. 'His conduct was unsophisticated,' said his lawyer, Hugh Davies. 'In payment he received suits which are of no use to him where he is now and will be out of fashion when he gets to wear them next. His motivation is source material for a forensic psychologist rather than his counsel. Perhaps he found it exhilarating to be involved with criminals.'

After his conviction, Fletcher sent a letter to his former colleagues attempting to explain why he had done what he had done. The letter read: 'I suppose you're wondering why it's taken me this long to write and offer some sort of explanation. To be honest, it's taken me this long to come to terms with the shame of my actions but most especially the betrayal of all my old colleagues. In answering "why?" I feel my greed, vanity and naivety were to blame and the fact I didn't have the strength or courage to face up to my wrongdoing and tell someone before the inevitable happened. I was blind to the consequences of my actions and chose to ignore them. So selfishness played a big part in my downfall as I showed no regard for how my actions would affect my family, friends and those close to me.'

Detective Superintendent Russ Foster, the head of professional standards at the force, said Fletcher had been less than comprehensive in his version of how Gunn had corrupted him: 'There are two hypotheses. One is that he has infiltrated Nottinghamshire Police purely to supply information to organised crime groups or the criminal fraternity; or, he joined the Nottinghamshire Police, he became vulnerable, susceptible, and was corrupted by these individuals while serving as a police officer. I'm not certain which of the two theories are correct. Fletcher has given us no indication.'

IN MAY 2007, it was the deadly John McSally's turn to face justice. He had been arrested after walking into his favourite pub drunk and waving a revolver around, saying he had a job to do that night. The landlady persuaded him to leave the revolver in the pub's safe and McSally drove off to his home in Plaza Gardens, Basford, with the bullets still in his pocket. The brave landlady then phoned the police and told them what McSally had said, adding that she had managed to persuade him to leave the gun. Armed officers were dispatched to McSally's home. They pounced as he got out of his Nissan 4x4 and seized the bullets from his pocket. They were .38 calibre and matched the .38

revolver later recovered from the pub safe. McSally could only say, 'You planted those on me.'

A jury at Leicester Crown Court did not agree. They convicted McSally, aged fifty, of the murder of a forty-six-year-old Patrick Marshall outside the Park Tavern in Basford in February 2004, and of the attempted murder of youth worker Derrick Senior in May 2003. The pub landlady, who had been in regular contact with police from the middle of 2004, gave vital evidence to help bring him to justice. McSally boasted that he had shot Derrick Senior for 'three bags of sand', which he explained was £3,000. He had even boasted about shooting Joan Stirland and, although later evidence emerged that he had been somewhere else that day, his phone was linked to the Lincolnshire area in the days leading up to the murder, suggesting that he may have been involved in the planning. The judge jailed him for life and told him he would serve at least thirty-five years. 'You are an incredibly dangerous man,' said Mr Justice Pitchers, 'ready, for money, to kill without a second thought.' McSally, who according to his boasts had carried out five murders and at least eleven punishment shootings, did not react to the verdict, other than to tell the judge the sentence would be 'no problem'.

Police believed that McSally had received some help with the getaway car on the Patrick Marshall murder from a man called Craig McKay. They recovered the Volvo used in the murder, which had McKay's fingerprints on it, shortly after the shooting. In the glove compartment was a bill addressed to Colin Gunn and three pictures of his brother David. After the shooting, McKay was found severely injured by the side of the A608, close to junction 27 of the M1. Police believed he had received a punishment beating with baseball bats for being sloppy and leaving material in the car. However, McKay, thirty-three, of Bestwood Park Estate, a heroin addict with more than forty offences on his record, denied any involvement and was cleared of Mr Marshall's murder, while his girlfriend was cleared of perverting the course of justice by allegedly giving McKay a false alibi.

In a message clearly aimed at a local populace traumatised by the constant gunplay, Detective Chief Superintendent Neil James, head of crime for Nottinghamshire Police, said afterwards, 'We would like to pay tribute to the courage of the witnesses and their willingness to support the investigation. A conviction would have been less likely without their evidence. I also want to reassure the communities of Nottinghamshire that we possess the skills, experience and the determination to continue to relentlessly pursue the individuals who have historically terrorised communities and committed serious acts of violence. We will leave no stone unturned. Our structures remain in place to tackle these issues and dismantle serious and organised crime to prevent it escalating. We will not tolerate a culture of lawlessness. Our objective is for people who live, work and visit the county to feel safe, reassured and enjoy a good quality of life. We are committed to providing a service we are proud to deliver and one that the public expects.'

The landlady, who is now in the witness protection programme, had her own share of tragedy to deal with as well as the stress of helping the police. Her son had unwittingly handled the gun in the safe and was himself arrested in connection with Patrick Marshall's murder. The young man would later commit suicide while still under suspicion for a murder he did not commit.

Charles Marshall, Patrick's brother, said on behalf of the family: "The last three years has been very hard for all our family. Today means we can start to rebuild our lives. We all still miss Patrick and only time will heal the wounds that we have from his death. Our dad was diagnosed with cancer about a year and a half ago and told that he had a limited time to live. At least he has survived to see justice done today. As it says on the plaque at our brother's grave – "Justice is thine."'

IN THE SUMMER of 2007, Colin Gunn, now more than a year into his life sentence, went back on trial for the corrupting of police officers. In an unusual move, the Crown Prosecution Service applied for evidence of his bad character – chiefly his conviction for conspiracy to murder – to be revealed in court, arguing that the jury needed to know about the deaths of the Stirlands to understand this case and his motivation for seeking police intelligence. At the start of the trial, Gunn sacked his legal team and refused to take part. He failed to appear in court for most of the case.

Not surprisingly, Gunn was convicted. 'The Crown's case was that using go-betweens, he asked for, and received, confidential information from Nottinghamshire police officers,' said reviewing lawyer Stuart Laidlaw, of the CPS Special Crime Division. 'Thankfully, the information he received had limited consequences, in part at least because the main police contact was under surveillance and the police were managing the risks that arose. Colin Gunn wanted to know what the police knew about various investigations which were of interest to him, such as the murder of the Stirlands, the shooting of jeweller Marion Bates in Nottingham and intelligence checks – or "MOTs" as they were referred to – on suspects. With this knowledge he hoped to keep one step ahead of the police.'

In August 2007, Gunn was jailed for a further nine years, the sentence to run concurrently with his life term. Only then could he finally be named in the media after previous legal restrictions, and the floodgates broke. 'Nottingham's "godfather of crime",' declared the BBC. 'Brutal ganglord who fell victim to his own drugs,' headlined the *Guardian*. 'Gangster No 1 finally unmasked,' blazed *The Sun*. The *Nottingham Evening Post*, which had been waiting for five years to expose the extent of Gunn's evil empire, produced a special thirty-two-page pullout which flew off the news-stands.

As the CPS lawyer Mr Laidlaw said, 'For a long time Colin Gunn stayed one step ahead of the law. The law has now caught up with him.'

CHAPTER 14
WITHIN THESE WALLS

B y the end of the first decade of the twenty-first century, it was clear that new technology now defined our way of communicating and interacting with the rest of the world – including the criminal world. Just as the birth of the pay-as-you-go mobile phone empowered the street drug dealer in his daily task of evading the 'feds', so cyberspace became a place where organised crime could prosper in relatively covert comfort and crime lords could galvanise and rally their soldiers more effectively. For law enforcement agencies, these same technologies offered a wealth of intelligence material; it was the mobile phone which convicted Colin Gunn and his cohorts. Nevertheless, by November 2009 it had become apparent to Gunn that the Internet offered him a chance to communicate with his friends and members of the Bestwood gang on a much wider level and with greater speed than the flow of letters he was constantly penning from his prison cell, some of which failed to reach their intended destination due to the high level of security imposed on such a notorious Category A prisoner.

Gunn enjoyed his letter writing and encouraged other prisoners to write to his family on the outside, which resulted in the letterbox of his mum Carol bulging with cards and greetings on birthdays and at Christmas, with regular postings from, among others, one Kenneth Noye, linked to the 1983 Brinks Mat gold bullion job and serving life for the so-called 'M25 murder' of Stephen Cameron. Gunn had become friendly with Noye while at Whitemoor prison in Cambridgeshire, where the two had found much common ground. Gunn's mum kept messages flowing to and from Colin and those he could not contact directly. She even relayed messages between Michael 'Tricky' McNee and John 'Jon Jon' Russell, who were in different prisons.

Both Colin and David Gunn were moved around the prison system regularly from the date of their incarceration in 2005. In Colin's case, it was unsurprising, given that he swiftly made a name for himself in prison. First, while on remand at the maximum-security Belmarsh Prison, he and a fellow inmate attacked nine Muslims remanded on terrorist charges after he felt they disrespected Christmas. Then at Frankland Prison he attacked a prisoner who had upset him in the gym, leaving him battered and bruised. In October 2007, he hooked up with fellow inmate David Bieber, an American who had shot dead a West Yorkshire policeman on Boxing Day 2003. The two men were gym fanatics. Bieber hatched an escape plan which involved a helicopter and firearms. Colin Gunn asked him if he could come in on it. The plan was scuppered before it got anywhere and ended up in the pages of the *News of the World*.

Yet in letters to friends on the Bestwood estate, Colin expressed deep frustration at having been moved several times between the top security prisons at Belmarsh, Frankland and Whitemoor, before finally arriving at Long Lartin prison, in Evesham, in October 2009. Police and prison security were well aware of the ability of both brothers to take over the wings of prisons and had been paying close attention to their activities on the inside. On the outside, representatives of the gang were said to be negotiating with the Turkish mafia to buy a twenty-plus-room property in Cyprus and even to set up a business running a brothel with the consent of local hoodlums. (During the late 1990s and early 2000s, Colin had become a company director of several firms he hoped would help him launder money. The companies have all since been dissolved and Colin was arrested before he had the chance to become a real-life Tony Soprano and take over a waste management company.)

When David came to be released on parole in April 2009, it was immediately clear that the authorities would not be giving him a free bus ticket back to his old haunts. As part of his licence conditions, he was banned from certain areas of Nottingham, including Bestwood, and from key potential meeting locations such as service areas on the M1 motorway. He was to reside at a bail hostel in Northampton until he had proved he was keeping to the terms of his licence. Gunn launched an appeal against these restrictions, claiming that the licence conditions imposed were unreasonably excessive, disproportionate in their impact upon his family and private life, and were not 'rationally connected' with the reason for which they were imposed: the protection of the public and his rehabilitation. He also argued that the high level of risk assessment on him that led to these licence conditions was not supported by evidence.

His appeal, however, was rejected by the High Court. So angered was he that he turned to the *Nottingham Evening Post* to publicise his plight. 'I have been unfairly treated,' he said. 'I was convicted of drugs offences, nothing more, and yet they have ranked me as a danger to the public. I think that is completely wrong.' He failed to point out that he had been convicted of violent offences in January 1993 and of threats to kill in November 1998, resulting in jail terms totalling more than five years.

He told reporters, 'I don't have any grievances against anyone. All I want is to have this ridiculous ban from my home overturned. If I have done anything else wrong, then why don't they arrest me?' He was particularly miffed by the argument that crime would rise if he was allowed back on the estate. "That is one thing they keep bringing up to use against me. It is wrong. If it wasn't for us, it would have been out of hand. And we never used the name "the Bestwood Cartel" either. You don't speak about your friends like that. We were just a group of school friends.' He said the restrictions placed on him made it difficult for him to see his six children and three grandchildren, and put forward the unlikely thesis that it was also preventing him getting a 'proper' job. 'I want more access to my kids,' he added. 'When they told me I was coming to the hostel, I said to them, "What is there to stop me from fleeing to Spain?" I think that's why they put the curfew on. I really do believe I was better off in prison. I had better access to my kids from there.'

The fact was within a few weeks of being out he had already hooked up with his old pal Darren Hayden (see Chapter Seven) and the two of them were seen together in a Ferrari visiting haunts in Eastwood and enjoying a meal with another former co-defendant, Shane Bird, who had been cleared with David of a murder conspiracy charge and who had visited him regularly in prison. David asked associates about a pub in Eastwood which he hoped to take over. However, neither he nor Hayden enjoyed freedom for long. Hayden was soon back in prison facing a seven-year sentence after setting up a £1 million amphetamine deal with supplies from associates in Liverpool. The drugs had been stashed away for two years awaiting Hayden's return from prison. A single fingerprint on the goods, and video surveillance, was enough to convict him at Nottingham Crown Court in February 2010.

Much as David Gunn talked of wanting to shrug off his past, it continued to haunt him. As a result of his appeal to the High Court in April 2009, information came to light about what he and Colin had allegedly been up to in prison. Police had been monitoring both brothers and amassing intelligence on their visitors: to Lowdham Prison in David's case and Whitemoor in Colin's case. A submission to the High Court included intelligence from both the prison and police that indicated both brothers were still a danger to the public, and a report from the public protection board MAPPA (Multi-Agency Public Protection Arrangements) outlined the intelligence they had been presented with:

A police representative reported that David Gunn was part of the Gunn Crime Group and that Colin and David were still working the crime group from within the prison with particular emphasis on Bestwood. There is intelligence to suggest that Colin is first in the hierarchy and that David is second or third in command. Anything that happens in Bestwood is attributed to the Gunns. Crime has decreased in the North of the city – GBH, abduction, control and supply of drugs – since the Gunns have been in prison. Community competence has grown on the estate and a sense of normality has returned. Now that it is known that David Gunn will soon be released the estate is closing down and there is an unwillingness to give police intelligence. Notts Police assess the Gunn organised crime group as being the top threat of harm to the community.

The court also heard prison security reports dating back to July 2007 which claimed the Gunn brothers were involved in 'gang forming, intimidating staff, had a vast history of drugs, mobile [phone] history, and were an escape risk'. In addition, police had carried out a new intelligence assessment in January 2009 which laid bare some of the fears of the authorities. The assessment stated:

> Intelligence suggests that upon his release that Gunn will resume a position of control within the organised crime group and will settle scores with witnesses and others involved in the trial against him and his brother Colin, and with others who he believes have acted inappropriately whilst David has been in prison. There are individuals who are believed to owe money to David Gunn and he will be enforcing these debts on his release. The Gunns are believed to have a contract out on Michael O'Brien, currently serving life and held responsible by the Gunns for the death of Jamie Gunn. David Gunn has close ongoing associations with individuals involved in the supply of firearms and class A drugs and who are believed to deal on behalf of the Gunn brothers. David Gunn is still receiving an income from this activity with some of this money being forwarded to him in prison.

The report stated that David Gunn was still considered a high risk to the public with regard to firearms and class A drugs and came to the conclusion that while in prison 'David Gunn has continued associating with known criminals and still exercises a significant degree of control within the community. Upon release it is his intention to make his presence more prominent by reasserting himself'.

Gunn, for his part, vigorously denied that he was a gang member or had been concerned with gang activity while serving his sentence. He called his risk assessment 'ill-founded and inaccurate' and his lawyer argued there was 'insufficient hard evidence' to support it. But Mr Justice Blake, sitting at the Royal Courts of Justice in The Strand, was not swayed.

David Gunn also announced his intention to sue Nottinghamshire Police after they mistakenly crushed his 3 series BMW car, which should have been used as part payment in the £18,000 assets recovery case against him. Police were able to retrieve £8,000 from the sale of jewellery and the remainder had been due to come from the sale of the now-obliterated BMW. But David's decision to go to the media appeared to have backfired. Within a few weeks of speaking to the *Evening Post*, on 12 August 2009, police arrested him at the bail hostel in Northampton. He was found with more than £3,000 but was able to explain the cash. He was recalled to prison on the basis that he had flagrantly disregarded his curfew and was placed in HMP Ranby, a former army camp at Retford, Nottinghamshire, where he remained until he was shipped out to the Category A prison at Full Sutton, North Yorkshire, the following April. The move to 'ghost' him out of Ranby coincided with reports that an inmate had been scolded on the orders of Gunn, though there had also been reports from staff that Gunn was at risk of being attacked himself.

Colin, meanwhile, was also finding that prison life was no holiday camp. In a series of letters sent out from Long Lartin, where he was being held in November 2009, he raged at the authorities' treatment of him, particularly over prison visits and the opening of his mail. 'All my visits are in a special room for high risk visits,' he wrote. 'The high risk is an escape classification which means there is far more security for me than other Cat A or B prisoners get. At our visit table a screw sits almost on it taking notes of all the conversations ... I'm trying to keep my head down here. I need to get off the Managing Challenging Behaviour Strategy they put me on. Its not a good look.'

He also revealed that he was glad he had been moved from Whitemoor, as the regime at Long Lartin was more relaxed. 'I was at Whitemoor for 18 months and was relentlessly pursued by the security department who seemed to think that I was the only criminal in there. My name was put up for anything that went off in there; assaults, drugs, phones – you name it. All this without one bit of evidence, all intelligence which we all know means "made up" and the word intelligence means we are never to see this on paper. Long Lartin was a good move for me, really. Things was only going to get worse at Whitemoor. Things got so bad for me there the security department started opening my legal mail ... I took none of this lying down and let my pen become my sword. I had lots of meetings with the security governor at Whitemoor, all along the lines of me being "influential" and the prison service getting lots of security reports about me, at one stage 70 per cent of the intel reports involved me. This is absolute crap. It was just a phrase to use to refer me to their ultimate goal of putting me in isolation. Early October I had the mufty squad at my door [MUFTI is the acronym for prison officers dressed in riot gear and expert in restraint techniques], videotaped and taken off to segregation for concerns of bullying. I asked who I had bullied and again it came back "intell". Ha, Ha.'

At the same time, some of Gunn's family members and associates in Bestwood were raided by the police as part of a money laundering investigation. By now even the guards at Whitemoor appeared to have had enough of Gunn's name turning up on their intelligence reports. 'Family and friends had the pigs raiding for money laundering ... coincidence?... yes right. Nothing was found, the pigs searching for masses of money took computers, phones etc ... Then on October 22, I was laying on my bed mid afternoon and they came and told me I was moving. As usual when I move anywhere its total secrecy, the whole prison gets locked down, phones turned off etc and then I am on the move flanked by armed police and helicopter, all overkill but what do you expect. So now I am at Long Lartin on a new wing. This is the 3rd time I have been here and about the 20th time I have been moved in the four and a half years since I have been locked up.'

Colin signed off his letter in the usual manner, 'Chin up, chest out. Thugz love.'

One of the reasons Whitemoor prison officials had come down on him was because Gunn's supporters had set up a website for him to put forward his case. He and his supporters viewed this book as a wholesale character assassination which had damaged his credibility. But the publicity the website received in the Nottingham media antagonised people on the outside, including Graham Allen, the MP for Nottingham North, who was outraged that such a prisoner should be allowed a public platform. The website was quickly frozen and Gunn was refused contact with the individuals running it. Nevertheless, he was so pleased that the website had worked – it had more than 15,000 visitors in the short time it was fully active – that he began to think more on the idea of using the Internet as a platform to get his message out.

In one of his first missives from Long Lartin, he was clearly in a cheery mood: 'Good news from seeing the security governor, he said he had no problem with me blogging and its [sic] not illegal to do. I have provided him with all the up to date laws on it. Unlike Whitemoor it does not concern them here.' By early December 2009, friends of Colin had set up a Facebook page and messages began to fly back and forth at such a rate it was hard to believe he was not responding on a mobile himself. The bulk of the material however was undoubtedly being exchanged on prison visits and through the normal mail channels, including further letters which were posted onto the website. On January 10, he posted a new letter on Facebook which revealed he had spent some time over Christmas brooding over the matters that had left him sat in a cell and feeling bitter about his predicament.

'I was blamed for most things that went on in Nottingham and of course without evidence. I have never had a drug charge against me and my criminal convictions before this conviction was in my younger years. I am no angel but I had fuck all to do with the murders and I aim to show fresh evidence this year. Cannot comment too much or the letter will be delayed or not sent at all. I'll admit I'm up against it but I will never give in … others out there who I thought was friends have already given up on me and I do not hear a thing from people who I honestly thought was friends. It turns out those people have no balls and was mere cowards who sought protection. Rats, they know who they are. I will bump into those people again I know that.'

He also had strong words to say about this book and its author. 'What a joke, shows what an idiot [Carl] Fellstrom is … my Gracie could have wrote a better book. Worst of all though, than Fellstrom himself, was all the gossipers, the people who believed it. Anyone who knows me knows I would never have done any of the shit Fellstrom wrote about … Anyone who believed it, fuck 'em, rats, I'd love anyone to have the balls to say it to my face. Cowards all chatting shit with a hooter full of Columbian ha ha. Still I suppose it gave the mugs something to chat about.'

In the later years of his criminal life, it was true that Colin Gunn played less of a direct role in the terror that was visited upon his enemies; instead he directed others to do it. But as the judge at the Stirlands' murder trial, Mr Justice Treacy, put it, 'To your gang, your word was law. You would, I am sure, do the same thing all over again if it suited your book.'

Gunn was particularly incensed by the implication that he had been helpful to some police officers and he published letters from Nottinghamshire Police that stated categorically that he had never been registered as an informant with them. He failed to mention the informal and covert meetings he had had with police officers, stretching over a number of years, in which he had sought to manipulate the criminal justice system to his own advantage, with some degree of success. During 2002, a detective constable under surveillance by Nottinghamshire's anti-corruption unit was seen meeting with Colin Gunn several times. The officer was subsequently questioned under caution but was never charged with any offence.

By Christmas 2009, Gunn's Facebook page was live and would become, in the opinion of the authorities, dangerous. He accumulated more than five hundred Facebook 'friends' in just a few weeks and posted on a regular basis. This was achieved by receiving the hard copy of messages sent to his Facebook page from friends on visits or through the post. He would then write out the messages to be copied back onto the site as replies. However, it did appear the speed of the replies indicated in some cases he was replying directly back onto the site and not using intermediaries. In one case he was replying to Michael McNee, who was at HMP Frankland in Durham and, at this point, certainly had access to a mobile phone to send out messages on Facebook. In one exchange between the two men on 13 December 2009, McNee, who was using the name Riley McNee, wrote to Colin, 'Yes my pal ... hope ur cool chin up chest out. U just remember who the best lukin 1 from Bestwood is (ur the second one bro lol) love ya mate tricky xx.' McNee even used Facebook to end a relationship with one girl and begin a new one with a young woman who changed her surname to his within the space of a few weeks.

Gunn was also using Facebook to communicate with the 'friends of ours' network from Mansfield, the Dawes Cartel, with whom he had been pally since the 1970s. One posting, from Helen Dawes, wife of Dawes Cartel general John, said, 'Hi hun ... just a little something to make you chuckle ... Hezza took out five screws [prison officers] yesterday and Johnny received your letters yesterday. He doing ok. Luv lots H x.' Colin also made contact with

Darren Peters, convicted for his part in the police corruption case against Charles Fletcher, who was now free and eager to visit Gunn at Long Lartin prison.

By February 2010, my own investigation was coming to the startling conclusion that there were hundreds of inmates now using Facebook through mobiles smuggled into prison. Other 'faces' mentioned earlier in this book were using the network to chat to people on the outside, including Ashley Graham, serving life for a brutal murder of Roy Henry, who was going under the names Jheezy De Niro and Mista J. Darren Kirby, a Bestwood Cartel runners caught with a huge shipment of ecstasy, went under the name Daz Kirby. Gavin Dawes, jailed for fourteen years for the biggest heroin seizure ever in Nottinghamshire. Dawes joined the Free Colin Gunn Facebook page and in his own posts boasted that life was 'cool ' inside HMP Lowdham, where he joked he had his own 'en suite cell, Sky television and an xbox'. Shortly after this posting, he adopted the surname Beeton, his mother's name, presumably to avoid detection.

The Ministry of Justice was not blind to the problem of prisoners using mobile phones. Years of poor wages for prison staff had led some officers to 'go native', taking bribes from prisoners in order to bring in phones, drugs and other contraband. During Nottinghamshire Police's Operation Utah into the Gunns, a number of prison officers had been identified as having taken bribes from the Bestwood Cartel to provide favours, though none was ever charged. Corruption has been a problem which has grown in the prison system in parallel with the pernicious black economy. Dealers could expect to get up to ten times more for drugs inside a prison than on the outside. The introduction of mandatory drug tests had led to more prisoners turning away from cannabis towards class A drugs, which could be flushed from the system more quickly, cannabis sometimes showing up on a test more than thirty days after last being used. Some prisoners were building up large debts from their addiction to drugs and would be subjected to bullying and threats which might even extend to their families on the outside. The nature of the relationship between prisoner and keeper places staff in a potentially vulnerable position whereby the tail can wag the dog, resulting in some prison officers being compromised. All these ingredients provided for a flourishing organised crime network within the system, where gang leaders could take over the wings of some prisons and not only continue to run their outside empires but also expand their networks to take in the prison community.

The upshot of all this is a prison system which is not only unfit for purpose but also creating more criminality. Over the past five years I have come across numerous examples of people sent to prison who had minor drug issues before they went in but left at the end of their sentence with full blown class A drug addictions. Often those people will be back in the system within a few months as they drift back into a life of crime in order to pay for addictions which first claimed them inside prison. In one case, a young woman who had been sent to prison for continual shoplifting walked out after twelve months with a substantial heroin habit. Before her fall from grace, 'Helen' had held a steady job. Then her marriage broke down and she began to drink too much, eventually getting sacked. Unable to pay her bills or look after her family, she resorted to shoplifting. After her prison sentence, she was desperate to kick her habit but it had such a grip on her that she not only sank from shoplifting to prostitution but also began to corrupt other young women, some barely sixteen, into her business, and they also became heroin users. Sitting in the squalor of a terraced house in Normanton, Derby, it was profoundly sad listening to her among these teenagers, as she confidently jacked up her veins and tried to kid herself that the following week she was 'going straight, getting off the smack and getting a proper job'. It was a pipe dream and she was soon back in prison.

THE FACEBOOK SITE was a fascinating cauldron of information which showed just how Nottingham's criminals and others further afield were connected to each other. Beefs or arguments regularly blew up over the pages of the site between rival gang members all over the country. Nottingham was no exception. On some pages, the colours and bandanas of the various gangs were displayed: red for St Ann's, black for Radford, blue for Meadows and green for Sneinton. Gang members paraded their homespun philosophies, rapping lines from well known songs and often using their street names with acronyms attached to denote their area or stance on life. MPR stood for either Money + Power = Respect or Make Paper Regardless. GWOP stood for George Washington On Paper, as in the US dollar bill. TOPV denoted someone from the Top Valley area; RAD, a member from Radford or NG7; SV, a gang member with affiliations to the St Ann's area or 'Stannzville'; WFG, the Waterfront gang from the Meadows or NG2 area of the city. Snentz meant Sneinton and BPG meant Base Pound Gangster from the Basford area of the city. MOB was also a favourite abbreviation. Taken from a song by Tupac Shakur, the US rapper gunned down by an LA gang in 1996, the abbreviation denotes 'Money Over Bitches', meaning money was more important to these wannabe gangsters than the love of a woman; without money the street dealer would not be able to keep the 'babe' on his arm. A favourite oneliner also culled, though not exclusively, from Tupac was 'only God can judge me', furthering the idea that they were operating outside the normal rules of society. The avatars that these young men used on their Facebook pages included the usual suspects: John Wayne, John Gotti, Tony Montana, the Cuban gangster portrayed by Al Pacino in *Scarface*, Tony Soprano, and Don Corleone from *The Godfather*. These were fictional characters in the main, yet in the eyes of the young gangsters they portrayed the values they aspired to.

It was apparent that we now had a generation of drug dealers growing up who were so influenced by the gangsta rap scene and fictional characters from gangland dramas that they were importing a fake ghetto into their lives, a way of life which in reality existed only in a very limited way. This was a life they had, in part, decided to embrace because they found little of any meaning in the world. Secondly the young 'gully' or street drug dealers were not just following the money trail in a random way; 'making paper' was their ideal, their religion. They personified the purest form of street capitalism. The hoodies were the new entrepreneurs, aggressively taking over the drug dealing markets with their commercial, albeit illegal, products. Supply and demand was their mantra and if necessary they would use extreme force to dominate those markets. Money was their God and would lead them to power and ultimately the respect of their peers, something they believed they could only achieve otherwise as a rap artist or professional footballer. Anyone who got in their way in the pursuit of this dream or 'dissed' their beliefs was to be regarded as the enemy. Universally, the Facebook pages within this group of young people showed contempt for the police and rule of law, often backing groups such 'I hate Police' and such like. Street life was their world and there a different rule of law operated: dog eat dog. Often the commentary on their pages would include 'shouts' on the status updates, like 'Free all my SV Niggas', referring to criminals from the St Ann's area who had been locked up. Elsewhere there would be a few lines about how 'the Feds' or 'snitches' were undermining their dealing activities. Homage was paid to firearms, often illustrated by pictures lifted off the Internet of an assortment of weapons. In many cases there were photographs taken on mobiles of young people in possession of firearms, whether real or replica, in locations in Nottingham.

The lingo deployed by many of these youths was often a mix of Jamaican patois and gangsta rap and sometimes bore little relation to the language of their own families in Nottingham; indeed some were from white European and even Asian backgrounds. Nevertheless they believed this was their voice. Video games like *Grand Theft Auto* and television dramas such as *The Wire* were also playing a powerful role in shaping this 'lost generation' in terms of how they perceived the world around them. In effect, the ghetto was now being defined by a fictional world and not a real one and the danger was that the more the young guns embraced that life, the more likely it was that someone would use a firearm or a blade to make the fictional life they were leading that much more real.

By January 2010, Colin Gunn's Facebook presence was about to be terminated. Having seen him accumulate more than 550 'friends' on his own page and another 2,000 on the Free Colin Gunn page, the authorities believed his continued use of the medium was a threat to their efforts to stymie his influence from within prison. On January 23, he wrote what would be the final letter posted onto the site. He was in a cheery mood and was keen to set the record straight on what had happened to his relationship with Victoria Garfoot, his long term common-law wife and mother of his children.

'Everyone knows me and Victoria fell out and I got rid about a year ago. Had to and I believe Victoria's mental state was suffering. I told her to go find someone else and she did. I have no problem with that at all, just so everyone knows. Nothing was done behind my back. I truly believe that Victoria deserves some happiness. Don't get me wrong, it was a tough decision, but there was nothing there for me or from me. Just clearing that up in case people was wondering why I allowed it. I won't comment on her new fellah, I think we all know the dance there, and all I'll say is "what a guy" ha ha fuck em. They deserve each other. There's certain rules that have to be kept and I'm happy for her then.'

Mysteriously, properties linked to Victoria's relatives and her 'new fellah' suffered a number of suspicious fires during 2009 and the early part of 2010. The fires were investigated and confirmed as arson attacks but there was no evidence that they were linked to Gunn.

Gunn carried on his missive, looking forward to the inquest into the Stirlands' deaths and remarking that he hoped more information would come to light which could help him appeal against his conviction. He also joked that he wanted more letters from 'the ladies' and asked that they include photographs as he 'needed something to work with' while alone in his prison cell. But it was the final lines of his letter which were to land him once more on the front pages of a national newspaper. 'I'm sound though, strong as fuck and plodding on,' he wrote. 'I will be home one day and I can't wait to see the look in certain people's eyes and see the fear of me being there, and those no good cunts who have done nothing for me. Of course I wouldn't do anything to these people, I'm too nice a man. A look would do. Til next time then when I will enlighten you as to the behaviour of certain individuals to a little plan I executed a while back, suckers. Chin up Chest out. Thugz love, Colin.'

Whether his bitterness had got the better of him or whether he intended the words to be taken as a joke among Cartel members, they were seized upon as evidence that he was intending to take some sort of revenge. On January 31 the *Sunday Times* published a story about it. Justice Secretary Jack Straw quickly became involved and negotiated a rapid response from the owners of

Facebook in the United States to get the pages shut down immediately, without any recourse to the complicated laws which govern such material over the Internet and which otherwise would have taken weeks to resolve. 'We have made requests to Facebook to remove thirty prisoners' sites and they have responded positively to that with no single refusal, within forty-eight hours,' said Straw. 'It's unlawful and it's against prison rules.' Gunn was reportedly fuming, not least because, in the aftermath of the exposure of the story, the prison's governor decided that he must also lose any privileges he had accumulated and should be placed in segregation without access to private phone calls. Michael McNee's site was taken down too but within a week he was back, having taken over the Facebook profile which had belonged to his mother.

The authorities had been considering the cellphone problem for some time, as well as other pieces of technology, such as gaming consoles, which provided a capability for communication with the outside world. In 2008 alone, prison staff in the UK seized more than 4,000 phones and SIM cards which had been smuggled in for prisoners. In August 2006, the power that such phones gave to prisoners became evident when nineteen-year-old Liverpool gang member Liam 'Smigger' Smith visited a friend at Altcourse prison on Merseyside. Smith, a member of the Strand gang from Norris Green, had a verbal spat with inmate Ryan Lloyd, a member of the rival Croxteth Crew, in the visiting area. When visiting time ended, Smith left the prison, but not before Lloyd, who was on remand for firearms offences, had made a call from an illicit phone to summon his crew to Altcourse. Within forty minutes, Smith had been shot in the back of the head at point blank range outside the prison gates. Lloyd, also nineteen, and four other young men were subsequently convicted for their part in the murder.

In May 2009, Bill Hughes, the director general of the Serious Organised Crime Agency, expressed concern that some gang leaders were also using games consoles to pass on coded messages in forums. Prisoners, he said, had also been using the consoles to charge up contraband mobile phones. An officer working at a prison in the north west of England told me that the contraband culture was 'endemic' where he was working. 'On the wing I have been working on, the prisoners don't even try to hide it,' he said. 'They can get pretty much anything in there and the officers just turn a blind eye to it even though there is also info about packages coming in. Some evenings when you are doing the rounds you can hear the mobile phones ringing and smell the weed they are smoking, it's that obvious. But no-one says anything because they all want a quiet life.' In May 2010, a Government study concluded that as many as one in every ten prison officers were corruptly accepting money to help gangsters flood prisons with drugs and mobile phones. The report, from the Policy Exchange thinktank, cited prisons in Nottingham, Liverpool, Birmingham and Manchester, among others, as having acute corruption problems and said eighty-five per cent of inmates interviewed found it easy to get hold of drugs.

The authorities changed tack and announced that they were considering signal-blocking technology. By the beginning of 2010, three prisons had been picked for a trial to see if the technology could be introduced without having an impact on people going about their normal business with mobile phones near the perimeter of a prison. At the time of writing, there was a plan to roll out the programme nationwide. Colin Gunn, meanwhile, had been forced back into the old 'snail mail' routine of handwritten letters, hoping that sensitive material sent through his legal channels as privileged documents would not be opened by the prison's security unit. His flirtation with the Internet was over for now and 2010 was looking a bad year for him in other ways. News reached him that in early March his close friend and a stalwart within the gang, Luke Scriven, had hung himself while on day release from prison after a bust-up with his estranged wife. Gunn organised help for the family for the funeral from his prison cell along with a personal message of condolence placed in the *Nottingham Evening Post*.

Indeed there had been a number of tragedies on the Bestwood estate in the preceding twelve months, including the death of Stuart Lownds, stabbed at a party by twenty-two-year-old Robbie Mather, who at the time was the boyfriend of Laura Gunn, David's daughter. Mather received an eight-year sentence for manslaughter in May 2010. Jak Gunn, Colin's eighteen-year-old son, was arrested after being involved in an incident in September 2009 in which an eighteen-year-old was stabbed by members of the Raiderz gang from Top Valley. A subsequent trial at Nottingham Crown Court resulted in Jak being convicted but walking free because the time he had served awaiting trial was enough to cover the twelve-month sentence he received for violent disorder. He was sentenced by Judge Dudley Bennett, who told him, 'I think to some extent you were taken advantage of because of the notoriety of your father. I'm satisfied you had no idea about this knife.' Colin, who had predicted that his son would be home by March in letters to friends some two months earlier, was very happy with the result.

However, by that same March, Colin had been told to pack his bags once more for a return to HMP Belmarsh. He told friends he was glad to be out of Long Lartin but the travel distance to Woolwich would inevitably mean fewer visitors. There was no appeal in sight, despite all the bragging, and the inquest into the death of the Stirlands would not deliver anything that questioned the case against him. His supporters continued to be overly optimistic, blind to the overwhelming evidence against the 'big man'. Their Free Colin Gunn page carried on until it was deemed to have breached Facebook's rules on offensive content, though the only thing of offence on the site appeared to be pictures of Colin Gunn posing bare-chested against the bonnets of various top-of-the-range cars bearing the GUNNY numberplate. Facebook took down the page in May 2010, on the day it announced its response to privacy invasion fears among users, but it re-emerged the following day under the name Supporters of Colin Gunn. Gunn's Category A status continued to be questioned by his supporters but it was appearing increasingly likely that his thirty-plus years future starring at the walls of a prison cell had been cemented.

CHAPTER 15
TWO LIVES

BERNARD Langton and Reece Staples had much in common. Though not friends, they had crossed paths amicably in their home city. Both shared a passion for football, both were fathers of two young children and, according to those close to them, both were rarely without a smile. On 25 May 2009, these two young men from Nottingham were 5,300 miles apart, but both were about to make fateful decisions that would lead to the same tragic destination.

Twenty-seven-year-old Langton, known as 'Nard', was a cheeky, outgoing young man who made his money as a medium level drug dealer, mainly running a string of houses producing hydroponically-grown cannabis. Originally from Liverpool, he had made his way to Nottingham, living in the Lenton and Bulwell areas of the city. He had a partner, Nadine, and two young children. He had been in trouble with the law in July 2004, serving four months in prison after running down and killing fifty-nine-year-old pedestrian Kevin Kent on his Yamaha motorbike and fleeing the scene. He eventually handed himself when his conscience got the better of him. Langton enjoyed clubland to the full and it was no surprise that in the early hours of that hot Bank Holiday weekend, he decided to visit a newly opened venue in the city's Lace Market called Paris, formerly Geisha, to finish off what had been a 'banging' night out.

It was about 1.45am in Nottingham and the neon lit streets still held an abundance of promise for young clubgoers who knew there was no work to get up for that Monday morning. Some of Langton's companions mentioned that Paris might be full of people that they had had an ongoing beef with. 'Nard' shrugged. He was up for a good night, not trouble – but he had his knife on him just in case. He walked in, nodding to the doormen. They didn't search him.

On the other side of the world, in the quiet Costa Rican coastal town of Talamanca, it was 6.45pm. Nineteen-year-old Reece Staples, nicknamed 'Dubbler', had ditched a promising football career in Nottingham. Now he was thousands of miles from home and planning to make a purchase of high-grade crack cocaine. He had told friends he was taking his girlfriend, Kylee, on a Caribbean holiday, but he was here to make a deal. He would buy enough crack that, once it was cut for sale, could bring in around £27,000. It still had to be transported back to the UK, but Reece knew what had to be done. It had all been planned before he had set foot in Costa Rica. Although he would not be the primary recipient of any profits – others who had bought the plane tickets for him would see to that – it would keep the wolves from the door. Sure, trepidation pulsated through his body and his heart beat faster when he thought about what he was doing. But that was all part of the game. Besides, he chuckled to himself, when it was done he could dine out for weeks telling friends about his smuggling vacation adventures.

Back at the Paris nightclub, Nards was clocked by a number of people as he walked in. Many 'hollered' to him, but there were others lurking who had history with Langton and his friends. It went back to an incident several years earlier, when a friend of

Langton's had been shot in the back near the city's Showcase cinema. One of those who had a beef with him, Alex James, now pushed his way through the teeming club. Without warning, James struck Langton over the head with a champagne bottle. Langton reacted instinctively, pulling out his knife and stabbing James in the leg. Someone close by the group then whipped out a handgun and fired off two shots. People screamed, 'Get down, someone's got a gun.' Friends of James, seeing the blood running from his leg wound and hearing the gun discharge, thought he had been shot. Even as people began running from the upstairs bar down the stairs and onto the street, a police armed response unit was being sent to the scene.

Among the crowd was thirty-four-year-old Dion Griffin, a braggart who had saturated himself in gangsta life for two decades. Griffin was another mid-level drug dealer, always looking to step up and leave his mark. He had been convicted previously in Operation Opal, which had focused on dealers being used by the Bestwood Cartel, and had also been suspected of ordering a number of shootings in the past. In one case, a twenty-seven-year-old man from the Aspley area who had displeased Griffin was kidnapped outside the Lord Nelson pub. The victim was beaten and tortured for three hours and then, while pleading for his life, was shot several times and left for dead on Moor Road. The man, who police said was 'very, very lucky' to be alive, managed to crawl to a phone box and dial 999. When medics arrived, they were kept back for several minutes while armed officers quizzed the victim about who had carried out the shooting, such was their belief that he would not survive. Whilst there was little doubt that Griffin had ordered the kidnap and shooting, he had distanced himself enough to avoid being charged.

Now, in the early hours of May 25, Griffin cemented his notoriety. He summoned Anthony 'Tony' Tirado, his personal enforcer.

Tirado was armed with a handgun and pulled on a pair of black gloves. Together they went searching for Bernard Langton, working their way through the Paris club as people spilled out onto the street. Griffin, Tirado and an associate from Birmingham went outside and spotted Langton, with blood streaming from his head wound, walking, then trotting, down the street. Still thinking Langton might be armed, Tirado hid behind a pillar, then walked out onto the street again as Griffin ordered him to 'take him down' from twenty metres. The sound of four gunshots erupted, and Langton was hit twice in the back as he fled down Pilcher Gate. He staggered before tumbling down a set of stairs near the Pitcher and Piano pub and Living Room restaurant. Griffin and his cohorts fled.

Armed police and ambulances, already summoned to Paris, arrived to find that stabbing victim Alex James had been put into a car by friends, arriving at the Queen's Medical Centre at 2.18am. Griffin, Tirado and others, in another car, made their way to the hospital to check on the condition of James, arriving at 2.22am. But in the city centre, paramedics arriving in the Lace Market were not given immediate access to Langton because the incident was still considered 'live' and no-one knew if gunmen were still around. By 2.35am, Langton was finally on his way to the QMC, already unconscious. His ambulance drove into the Accident and Emergency bay of the hospital at 2.45am, followed by a police van, only to be met by a distinctly unwelcoming crew led by Griffin. They were intent on preventing the young man getting into the hospital for treatment. Even as Langton was taking his last breaths, Griffin stood at the centre of the group screaming at the paramedics and security staff at the hospital.

'Hope you're dead.'

'If he comes out, we'll finish him off.'

'He is going to die.'

'He's not coming in here.'

Eight minutes elapsed before staff could get Langton into the hospital. By then it was too late. He was officially declared dead just before 3am.

IN COSTA RICA, Reece Staples was having problems confirming his flight to the UK. He was also trying to judge the right time to swallow the crack cocaine he and Kylee had bought. When the couple eventually arrived back at Luton airport on June 5, they were greeted at the airport by the man who had sent them on their mission, Stanley Leach, a Jamaican national living on the Broxtowe estate. Leach was married, but was having an affair with Kylee and clearly had some kind of hold over her to demand that the pair become drug mules for him. Reece insisted that he take the risks and swallow all the drugs himself. The twenty-two pellets of crack had been secured inside the cut-off fingers of latex gloves which were then sealed with wax and wrapped in cling film. The disrupted stages of the flights back to the UK meant that Reece had had to re-swallow some of the packages he had first swallowed twenty-five hours earlier, but nevertheless he and Kylee walked unhindered through customs at Luton airport. Reece was able to give Leach three of the cocaine packets he had excreted, but the constipating agents he had taken to make sure the drugs did not pass through his body too quickly meant a further nineteen packets remained inside him.

The day after arriving back, Reece was on the streets around Radford and Basford, his home turf. He didn't feel well. He told Kylee he suspected some of the drugs were now leaking into his body and said he thought he might be dying. Desperation began to boil over in him and in the early hours of June 7, he was picked up by a routine police patrol in the Basford area on suspicion of causing criminal damage to a car. At 1.15am he was arrested and taken to Oxclose Lane Police station where he was placed in a cell. What took place during the next three hours is still not clear but at 5am, officers in the custody suite area were alerted to their prisoner suffering some sort of seizure in his cell. Like Bernard Langton, Reece Staples died in the ambulance on the way to hospital.

Nottinghamshire Police, in line with policy on deaths in custody, immediately called in the Independent Police Complaints Commission to investigate whether any officers had failed in their duties. The outpouring of grief among those who had known Reece was overwhelming. More than 4,000 people signed up to a Facebook page in tribute to him and hundreds attended his funeral, many wearing tee-shirts emblazoned with his smiling face. Few could understand what had led a nineteen-year-old away from a path as a talented promising footballer to become a drug mule. Unfortunately part of the answer was there in the double lives being led by many young people in the deprived inner-city areas. The aspirations these youngsters had set themselves were often so unrealistically high – a lucrative career in football, music, modelling – that when those dreams were dashed they saw few other options but drug dealing and gang life.

Reece Staples had first come to prominence in 2004 when, as a fifteen-year-old from the city's Trinity School, he played for Nottingham Forest Under-16s, then signed for their rivals Notts County. It wasn't long before Premiership clubs lined up at Meadow Lane to secure the signature of the surging, goal-scoring midfielder. He was potentially the best thing to come out of the club since Jermaine Pennant, who went on to play for Arsenal, Leeds United and Liverpool. Manchester United, who had been on the receiving end of Reece's talents when he was with Forest, won the race to sign him, ahead of Aston Villa and Blackburn Rovers, after he impressed on a trial. But things did not work out at Old

Trafford and less than a year later Reece was on his way back to Nottingham. He returned to Forest's youth academy and was given the number thirty-four shirt of the full squad. By 2006, he seemed back on track with the Forest youth team, regularly turning in key performances which helped take them through to the fifth round of the FA Youth Cup and, during the 2007/8 season, to a fifteen-match unbeaten run.

But it appeared he had two personalities. There was Reece, the promising young footballer. And then there was Dubbler, the Radford gang member, wearing his black bandana and drinking brandy. In the early hours of New Year's Day 2007, as Dubbler, he was involved in mass fight at private party at the Variety Club in Radford. Three people, including Reece, suffered serious stab wounds. He was rushed to the QMC by friends who acted quickly enough to save his life. The violence he suffered that night seemed to sap his self-confidence. He continued with Nottingham Forest throughout 2007/8 but his head was somewhere else. In October 2008, he was released by them and snapped up by town league team Carlton FC. Away from the pressure of professional football, Reece's confidence and passion for the game returned, but he could not stop Dubbler dragging him back into the gully life that crackled in the streets around him.

It was no different for Bernard Langton. Both were victims of a lifestyle which, had they the strength of mind, they would surely have wished to escape. Instead they were lured to their end by the intoxicating draw of another life, gambling on the promise of street credibility and financial security. Both men would be remembered by those closest for the smiles and brightness they beamed into others in their short lives. But there was also the terrible legacy of sadness they left; that of unfulfilled hopes and, not least, the tragedy that two sets of children would now have to face growing up without knowing their dads.

In May 2010, the individuals identified by the police as playing a part in pulling Reece Staples back into the ghetto were jailed at Nottingham Crown Court. Stanley Leach, thirty-eight, was sentenced to five years and three months for conspiring to import and supply cocaine. Kylee Hodgson, twenty-four, who had a child by Reece, was sentenced to three years after admitting importing the drug, which police estimated would be worth up to £27,000. The 135 grammes of high-grade coke that made up the shipment was not a large amount and may have been a test run in preparation for regular excursions. The authorities seemed as perplexed as anyone about why Staples chose drugs over football. Judge Milmo, QC, said, 'It's impossible to work out why a lad of nineteen, who spent time with Nottingham Forest Academy, got involved, to put it bluntly, in drug smuggling.'

BERNARD LANGTON'S DEATH was the first gun fatality in 'Shottingham' in three years, since the killing of seventeen-year-old Nathan Williams in September 2006. Drug dealer Courtney Hunt, aged twenty-one, was later jailed for life for shooting Williams through the heart in the Meadows Bridgeway shopping precinct after the teenager had taunted him for being fat. The introduction of airport-style scanners at the entrance to some city centre clubs offered reassurance to some, but there was criticism from owners that it put people off coming into their clubs. The fact was that gang members were increasingly treating clubs as their own offices and extended cribs. Questions were rightly being asked about how two people had managed to enter the clubs that night carrying firearms. One club plagued by gun problems on the outskirts of the city had its licensed revoked after testimony from police that the licensee had been 'cleaning up' evidence after one particular clash in which a car was shot up.

It did not take police long to arrest those responsible for Bernard Langton's death. Thanks largely to CCTV footage from outside the Queen's Medical Centre and around the Lace Market, which had caught the flashes of the gun being fired, eight people, including Dion Griffin and Anthony Tirado, were arrested. Their trial got underway at Birmingham Crown Court in May 2010, with experienced QC Peter Joyce leading the prosecution. The full scale of the terror visited upon Nottingham that evening emerged in what was described by the judge as something akin to 'the Wild West'. One of the four shots fired by Tirado had gone through the window of a pub, hitting the optics behind the bar. It was only luck that no passing revellers were gunned down that night. The court heard how Griffin had a hold over Tirado, appealing to the younger man's perverse ambitions to become a fully fledged gangster. Griffin's word was law to Tirado, who was more than happy to carry out the demands of his ego-fuelled boss.

The evening after the shooting, the two of them had fled to Skegness, where Griffin, like Colin Gunn, kept a caravan for holing up in. After a couple of days, Tirado was feeling the heat, not least because Skegness was full of people from Nottingham. He sent Griffin a text saying, 'Ask what time I'm getting off it's flaming here. T.' Griffin replied with the calculated coldness of a man who had been there before. 'No drama,' he texted Tirado. 'Just chill. No more texs.' Shortly after, a third man, Andrew Pleasance, aged thirty-three, organised £100 for a taxi for Tirado to disappear down to Gloucester, where he intended to hide out. Despite dumping more than ten mobile phones they had used before and after the murder, the three were convicted on the basis of the CCTV footage and the ability of police to forensically map signal movements through mobile phone masts and calls made between the missing phones. After a trial lasting more than six weeks, the jury found Griffin and Tirado, who both lived in the Top Valley area, guilty of murder. Pleasance was found guilty of assisting an offender and was sentenced to four years. The jury failed to reach a verdict on a third man, from Birmingham, accused of murder. Sentencing Griffin and Tirado to life with a minimum twenty-eight years each, Mrs Justice Sharp said the scenes at the hospital were 'utterly disgraceful'. She added, 'This was nothing less than a cold-blooded execution motivated by revenge. Innocent passers-by could easily have been struck by a stray bullet and the public could have been caught up by something that resembled something from the Wild West.'

After the case, Langton's mother, Christina, recalled her son's good nature. 'I really miss his cheeky smile,' she said. 'He was always laughing and had a very bubbly character. He liked to make us all laugh and was a brilliant dad. His daughter was only one when he died. He would always be spending time with his son, going to the park and taking him to the cinema. It is hard to believe he is gone and they have to grow up without him. The people who did this have taken my son from me and ruined my life. Everyone needs to wake up and know what is going on around them and to understand gun crime devastates families.'

CHAPTER 16
LOOSE ENDS

One man who has not featured yet in the pages of this book remains the most powerful organised crime figure in Nottingham. For legal reasons we shall call him the Taxman. The Taxman is a legend in his own right, controlling the money end of drug dealing throughout the East Midlands. He also has legitimate business interests stretching across the country. Many drug dealers who need collateral for the products they will smuggle into the UK will go to the Taxman for funding. It is a profitable route for them if they believe they can turn around their drugs quickly to beat his extortionate interest rates. If their shipment gets busted they know what to expect: they may be in hock to the Taxman for the rest of their lives. The Taxman prefers his borrowers not to pay up in full so the bill keeps going up and up with the interest. He is known to take protection money when business executives come to him seeking help after being pursued by other crooks. On one occasion a businessman who was being threatened by the Bestwood Cartel approached the Taxman to sort it out, saying he was not prepared to pay the Cartel but would pay the Taxman if he could deal with it. The Taxman said it would cost a couple of grand to do it and, true to form, the matter was sorted. What the businessman was not aware of was that the Taxman split the money with the Bestwood Cartel.

The Taxman has had business dealings with other villains such as Wayne Hardy, Dave Francis and members of the Dawes Cartel. He is probably worth in the region of £50 million. Most of all it is the climate of fear that he generates, and not his wealth, which enables the Taxman to consolidate his power. The police have questioned him several times but they have never yet managed to nail him; he has the ability to slip from their grasp every time. On one occasion, National Crime Squad detectives came close after they stumbled across what they believed was a multi-million-pound money laundering exercise. It had involved a major land development that went bust after large amounts of money had been invested, not least several million pounds of his. At least that was what the paperwork showed. Detectives believed that in reality he was probably 'losing' money that had come in to him in cash from trade in illegal products. After a two-year investigation sifting through all the financial records for the deal, they had enough, they believed, to put a file together for the Crown Prosecution Service. It was not enough for the lawyers and because no one was talking, they didn't have a case.

He has taken over companies which have been about to go to the wall owing money to him and has used these companies to launder some of his illegal millions. The wall of silence that pervades his everyday work means that he can go about it safe in the knowledge that it is highly unlikely that anyone will squeal on him or get close enough to be able to hurt him. The other major factor that prevents law enforcement agencies getting close to him is that he has friends in the police. The Taxman has a number of former police officers who he can call upon for help and some of them have even gone on to work for him. One senior officer told me, 'I'm getting sick and tired of losing officers and the following day I find out that he has gone to work for [the Taxman]. It often means that he is aware whether we are snooping around him and he can then adapt to any investigation and close up any chinks in his armoury.'

He is able legitimately to have large amounts of cash going through his books at any one time and that is the kind of business that drug dealers like best of all. It means that they can wash the money and it will not be traceable without an extremely determined investigation. The Taxman also knows that senior police officers are loathe to sanction any major investigations into him for fear of failing and falling foul of the expensive lawyers he can afford to hire. He is well respected and known by almost all the major villains in Nottingham and by many legitimate businessmen as well.

He does not overtly display his wealth but lives comfortably with his wife and children just a few miles from the city in a house worth around £750,000. He also resolves disputes such as problems between rival criminal gangs and has a huge influence within the criminal traveller community. On one occasion, a man charged with killing a member of the travelling community was under threat after the court case against him collapsed. He went to see the Taxman to sort it out, otherwise he would be looking over his shoulder for the rest of his life. The dispute was resolved but for twelve months the man was forced to carry out money collecting duties for the Taxman, visiting poor families who had been so desperate they had borrowed money and had fallen behind with payments.

The authorities continue to keep a close check on the Taxman and he was arrested again in the spring of 2008 as a major drugs trial involving members of the Dawes Cartel was being prepared. The Serious Organised Crime Agency wanted to question him about transactions with Gary Hardy, the business partner of John and Rob Dawes. They believed Hardy sent him money for the sale of drugs in city nightclubs. The Taxman had already given officers from SOCA his explanation and they went on their way. He remains as elusive as ever.

No sooner had police dealt with John Dawes than they began to set their sights on Hardy. He had been spotted at the scene of a drugs deal involving Dawes and police suspicions grew that he was a senior member of the Dawes Cartel. On 23 May 2005, Operation Normality was about to be brought to its conclusion with the arrest of John Dawes. With a decision having been made to arrest Dawes at the earliest opportunity, undercover police followed Dawes diligently that day. They knew Dawes had a meeting that day to pick up some money but they were not sure who would turn up at the liaison. Dawes hung around at a junction in Sutton-in-Ashfield town centre until a black Porsche appeared at high speed. It stopped at the junction long enough for John Dawes to get into the passenger seat. Gary Hardy was the driver. A plastic bag, which it later transpired contained £14,000 in cash, was handed to Dawes by Hardy, who promptly sped off in his Porsche without looking back. The police officers had been given no instructions as to what to do as far as Hardy was concerned, so they let him go. Dawes was arrested with the money. In interviews later Dawes refused to admit that Hardy was the man in the car who had given him the money, save to say that the money was for Apex Windows.

Hardy was, on the face of it, a successful businessman with his company, Apex Windows, showing more than £1 million of assets and enjoying ever-increasing profits. He was also a former chairman of local football side Eastwood Town FC. Hardy went to trial in June 2008, along with his brother Paul and mother June Muers, accused of conspiring to supply heroin, cocaine, amphetamines and cannabis. Also accused was Carl Busby who faced money laundering allegations. The trial was held under the tightest security ever seen at Nottingham Crown Court, with a procession of police cars carrying secret witnesses under the protection programme, one of whom was Jonathan Guest, one of the gang's lieutenants. The witnesses were ferried in and out flanked by police motorcycle riders and a helicopter which brought traffic to a standstill at the beginning and end of every day at court. Guest had pleaded guilty in 2002 to conspiracy to supply amphetamines and cannabis and possessing £150,000 of heroin. He was still serving his twelve-year sentence in 2006 when he decided to approach a solicitor in London and then got in touch with *Crimestoppers* from prison. He spoke to Notts Police in November 2006.

Guest told the courtroom how he was kidnapped and 'moulded' into the organisation, sent on drug runs and left in charge of an amphetamine factory in Colwick. The former university student became involved in the drugs trade over an unpaid business loan to Rob Dawes. He told how Dawes had pointed a gun to his head because he could not sell a Range Rover to pay off the debt. Guest then became desperate, stole one of his grandparents' cheques, wrote it out for £15,000 and gave it to the man. Dawes told Guest the cheque had better not bounce as he was going to put it through a car dealership in Kirkby-in-Ashfield belonging to Gary Hardy. When the cheque did bounce, Guest knew he was in deep trouble and his debt continued to increase. 'As the problem developed, I ended up taking more money from my grandparents to pay off the debt,' Guest told the court. 'I believe it was forty thousand pounds in total. That was just a figure they came up with. I was in debt to them ... they owned me.'

Returning from a holiday, Guest knew Dawes would be waiting for him. 'They took me away in a car. I spent six months in an attic, in a house, more or less under lock and key.' Dawes would also pick up Guest from the house and use him as a 'bar prop', ordering him to get drinks at a bar and then taking him back to the house. As their trust grew in Guest, he was given a Renault Clio and trusted to deliver cash, sometimes to Rob Dawes and sometimes to John Dawes, in bundles of £1,000 notes. 'On one occasion I was asked to go to London with a holdall and I believe I had a hundred thousand pounds in it.' Guest often used to meet drugs contacts at motorway junctions. He would be given their name and a description of their car and was ordered to make a quick cash exchange. He also started delivering drugs to Matlock, where he would be told to go to the car park of a garden centre. A man in a Toyota pickup truck would oversee the exchange. 'His soldiers came on motorbikes and collected the drugs off me and drove off on the bikes at speed,' said Guest. 'It was literally pass the drugs to the person on the motorbike with his visor down.'

Guest had first met Gary Hardy in the Devonshire Arms, Sutton-in-Ashfield. Guest came to believe that Hardy was one of the three drugs generals operating in the area. Each would receive £8,000 from the £40,000 that one kilo of heroin would bring on the streets. Guest, who would hide the heroin in buckets in the ground in woodland, said he was collecting a kilo every seven to ten days. Gary Hardy had also held a 'drug dealer's lottery' for a Mercedes car he owned. Thirty tickets were sold for £1,000 each and among those who bought one each were David and Colin Gunn. The winner was determined by the bonus ball number each week on the National Lottery.

The trial heard how Hardy was one of the three generals of the Dawes Cartel. Witnesses who had been part of the gang told how they were often asked to keep watch over lorry trailers containing cocaine worth up to £30 million and hundreds of kilos of amphetamine and cannabis. Hardy himself had a fleet of luxury cars which could not have come from his legitimate business dealings.

Richard Latham, QC, prosecuting, said, 'Gary Hardy, we suggest, for at least ten years leading up to his arrest on January 4, 2007, was a major player in the drugs scene in Nottingham and the area north of Nottingham. He had a cash-rich lifestyle, a stable of hugely expensive cars – Porches, Ferraris and Mercedes – and he bought and sold properties and his children were educated privately. To the outside world he had a legitimate source of funding for his lifestyle. He was a director of a number of companies, but the companies were not successful and incapable of paying for his very expensive lifestyle.'

In August 2008, after a three-month trial, the jury came back with verdicts against Hardy. The forty-five-year-old was found guilty of conspiracy to supply heroin and amphetamines. Nottingham Crown Court also convicted him of money laundering, and possession of criminal property. His mother, June Muers, aged sixty-six, of Pearl Avenue, Kirkby-in-Ashfield, was found guilty of conspiracy to supply amphetamines and conspiracy to supply cannabis and his forty-seven-year-old brother Paul was found guilty of conspiracy to supply heroin, amphetamine, cannabis resin and possessing criminal property. Paul Hardy's girlfriend Zoe Chapman, twenty-nine, of Willow Avenue, Kirkby-in- Ashfield, was convicted of conspiracy to supply amphetamines. Carl Busby was cleared of money laundering charges.

Gary Hardy was jailed for twenty years, Paul Hardy for twelve years, Muers for three years and Chapman for three-and-a-half years. Before Gary Hardy was led away, still maintaining the jovial façade he had throughout proceedings, Judge Henry Morrison told him, 'Those who deal in drugs are dealing in the misery of addicts. Heroin has a devastating impact on addicts, their family and society. You dealt in large quantities of heroin and amphetamines and made large sums of money. It was easy profits for you but it also means a long sentence. However you are not in the same league as John Dawes. You will serve twenty years in prison.'

IN AUGUST 2008, two more Dawes Cartel members were jailed. Gavin Dawes, a thirty-year-old cousin of John and Rob, was jailed for fifteen years for involvement with a £14 million heroin consignment found in a garage in Ruddington, just outside Nottingham. Nottingham Crown Court heard that Dawes was laundering at least £1 million a month for his cousins. Fellow gang member Brian Peck was jailed for twelve-and-a-half years after both men pleaded guilty. It followed a joint investigation by SOCA and Nottinghamshire Police. The haul included sixty-five kilos of heroin, 89,000 ecstasy tablets and ten kilos of amphetamine and had been stored in the garage by Peck. Assets recovery investigators, however, failed to locate all the millions which the Dawes Cartel have earned from their drug dealing. At a hearing at Southwark Crown Court in September 2008, Judge Michael Pert placed an assets recovery order of just £355,000 on John Dawes, concluding that, although it was accepted during court proceedings that Dawes had made over £8 million during the course of his criminal activities, most of the assets could not be located.

Another trial linked to seizure of the heroin in Ruddington revealed that, at a conservative estimate, at least £1 million in cash was being washed every month by the Cartel. A doctor from Leicester, Mohammed Aziz, was convicted after helping Gavin Dawes wash the fruits of drug dealing through a series of money transfers at exchange bureaus. Police discovered Aziz's phone was hot with texts confirming regular cash transactions of £150,000, which were often heavily coded or encrypted. Aziz, who was code-named 'Spac' by the gang, was trapped when police discovered a ledger of transactions in Dawes's car, which implicated Aziz. Along with a number of others involved, he received three years jail time.

In January 2009, another one-time associate of the Dawes Cartel who had built up his own drug smuggling operation was caught by Dutch police as part of a British-led operation. Anthony Spencer, a sixty-one-year-old career criminal from Coventry, had spent forty years of his adult life behind bars but was still organising shipments of amphetamines and cannabis to Britain. SOCA and the Dutch monitored his Midlands-based gang on bugged mobile telephones as they talked in code about the 'product' being moved from Amsterdam to the UK. They used the words 'garden work' and 'green paint' for cannabis, 'paperwork' for money and 'DVDs', 'CDs' or 'film' for synthetic drugs such as amphetamine. They also used the words 'horse and jockey' to discuss when the drugs were being transported or when their couriers were arriving or leaving. As Spencer made one more trip to finalise details of the shipment, armed Dutch officers moved in on him and the drugs stored in the farmhouse just outside Amsterdam.

During Spencer's trial, details emerged of the technologies now used against organised crime. Spencer's defence team presented the trial judge with a skeleton argument claiming that a 'roving' bug had been utilised by the Dutch at the request of SOCA, and planned to argue that the intercept evidence so gained was inadmissible. Dutch investigators and telecommunications experts were flown into the UK in preparation to defend the intercept evidence. Under the Regulation of Investigatory Powers Act, which governs surveillance and eavesdropping in the UK, telephone intercept material is inadmissible as evidence in a British court unless it is recorded overseas, and then only with the proper authority of that foreign state. Telephone bugs usually intercept audible material while a phone call is in progress, but anomalies in the material received by defence barristers in the Spencer case indicated that police were able to record conversations taking place even when a call did not appear to be in progress. In a legal argument to the trial judge, defence barrister Charles Benson, QC, stated, 'We are aware that a different technology now exists, known among other things as a roving bug. This enables a prospective eavesdropper to access the handset of the telephone in question and use it as a transmitter or microphone whether or not a call is actually in progress. Indeed, any conversation within some ten feet of the handset can thus be overheard.'

Mr Benson alerted the trial judge to one conversation between Anthony Spencer and a member of the gang which had purportedly been bugged by 'the Dutch authorities when both men are known to be in England'. However, despite having flown in the Dutch telecommunications experts in preparation to defend the use of the bugs, late guilty pleas were accepted by the prosecution, which meant the issue was not debated in open court. Benson's proposition to the trial judge, and one which was accepted as wholly possible by security experts, was that the mobile phone can be controlled by remotely infecting it with a piece of software either by text or other message not visible to the target. The method had been considered urban myth until, in 2006, a court application made by the FBI in a case against two Mafia families revealed that roving bugs were being used in the United States. In 2009, the US National Security Agency voiced fears that European-based terrorists and organised criminals had been turning to Skype, software that allows phone calls to be made over the Internet, as a way of thwarting state eavesdropping. Mobile telephones, unlike personal computers, have no firewalls, making them easy targets for the implanting of rogue software through texts or other means.

'The technology has been available for a number of years and to my knowledge was first used by the FBI against Mafia targets,' one security expert told me. 'Basically if you have the phone number and the IMEI [International Mobile Equipment Identity] number of the target and you then have the collaboration of the phone network service providers, a piece of software can be installed which turns your mobile phone into a roving microphone or a roving bug as it is known. That software can be installed physically or remotely without the knowledge of the target. The software can then be used to trigger the phone as a mike at will or by voice activation so you can not only hear two sides of the conversation on the phone but also any activity within a few feet of the infected telephone.'

One recently retired head of a UK CID force confirmed, 'The technology has been available to the Security Services and SOCA for a number of years now. I can only tell you that it was never used or made available to my own force.' While the debate over the inadmissibility of bugging material in British courts is ongoing, it may be only a matter of time before the authorities are forced to concede that they only have the prospect of a conviction in some gang-related cases if such intercepted material is allowed into court.

Anthony Spencer pleaded guilty, along with his lieutenant, former prison governor Jogendranath Rajcoomar, aged fifty-nine, also of Keresley, Coventry. Spencer was jailed for five years and three months, Rajcoomar for three years and nine months. Six other men also pleaded guilty to their role in the conspiracy to import and supply 140 kilos of amphetamines and cannabis.

ROBERT DAWES, JOHN'S brother, was proving a more difficult catch to land. Intelligent, ruthless and with powerful connections, but wanted in three countries – the UK and Spain, for drug smuggling, and Holland, for questioning over the execution of teacher Gerard Meesters – he esaped arrest until June 2008, when he was caught as he flew into Dubai airport from Spain. The Spanish authorities had been after him for several months in connection with a multi-million-pound haul of cocaine. Caught up in the Dawes sting, which had been conceived, planned and executed by officers from SOCA, was an innocent British pensioner.

Trevor Wade wakes every morning in the small cell in Leon, northern Spain, which has been his home since September 2007, and wonders what he has done to deserve his misfortune. Trevor is no spring chicken. He is entering his late sixties and has a history of poor health, including prostate cancer, angina and a crumbling spine. He, his wife Anne, and their two children were looking forward to a quiet retirement when Trevor's ill-health forced him to give up first his work as a lorry driver and then his work for a firm of private investigators. When a supposed friend asked him to accompany him to help out with some driving on a four-day trip to Spain, he worried about leaving his family for a few days but Anne convinced him that a break would do him good and would get him out from under her feet. But the decision was to propel Trevor and his family into a nightmare of Kafkaesque proportions. Trevor had known Karl Hayes for some eight years through the haulage business and thought he knew everything that he needed to know about him. But he had no inkling that Hayes had become indebted to the Cartel run by Rob Dawes and had been working for them for more than five years, helping to smuggle drugs and launder money. As far as Trevor was concerned, when he set out from his Lincolnshire home on September 5, he was simply helping out Hayes by doing a bit of driving from England to Spain so that Hayes could pick up some payments due for the fruit and vegetable transports he carried out between Valencia and the UK. After an uneventful journey through France, the Mercedes car the two men were travelling in began its journey into Spain. As they approached Madrid, Mr Wade was told by Hayes that the car was overheating and he needed to pull over to allow the engine to cool.

In a letter from his cell in Leon, Spain, Wade explained what happened next.

When we pulled up I got out of the car to stretch my legs and then saw this man approach Karl, who was still in the car, and began talking to him. All of a sudden Karl got out the car and handed his car keys to the man who then got in and drove off. I couldn't believe what I was seeing and asked Karl what it was all about. He said 'It's okay he's English and he is going to check the water system for me'. I told him he was crazy and he would never see the car again. I was puzzled but he assured me the car would come back so we then went into the bar for a coffee to wait. After about 45 minutes the car came back and the English man now had another man with him travelling in a red Ford Kia The three of them all began talking and I just kept out of it, thinking this was none of my business, but when I got back in the Mercedes I noticed a large carton on the back seat of the car which was not there before. I alerted Karl to it and he said it was nothing to worry about that it was just cigarettes which the other man had asked him to take to Valencia. I knew Karl transported fruit and veg from Valencia so I assumed that must be where he was going to pick up the money owed to him. We drove off from the coffee bar and the Red Kia was in front of us. Karl said the other two men were going to show us the road out towards Valencia as far as a service station a few miles away. I knew we needed some more diesel so I said no more. When we got

to the service station Karl got out to fill up the car while I
went in to the service station to pay. After paying, I walked
back out and then just as I was about to get in the car I was
grabbed from behind and pushed against the car. I could see
Karl on the floor surrounded by other men and they were all
armed. At first I thought the petrol station had been robbed
and they wanted our car as a getaway but then I realised as
they handcuffed us, as well as the men in the red Kia, that
they were plain clothed policemen.

Unbeknown to Wade, the carton in the back of the car and five
others in the boot contained 200 kilos of cocaine with a purity of
eighty-two per cent. It was worth £7 million wholesale or approx-
imately £22 million at street value. Wade, along with Karl Hayes,
Andrew Cunliffe, another British subject, and a Columbian, was
charged with conspiring to distribute cocaine. SOCA had had
Hayes on their radar for more than a year and, having allowed one
shipment through, had tracked the Mercedes car electronically
from Boston, Lincolnshire, to Madrid. Also in their sights was
another British lorry driver, Brian Kelly. As the job progressed
SOCA investigators sent communiqués to the counterparts in
Madrid detailing what they knew about Hayes and Kelly and
linking both of them to Rob Dawes. In one, SOCA officers stated,
'Our information indicates that Brian Kelly born 20 April 1954 is
on route to collect 100 kilos of cocaine from Spain and to transport
it to Belgium. After receiving a legitimate cargo Kelly will go to
meet one of Dawes partners in Madrid to collect the 100 kilos of
cocaine. We have received information that Karl Hayes, on behalf
of Dawes, has travelled by car to Spain this afternoon to be able to
see that the lorry meets its destination.'

The following day, a new note was sent by SOCA to Madrid: 'Our
information indicates that Hayes is travelling to Spain to super-

vise the delivery of a quantity of cocaine to Brian Kelly. We suspect that given the distance of travel that Hayes has a travel companion. We suspect that the last time Hayes did this journey he collected the drugs and passed them on to Kelly.'

Wade's case was backed by statements made to SOCA by Karl Hayes and his partner Paula Sharp, who ran the transport firm SOCA suspected had been used by the Dawes Cartel. Hayes claimed he was acting as an *agent provocateur* to try to nail members of the drugs gang after his son had died from a drugs overdose. He has been visited in the Spanish jail at least five times by SOCA officers who have offered to help him get a reduced sentence from Spanish prosecutors in return for information about Robert Dawes. 'I have made it clear in my statements that Trevor's involvement in this situation was as a favour to me to help me drive from the UK to Spain,' says Hayes. 'As a friend I should have made all the facts and my full intentions known to him. Had I done so, I am sure that Trevor would not have been in my car that day with me. Trevor and his family don't deserve this to happen and if he were to die in prison the damage to his family would be immeasurable.' More corroboration that Wade was innocent came from Paula Sharp, Hayes's partner at Sharp's Haulage. She stated, 'Karl was needed back in England for the weekend for other duties and so I made a suggestion that he took Trevor Wade with him to share the driving and hence get back for the weekend. This is indeed what happened and Trevor Wade has been innocently caught up in the consequences.' SOCA's own communications to Spanish investigators indicated there was no intelligence that Wade was involved in the drugs deal. Indeed, a communiqué stated that there was an unknown man in Hayes's car who they presumed was merely 'a travel companion for Hayes given the distance of travel'.

Wade's wife, Anne, has been campaigning for his release

through Fair Trials International, the Foreign Office and her MP. She is the only breadwinner in the family now, working long hours to keep the family afloat financially as well as mentally. Every day she tries to find a way through the mountain of bureaucracy which is preventing the truth coming out.

'I have only been able to go to Spain to see Trevor once and I fear that he will die in prison without being able to see his two children again,' she told me. 'I am at the end of my tether. There is no way that Trevor would have agreed to accompany Karl Hayes if he thought there was anything dodgy about it. I just can't believe this has happened. I keep thinking I will wake up and it will all have been a bad dream but this has been going on for two years now. Now Trevor has been told it will be another year in prison before a trial starts. He is just being left to rot in prison while the guilty ones are either going free or are being offered cuts in their sentence. The Foreign Office and Fair Trials have been doing what they can but SOCA have not been very helpful. SOCA officers have been to visit Karl Hayes at least four times in prison in Spain and have told his ex-wife they have agreed a deal for him which will give him a reduced sentence in exchange for information. I have asked them why they have not been to see Trevor and they have told me it's because he is not involved and has nothing to offer them. The whole thing stinks, particularly when you look at the way the British Government did everything they could to help free the Lockerbie bomber to get him back to Libya because of his prostate cancer, when he has been convicted of killing hundreds of people.'

Stranger still was the languid response of the law enforcement agencies in both countries towards the main target, Rob Dawes. There was a huge intelligence file on Dawes, including identification of businesses he had on the Costa del Sol, properties in Mijas and business interests in Dubai, where he sometimes based himself. He was being tracked all over the globe. Trevor Wade had been arrested on 6 September 2007 and yet it took another nine months for the authorities to track down Dawes. He was only arrested because he made the mistake of thinking he was immune from an international warrant in Dubai. And as of July 2010, two years after his arrest, there was no sign of him being extradited to any of the countries which had accumulated so much information about his brutal methods and drug smuggling.

Meanwhile Trevor still sits in his cell wondering what has been going on. At worst, like Kevin Musgrove (see Chapter Five), he was a victim of his own naivety, guilty of trusting someone whose background and intentions were concealed from him. He learned the hard way that no matter how closely one follows the letter of the law, it sometimes pays to be more careful about who your friends and business associates are. Prison life in Leon would have broken many lesser men but what he lacks in physical strength he makes up for in mental fortitude, and he and his supporters are determined to see him back home with his family.

Every evening, he gets to make a five-minute phone call. During one of these calls, he told me his daily routine. 'We get up at 7.30am, then it's down for breakfast, which is usually a cup of coffee and a two-inch piece of sponge cake. Lunch can be anything from a bowl of soup, which is usually tinned French beans mixed up with water and a roll. Two days a week we get some fish, which is boiled to nothing and in a bit of liquid which is usually cold and slimy. We don't get any fresh vegetables ever, everything is army surplus tinned stuff, which comes from the barracks nearby, I guess. If we are lucky we get a sausage sometimes or a slice of fatty belly pork at the weekend. The only thing I can honestly say I look forward to is the bit of Spanish tortilla we get sometimes. There is no kind of work or education regime here like you might get in a British prison. They stick us outside in the yard for a few hours every day, and in winter and spring it's bloody cold sometimes. There is nothing in the cells except for a bunk and chair and table I am sharing with three other people. There is no distinction between prisoners in here. I am in with terrorists on one side and paedophiles on the other, bloody scary at times.'

Trevor's situation contrasts sharply with that of Gavin Dawes, cousin of Rob and John Dawes. He is, at the time of writing, residing in HMP Lowdham Grange in Nottinghamshire. He has good meals three times a day, access to an Xbox, Sky television and a phone in his en suite cell. Dawes is serving fifteen years. Amazingly he has access to his own Facebook page from his prison cell and, in his own words, is living the life of Riley. He may well be out in five years and allowed to go on home visits in three to four years.

Meanwhile SOCA insists it cannot extend any further help to Trevor Wade. 'SOCA has an obligation, under the relevant statutory disclosure provisions, to make available to the Spanish prosecutor any material in our possession that would assist in Mr Wade's defence or undermine the prosecution case,' said a spokesman. '[But] the proceedings in relation to Mr Wade and Karl Hayes lie firmly within the jurisdiction of the Spanish authorities. We do not have the authority to offer a benefit to any prisoner on behalf of another jurisdiction.'

As in the case of Kevin Musgrove, it is to be hoped that justice will one day be served.

MYSTERY CONTINUES TO surround the disappearance of James Brodie, the man who pulled the trigger in the Marian Bates murder. Rumours, some wild, circulated regarding Brodie's fate from the day he disappeared, including: that he was shot dead on Colin Gunn's orders twenty-four hours after the botched jewellery raid and then was fed to pigs, or that he was buried under new buildings on the site of the old Sporting Chance pub, or that he fled and is safely hiding out in Portugal, Spain or Ireland. In October 2007, there was a fresh appeal for his whereabouts but all enquiries – which even had police digging up land in Flintham – drew a blank. Rumours also circulated that an extensive dig carried out on land in Blidworth was connected to the search for Brodie's remains. Either way, police remain convinced that Brodie was executed within forty-eight hours of Marian Bates's death because it was feared his capture would bring down the rest of the gang.

Arrests were made in April 2010 for the murder of David Draycott. Police had been able to use new technology to recreate the scene of the shooting which they said provided significant new evidence. But after a few days' questioning, the two men arrested, aged twenty-two and thirty-three, were released without charge.

In June 2008, Vincent 'PG Man' Robinson passed away after a long battle with cancer.

In September 2008, Kevin Warsop, who had been been arrested with Colin Gunn back in 1998 over an incident outside the Astoria nightclub, threatened to shoot police officers and blow up his house during a twenty-four-hour siege at his home in Raymede Drive, Bestwood. The stand-off began when the thirty-nine-year-old Warsop refused to let officers into the property after his wife had dialled 999 following a domestic incident. Warsop made a gun gesture at the officers and said he had a firearm. 'Just see what happens if you come in,' he told police. 'Just see what happens to the first one of you through the door.' A nearby school was closed the next day as the siege continued, homes were evacuated and the gas supply to his house was cut off. The siege eventually came to an end when five officers entered the house and arrested Warsop after a struggle. No gun was found. Warsop was subse-quently jailed for twenty-one months after admitting making threats to kill and threatening to damage property with intent to endanger life. Nottingham Crown Court heard that the father of two young children had taken parenting courses while in prison and intended to move away from Bestwood to avoid criminality. 'He recognises, even knowing where his roots are, that he is going to have to move away if he is going to put his past behind him,' said his barrister.

ON 1 FEBRUARY 2010, the inquest into the deaths of Joan and John Stirland finally got underway, five-and-a-half years after they had perished so brutally on that sunny day on the east coast. Nottinghamshire Police had already agreed to pay the Stirlands' children compensation, amounting to less than £20,000, in recognition of its failings. Given the circumstances of the couple's death, it came as no surprise that this was not an ordinary inquest. There was tight security at Lincoln Crown Court, with members of the public and press barred from the building and instead directed to the local magistrates court a mile away, where a video link had been set up to view proceedings. Michael O'Brien, Joan's son, who was serving a life sentence for the murder which sparked the killings, was also allowed to watch proceedings over three weeks from a room in prison. Almost all the police witnesses in the case were given anonymity, being referred to by letters of the alphabet.

The outcome would be decided by a jury and the members of that jury were directed not by the usual coroner for Lincolnshire but by barrister Karon Monaghan, a QC from London law chambers Matrix, who had been called in to oversee the complexities of the case as a human rights law specialist. Monaghan made it clear that the jury would have to consider a number of specific allegations when considering the evidence, key of which were whether police corruption had played a part in the deaths of the Stirlands and whether police had failed in their duty of care towards the couple.

From the outset it was clear that the covert nature of the investigation into the Bestwood Cartel had hindered the normal flow of information and intelligence within the police force about any threat to the Stirlands. Secrecy had been so tight that the senior investigating officer heading Operation Utah, the probe into the Gunns, did not even know who the Stirlands were until news reached him of their murder. Other police witnesses said the belief within the force was that the murders were beyond the capability of the Bestwood Cartel. As one senior officer put it, 'Gunn usually sought out and injured those who were involved in organised crime.' As far as they were concerned, the punishment shootings being carried out on the estate at the time were a case of 'bad on bad'. Yet one former detective superintendent pointed out that early on in the investigation into the crime empire, intelligence suggested Gunn had a team of hitmen, at least six 'shooters', who were willing to carry out jobs in return for payment or drugs. The list included Michael McNee and John Russell. Added to this, the intelligence log revealed more than 100 snippets linking Gunn to the procurement and use of firearms over the period of a year. All this was information available to some senior officers many months before the slaying of the grandparents.

Other information to emerge from the inquest included a more detailed account of just how much danger Joan Stirland had put herself in in order to help police nail her own son. One of Colin Gunn's original motives for sending shooters after the couple, when they were living in Carlton, Nottingham, was that Mrs Stirland had not 'given up' her son. However, it emerged in evidence that in fact Mrs Stirland had received a phone call from O'Brien in which her son had demanded £50 for food and drugs and confessed to the murder of Marvyn Bradshaw. Mrs Stirland duly related this to police and a meeting was set up in a super-market car park in Bulwell. Unknown to O'Brien, armed police maintained watch as the money was handed to a friend of O'Brien and, by following his car, police were able to arrest O'Brien a few days later in Leicester. After her own home in Carlton was shot up, Mrs Stirland asked Nottinghamshire Police officers to make it known to Gunn that she had helped police to trace her son. Officers refused the request, saying it was 'not appropriate'. Perhaps most controversially, it emerged that the police told Joan Stirland they could not give her protection because she had refused to give them a signed statement implicating her son.

Nick Gargan, deputy chief constable at the National Policing Improvement Agency, told the inquest that the witness protection arrangements for the couple were 'poor and inadequate'. He said it was wrong that officers had given Mrs Stirland the impression that she could only get protection if she made a statement against her son, and other solutions had not been sought by senior officers. Command level officers had not considered the option of a 'threat to life' policy, something in place at the Metropolitan Police, which could have given the Stirlands more protection without going into witness protection. Not only did they not offer the required level of protection, it emerged that there was a record of the new Lincolnshire safe house address on a Nottinghamshire Police computer at least three weeks before the murder. A prison inmate who had drug dealings with the Gunns claimed the address had been compromised by DC Charles Fletcher, but anti-corruption officers stated that although Fletcher had logged onto details about the Stirlands old address at Carlton after the shootings in 2003, he had not accessed the computer for the Trusthorpe address. It was conceded that the information about the address eventually came from a British Telecom employee making a reverse ex-directory number check.

When the jury returned with its verdict, after more than three weeks of evidence, there was an inevitability about the result. In all six major failings by Nottinghamshire Police were identified by the jury, which also found British Telecom had failed the couple. Police had: failed to take reasonable steps to protect the couple; failed to put adequate protective measures in place at their Trusthorpe home; failed to manage intelligence and information properly; failed to investigate the reprisal attacks after the murder of Marvyn Bradshaw; failed to perform a proper risk assessment on the couple; and failed to warn them of Gunn's links along the Lincolnshire coast.

It seems perverse that the design of the operation to bring down the Bestwood Cartel – in particular its inherent secrecy – prevented some officers from passing on and receiving vital information. This information indicated that the Stirlands were in extreme danger. The failings highlighted by the inquest gave heart to Gunn and his supporters, who felt it would help in any bid for an appeal. But an important fact had become lost amongst all the backslapping of the Cartel supporters. Colin Gunn was not arrested and convicted on evidence submitted by Nottinghamshire Police; it was Lincolnshire's Operation Karoo, the biggest inquiry in the history of the force, headed by its most senior detective, Graham White, his team of officers and Lincolnshire Crown Prosecution Service, which had finally brought the crime lord and some of his henchmen to justice.

After the termination of Steve Green's contract as Chief Constable in June 2008, Nottinghamshire Police looked to improve its poor standing in the league tables of crime prevention and detection. But by the time of the Stirland inquest, the force was in turmoil. Following Green's departure, the police authority selection panel once again went for a successor who had no background in crime detection or CID. Julia Hodson, the daughter of a Derbyshire coal miner, was variously described as 'well-liked' and, when she needed to be, 'feisty'. A former acting chief of West Yorkshire Police, she was the first woman to be appointed to the Nottinghamshire post. She inherited a difficult situation, with the county force still lying at the bottom of the league tables for many areas of crime. Added to this there were Machiavellian goings-on in the background, with several councillors looking to remove police authority chairman John Clarke.

The lack of unity, both within the police authority and at command level within the force, became public knowledge in December 2009. First came the resignation of police authority chief executive David Wilcock, who had been in the job only two months. His leaked resignation letter shook the authority to the core. 'Whilst it is not unusual to find multiple challenges running in parallel in the public sector,' wrote Wilcock, 'to find so many in one organisation with no inherent capacity to support self-improvement is extraordinary. In my experience, the current situation has not happened overnight and seems to have accumulated without action over a period of time, without being tackled.' John Mann, the MP for Bassetlaw, publicly criticised the force in the same week during Prime Minister's Questions in the House of Commons, suggesting that an 'organisational malaise' was hindering Nottinghamshire's crime-fighting abilities.

The day after the Wilcock revelations, documents leaked to the city's daily newspaper revealed that Deputy Chief Constable Howard Roberts had been embroiled in a private clash of personalities with the head of HMIC, Dennis O'Connor, the Chief Inspector of Constabulary. It was a dispute that Roberts claimed went back to 2005, when Nottinghamshire was under public scrutiny following Steve Green's declaration that the force couldn't cope with the murders on its patch. The public nature of the spat, which only came to light after it was discussed at a closed police authority meeting, was a huge embarrassment and led to the inevitable witch hunt for the person who had leaked the material. The dispute centred on Roberts' belief that his career progression was being impeded because he had 'stood up' to criticisms from O'Connor when the Home Office called in investigators to probe Green's 'can't cope' comments. Roberts suggested HMIC had subsequently taken to sabotaging his applications for various high-profile police posts. He also believed HMIC had played some part in blocking a twelve-month extension to his contract at Nottinghamshire, which had been rejected by police authority members. O'Connor and Roberts declined to comment on the revelations.

The fact was that HMIC was already taking a keen interest in the running of Nottinghamshire Police, indeed it had been gazing over the shoulders of the Nottinghamshire police authority and command team since 2005. Some even felt its presence was hindering the ability of the Chief Constable to make robust decisions and resolve some of the problems besetting the force. 'I think Julia [Hodson] has got her work cut out to deal with the mess she was left with,' one former senior officer told me. 'She could not have foreseen the malevolent political landscape which has been building around the force for the last few years ever since Steve Green's ill-advised outburst. It's a chapter devoted to meddling and muddling by outside influences, all of which appear to be speeding up the march towards a crisis.'

HMIC finally showed its public hand when a *Daily Telegraph* article speculated with some authority that Julia Hodson's job was on the line and that the force was locked in a cycle of underperformance. HMIC admitted it was monitoring Nottinghamshire closely and was working with it to produce an improvement plan.

Before the end of January 2010, HMIC declared it was facing an 'enduring issue of Nottinghamshire Police's under-performance' and that a team of experts would be sent to the county to plan improvements which could be enacted within ninety days. It was an unprecedented move in policing terms and one which placed a question mark next to Hodson's long-term future. The team of experts included two current chief constables and a police authority chairman from outside forces, a chief executive from British Transport Police authority and a captain of industry in Tony Wilkinson, former chairman of the Wilkinson hardware stores. It would be headed by Adam Pemberton from the Cabinet Office, who had recently overseen the biggest shake-up in the history of the civil service.

Before the team had completed its findings, the police authority chairman of ten years, John Clarke, announced he would be stepping down. At the same time, he denounced the leaks from the police authority, which he said had been referred to Derbyshire Police to investigate for offences under the Data Protection Act. 'I'm fed up with information getting out and being blamed for poor performance when I'm in a non-operational position,' he said. 'I can't work with information I'm given, be it details of counter-terrorism or organised crime, if someone within the organisation is leaking information. I'm proud of my record in helping achieve the reduction in crime in Nottinghamshire but on a day-to-day basis, there are people out there trying to undermine. The way I've been treated by some people, I believe, has been absolutely scandalous.' He didn't identify where he believed the mischief was coming from but the HMIC review team, when it made its findings public two weeks later, stated poor leadership from the police authority was impeding the progress of the police force. 'The leadership of the authority is ineffective ... The authority is not seen as adding value to policing in Nottinghamshire. By virtue of the long standing positions the chair and chief executive must accept primary responsibility for this.'

Alongside this criticism, the review team declared Julia Hodson unable to push through her vision because she lacked a capable chief officer team. 'It is a precondition for the authority's and force's future success that these issues are resolved,' the review team added. With Clarke's departure announced, the usual jockeying for position began with city council leader Jon Collins taking the reins as chairman, elected in a secret ballot. Vacancies for a deputy chief constable and two assistant chief constables were filled to strengthen Hodson's team in the top corridor.

Before that had happened, the latest HMIC report into Nottinghamshire branded the force the worst in the country. It could not sink any further.

Some officers speak of a deep malaise in policing in this country, one that may have much to do with social changes that have taken place among police officers and the law-abiding public in the past four decades. A former head of CID from a force close to Nottinghamshire told me that he had begun his thirty or so years in the force living among the community he actually served, pounding the streets as a beat bobby as many officers did. He got to know his community, he drank in the local pub most evenings and he gathered intelligence on who was who and who was doing what. He made sure he was a presence in the community he lived in, as an individual, as a family man, as a neighbour but above all as a police officer, and he was respected even if he had to arrest someone he had been talking amicably with the previous day. He told me, 'What happened was, as time went on police officers' pay got better and officers stopped living on the estates, they didn't want to live there because they could afford to live somewhere else and all the police houses that were on the estates got sold off and suddenly the connection between the police officer and the community had been eroded. The police officer wasn't someone who you could relate to or connect with any more. That also meant police didn't know what was really going on on the estates as well.'

The changes in the way Britain's streets are policed, the reduction of foot patrols and expansion of vehicle patrols, has exacerbated that feeling of detachment, creating a gulf that can easily be exploited by organised crime and gangs. The growth of the black economy has also seen otherwise honest people increasingly both at risk of being criminalised and of becoming victims of crime. Faith in both the criminal justice system and the police to deliver what the public demand is at an all-time low. In Nottinghamshire, at least, it seemed the bottom had been reached. In 2002, HMIC inspector David Blakey had stated, 'If you lived, worked or visited Notts, you are more likely to have a crime committed against you than anywhere else in the country.' Eight years later, HMIC assessed Nottinghamshire as the worst force in the country, and only in Greater Manchester or London were you more likely to be a victim of crime. It seemed that Nottinghamshire's outlaws still ruled the roost.

IN MARCH 2010, Janice Collins, the mother of Brendon Lawrence, finally saw his killer brought to justice. After eight 'horrendous' years, she watched as Rene Sarpong, aged twenty-nine, a gang member from the St Ann's area, received a life sentence with a minimum twenty-two-year term. The judge, Mr Justice David Clarke, was minded to reflect on how Brendon's death had been the start of so much pointless tragedy for the city. 'This killing, in February 2002, was the first killing by shooting of a young black victim on the streets of Nottingham,' he said. 'It was not the last. The killings that followed gave this city a reputation as a lawless place. Men are now serving long sentences for those offences and Nottingham is throwing off that unfortunate reputation.'

It had taken a long time to get a conviction. The jury had failed to reach a verdict at a previous trial of Sarpong and had found another defendant not guilty. This time the relief for Janice Collins was evident as she shouted 'Yes' and punched the air as the jury returned its verdict. 'It has been horrendous,' she confided afterwards. 'I've never slept through the night in eight years. You are walking the streets and going to the shop and doing what you are doing and it is constantly on your mind; you know, who shot Brendon? Well, we know now. It's taken eight years ... but we got there.'

Organised crime continues to flourish in Nottingham, despite the work of all the agencies tackling the problem. Alongside home-grown gangs there are now Chinese and Vietnamese gangs running cannabis hydroponic factories in empty houses and industrial units. Law enforcement agencies fear that foreign, particularly East European, gangs are making an impact in our cities, sometimes filling the gaps created by the successful prosecution of local drug lords. Drugs, prostitution, credit card fraud and people trafficking are their areas of expertise and they appear more adept than British gangs at laundering their gains. Meanwhile firearms and knife crime remain huge problems among the youth of Britain.

The answer lies not in the number of arrests to be made but in the offer of a positive future for the young, a future that does not involve them becoming drug dealers or gang members. There is hope in groups such as the Unity football team, set up by Morris Samuels in 2005 after the murder of Danielle Beccan and made up from youngsters from the three areas of the warring NG triangle: Radford, the Meadows and St Ann's. There is also the No Gun Organisation, set up by Clayton Byfield, which is continuing to get the message out to young people that guns and knives do nothing but take lives away. These groups offer something positive to young people despite a lack of support and funding. From little acorns great oak trees grow, as they say, and these projects offer some hope that there is a brighter future than one in which individuals and communities have too often in the past been ready to give up doing the right thing and tacitly accept the rule of the gun.